Off The Beaten Track
Greece

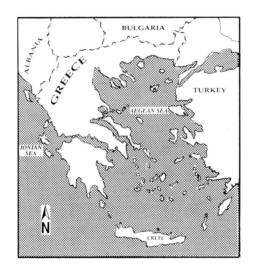

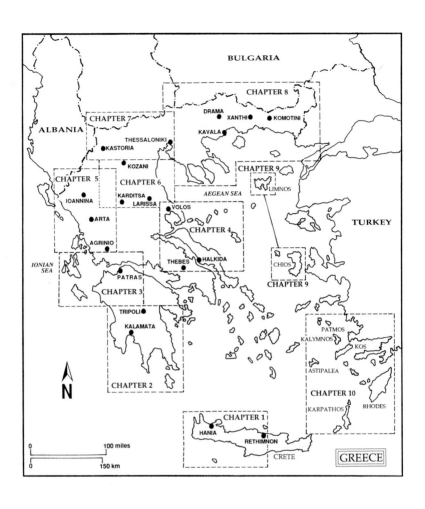

BULGARIA

CHAPTER 8

ALBANIA

CHAPTER 7

DRAMA
XANTHI
KOMOTINI

KAVALA

THESSALONIKI
KASTORIA

CHAPTER 9

KOZANI

CHAPTER 5

CHAPTER 6

AEGEAN SEA

LIMNOS

IOANNINA

KARDITSA
LARISSA

VOLOS

TURKEY

ARTA

CHAPTER 4

AGRINIO

IONIAN
SEA

THEBES
HALKIDA

CHIOS

PATRAS

CHAPTER 9

CHAPTER 3

CHAPTER 10

TRIPOLI

KALAMATA

PATMOS

KALYMNOS

KOS

ASTIPALEA

CHAPTER 2

CHAPTER 10

KARPATHOS

RHODES

CHAPTER 1

HANIA

RETHIMNON

CRETE

GREECE

N

0   100 miles

0   150 km

Off the Beaten Track

GREECE

Geoffrey Brown

MOORLAND PUBLISHING

The
Globe
Pequot
press

Published by:
Moorland Publishing Co Ltd,
Moor Farm Road West, Ashbourne,
Derbyshire, DE6 1HD England

ISBN 0 86190 496 6 (UK)

The Globe Pequot Press,
6 Business Park Road,
PO Box 833, Old Saybrook,
Connecticut 06475-0833

ISBN 1-56440-299-1 (USA)

First published 1991
Revised 2nd edition 1994
© Geoffrey Brown 1994

Front Cover: Skopelos (*B. Haines*)

Illustrations have been supplied by:
Geoff Brown; Greek National Tourist
Office; MPC Picture Collection;
C. Whitaker.

Printed in Hong Kong by:
Wing King Tong Co Ltd

British Library Cataloguing in Publication Data:
A catalogue record for this book is available from the British Library.

Library of Congress Cataloging-in-Publication Data
Brown, Geoffrey.
    Off the beaten track. Greece/Geoffrey Brown. — Rev. 2nd ed.
    p.   cm.
    Includes Index.
    ISBN 1-56440-299-1
    1. Greece — Guidebooks. I. Title.
DF716.B76 1994
914.9504'76 — dc20   93-10708
                                                            CIP

Contents

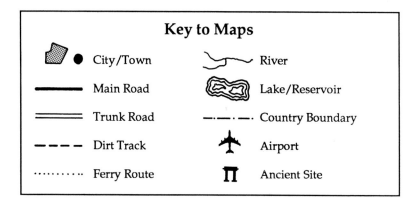

Key to Maps

City/Town		River	
Main Road		Lake/Reservoir	
Trunk Road		Country Boundary	
Dirt Track		Airport	
Ferry Route		Ancient Site	

Note on Maps
The maps for each chapter, while comprehensive, are not designed to be used as route maps, but rather to locate the main towns, villages and places of interest.

Acknowledgements
This book owes much to the moral and practical support of Joanne Kenning. For this reason and for countless others, this book is dedicated to her.

Introduction

For many visitors Greece has a timeless, enchanting appeal; the whitewashed houses of the islands set against a beautiful blue sky; ancient sites that trace man's history back to the earliest civilisations; thousands of gorgeous beaches and a fantastic climate. The country has all the ingredients for a wonderful holiday location, either for the avid sightseer or the devoted sun-seeker.

It is not surprising, therefore, that Greece is one of the most popular countries in Europe amongst tourists and that visitors are likely to share their experiences with countless others. In season, the established 'tourist towns' will be full of holidaymakers, and sunbathers will have to search hard for a spare square of sand where they can lay out their towel. In places, the authentic Greek atmosphere is submerged under a wave of mass tourism.

For many travellers this will not be the Greece they came to discover. These people will yearn for the Greece the travel agents and developers have left unmolested. They will want to get off the beaten track. It is for such people that this guidebook has been written. In its pages are outlined those areas where the mainstream tourist rarely ventures, where the sight of a stranger is still enough to raise an eyebrow or two among the locals.

Travelling off the beaten track in Greece is likely to be less comfortable than staying in the 'tourist areas'. English-speakers can sometimes be hard to find; beaches will have fewer facilities; and restaurants will be clean but often very basic. Yet the traveller will experience a feeling of adventure that is usually combined with a sense of personal discovery.

Not everyone knows, for example, that some of the finest beaches in Greece are on the mainland, around the beautiful Mount Pelion peninsula, to name but one area. One can visit the birthplace of Alexander the Great at Pella, and there is the stunning sight of Byzantine monasteries perched on top of sheer granite rocks at Meteora. Large areas of northern Greece offer captivating hikes across astounding, snow-tipped mountains and, on the gorgeous island of Patmos, one can visit the cave where St John wrote the Book of Revelations.

This book provides the historical background information that can make a town or monument truly fascinating. Yet the Greece of sun, sea and sand is by no means neglected and hundreds of beaches are covered here; it is just that they will be quieter, more secluded and often as lovely as the more popular beaches. To travel off the beaten track in Greece is to discover these beaches, and to discover a Greece of Macedonian power, of Byzantine mysticism, of medieval grandeur and of fierce national pride. In short, it is to taste the true flavour of Greece.

1 • Western and Central Crete

Introduction

Crete, the land of the fearsome Minotaur, is the largest of all the Greek Islands and is absolutely jampacked with attractions; a pulsating nightlife in the towns and resorts; archaeological sites and superb museums that trace Cretan history back to the earliest civilisations; quiet and attractive villages in a mountainous and green interior criss-crossed with gorges and rivers; and a coastline lined with glorious beaches. Add this to a summer that stretches from April to October, and one has an island with something for everyone; a miniature mainland Greece.

Taken as a whole, the island is not off the beaten track. On the north coast, particularly towards the east, resorts have sprung up at the merest glimpse of a strip of sand and many of the charming backwater resorts of the south are now the property of travel agents and developers. However, there are still two great chunks of the island blissfully free of the crowds and commercialism — western Crete, covering the county of Hania, and the villages of central Crete that are spread out around the foothills of Mount Ida. In both regions the traditional character of Crete still thrives.

Western Crete is stacked with wonders. Beginning at the capital of Hania, the routes outlined here visit the monasteries and beaches of Akrotiri; the Samaria Gorge which, at 16km (10 miles), is the longest ravine in Europe; the tiny coastal villages of the south (completely inaccessible by road) and the delightfully quiet and pretty Imbros Gorge. It then moves on to the extreme west coast with its stunning and rarely-visited beaches and a gorgeous, rolling interior where the sight of a visitor is still a rare occurrence.

Central Crete offers ancient Minoan and Roman archaeological sites and beautiful, isolated walks around the foothills of Mount Ida, passing agricultural villages that are completely untouched by tourism. One has to work hard to get off the beaten track in Crete but the rewards are worth the effort, particularly in the opportunities offered to experience the spontaneous hospitality of the Cretans. The islanders are understandably proud of their history and heritage, which shows them to be a strong-willed and fiercely independent-minded people. The Venetians and the Turks must sometimes have felt that it would have been better to have left the island alone — over 400 Cretan revolts were recorded against the Turks during their occupation, an average of one every 5 months. However, it was during World War II, in March 1941, that Crete really gained glory. While much of northern Europe fell in less than a week, the Cretans, backed by only a handful of Allied troops, held out against an elite German paratrooper division for 10 days before falling, having inflicted heavy losses on the Germans. The Cretans kept up their resistance throughout the war, assisting a British commando team (led by Hellenophile Patrick Leigh-Fermor, then a 22 year old Captain in the British Army) in the audacious kidnapping of the German Commander of Crete, General Von Kreipe.

Many of the most famous Greeks are Cretans; Eleftherios Venizelos, the first great statesman of Greece and prime minister several times during the early twentieth century; his son, Sophoklis, prime minister during the dark days of the Civil War; and the painter and iconographer Domenicos Theotocopoulos, better known as El Greco. Another famous Cretan is the author Nikos Kazantzakis — look no further than his *Zorba the Greek* for a sometimes chilling picture of the hard Cretan village life. The list omits the current Prime Minister of Greece, Konstantine Mitsotakis, who is related to the Venizelos family.

Some of the best-known tales of Greek mythology feature Crete which was, after all, the birthplace of Zeus. The great King Minos had his palace at Knossos, 5km (3 miles) south of what is now Iraklion and the half-man, half-bull Minotaur lived in the labyrinth below the city. The monster's special treat every 9 years was to be allowed to gobble up fourteen young and tender Athenians, given to King Minos by the city of Athens as part of a tribute. After Daedalus, one of the trusted servants of Minos, helped in the slaying of the Minotaur, he and his son Ikaros were jailed but managed to escape by making wings held together by wax and flying away. Ikaros, of course, flew too near the sun, the wax on his wings melted and he fell to his death in the sea below.

Knossos, where King Minos had his court, is Crete's most important archaeological site, revealing as it does that the island was home to one of the first great civilisations, the Minoans, who ruled Crete for 2,000 years from around 3000BC. By around 1450BC, this civilisation

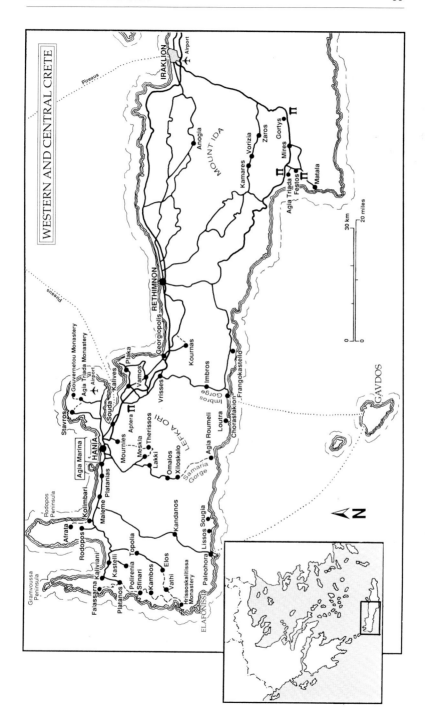

WESTERN AND CENTRAL CRETE

was at its peak, with beautiful palaces and such 'mod-cons' as flushing toilets but all was destroyed by a huge natural calamity, popularly believed to be the same volcanic explosion that blew the island of Santorini to pieces. The Minoans tried hard to re-establish themselves but, by around 1100BC, had been routed by the Mycenaeans. Crete remained quiet through the Hellenic era with only a few cities establishing themselves as important trade centres but staged a revival of sorts under the Romans who made the town of Gortys capital of their province of Crete and North Africa.

Christianity came early to Crete, due to the Apostle Paul's brief visit in the first Century and the Byzantine era saw the new religion establish itself. Hundreds of churches and chapels were constructed although many were destroyed by the Saracens who ruled in the ninth century. The Genoans captured the island in the early part of the thirteenth century but it was soon purchased by the Venetians who were to rule here for 459 years. Under the Venetians, the island flourished economically and culturally and a number of traces of their rule can be seen, particularly around Hania. The Turks took control in 1669 and Crete entered a sullen and stagnant age, punctuated regularly by rebellions against the occupiers who did virtually nothing for the island. By 1898 Crete had gained independence and was incorporated into the Greek state in 1913.

The island has excellent transport connections with the rest of Greece and further links with Europe as a whole. It has three airports, several ports and, in recent years, even a bus service from Thessaloniki in the north of the mainland. The airports are at Iraklion, Hania and Sitia and offer Olympic Airways flights to Athens several times daily, as well as to a number of islands and to several major European cities such as London and Amsterdam. By ferry Crete is linked to Cyprus, Israel, Egypt, Turkey and Italy, all boats bound for these destinations docking at Iraklion, the main port. There are daily services from Pireaus to both Iraklion and Hania, services three times a week between Kastelli and Kythera and the Peloponnese and the eastern port of Sitia is the gateway to the small islands of the Dodecanese. Two boats a week make the 12 hour crossing to Rhodes and the Cyclades can be reached via the daily sailings to Santorini.

Crete has no trains but does have an extensive public bus network which, while sometimes slow and erratic in the interior, is quick and frequent along the island's main artery, the northern coastal road. All of Crete's major cities stand on this road, each one being the capital of its own *nomos* or county — Hania, Rethimnon, Iraklion and Sitia.

A stretch of Crete's rugged coastline, between Chorasfakion and Loutra

Car and moped rental agencies abound in these cities for those unwilling to rely on the bus service; if you are hiring a moped for travel in the interior make sure that the engine is powerful enough to handle the hills (at least 50cc per person). On the southern coast of western Crete, between Paleohora and Chorasfakion, caiques (small boats) are the only possible means of transport besides walking.

Wildlife enthusiasts will enjoy Crete. Its three mountain ranges are home to many swooping birds of prey such as kestrels and eagles and along the lower slopes of the peaks are beautiful wild flowers and plants. Crete has over 1,500 different species of plants and 130 of these are unique to the island. The Samaria and Imbros Gorges are particularly rich in flora and fauna and on the west coast around Kastelli the tiny camomile flowers grow wild; they are fine for making your own tea. The best-known animal of Crete is the kri-kri, a long-horned mountain goat found only on Crete—it has inhabited the island since the Minoan age. Until recently, the kri-kri was facing extinction and so has been made a protected species, living around the rocks of the Lefka Ori National Park and on the tiny islet of Agios Theodoros.

Cretan music is very different from that popular in the rest of the country but those unschooled in Greek folk music will have a tough time telling the two apart. Performances will nearly always feature a lyre, a variation on the violin. If you get a chance to hear the music accompanied by traditional Cretan dancing, take it, even if it is part of one of the many 'traditional Cretan evenings' organised by travel agents. The steps may seem slow at first but soon erupt into a frantic riot of high-kicking and ankle-slapping.

Western Crete

In all probability, any tour of western Crete will either begin, end or, at some stage, pass through **Hania** (Chania, Xania), a city which has considerable charm and appeal. It stands head and shoulders above the three other rather bland cities of the northern coast in terms of attractiveness; its fine old harbour and the Venetian quarter's narrow network of alleys are enchanting and even the new town, although noisy, is hardly uninviting. Be prepared, however, to mingle with the crowds while enjoying Hania for, although it is not as commercialised as some of the other towns and cities of Crete — probably due to it lacking a good town beach — it still lures many visitors, particularly during Nautical Week. Held between the end of June and the beginning of July, this offers an endless series of tours, exhibitions, demonstrations, competitions and dancing and draws participants from across the island.

Evidence suggests that Hania was inhabited during the Minoan era and it is a city that has prospered since then, be it under its ancient name of *Kydonia* or its Venetian title of *La Canea*. Under the Turks it became the capital of Crete and remained so until 1971 when Iraklion took over the mantle. Today, little remains of Hania's ancient past but the legacies of the Venetian and Turkish occupations are everywhere, particularly in the old city or Venetian quarter that begins at Scalidi Street in the new city and stretches up to the harbour.

The scythe-shaped harbour — not the main port of Hania, that is at Souda, 10km (6 miles) east — is small but colourful, much of it sealed in by a long jetty. At the end of this stands a lighthouse built by the Venetians. The object of this closing off of the harbour, leaving only a slim gap for ships to pass through, was defensive. At the time of its construction in the early sixteenth century, the Venetians were becoming increasingly alarmed by the ever-encroaching Turks; a massive wall was built around Hania for the same purpose.

The multi-domed, arched-windowed building on the east side of the harbour is a mid-seventeenth-century mosque, one of the first Turkish constructions in Hania. Nowadays, the mosque is visited for tourist information rather than spiritual cleansing. At the quieter, western end of the harbour, passing under stone Venetian arches into a maze of steep cobbled streets surprisingly free of tourist boutiques, you come to the naval museum. This is an exhibition/ collection of artefacts and models devoted to Cretan sea-faring history; two huge naval cannons front the otherwise discreet entrance. Parts of the old Venetian walls can be seen in the area, looking towards the sea.

Moving east along the harbourside, one can bear right at Sindrivani Square and head inland up Halidon Street, the main street of the old city. Lined on both sides by souvenir shops, moped rental agencies, bookshops etc, this is the place to buy gifts. Many of the shops specialise in leather goods, one of the old staple industries of Hania; sandals are especially popular. Halidon Street is also the home of Hania's small but educational archaeological museum, displaying the finds from ancient Kydonia and an excellent collection of grave steles. The museum is housed in the largest church the Venetians built in Crete, the church of St Francis. Later converted to a mosque by the Turks, it has a fine, grand interior although its exterior, as with a number of Hania's Venetian buildings, suffered war-time damage from German bombs.

From the archaeological museum one can either continue down Halidon Street to the main road that marks the old city/new city divide or just spend more time wandering the streets of the old, with its high, wooden-fronted and balconied houses. Many of the houses offer rooms to let, most of them of good quality and with attractive prices. There is no shortage of places to eat, including a few tavernas, patronised mainly by Greeks. However, it is at night that the old city can really be enjoyed; the harbour lights glow and good jazz music seeps atmospherically out into the town's alleyways from the many bars and clubs that are dotted around.

It is only to be expected that the new city has rather less to attract the visitor than the old. However, the municipal market, housed in a large and grand cruciform building, is well-worth a visit, even if only to buy a Cretan speciality, the ring-shaped and ornately decorated bread that is a popular gift at Cretan weddings. A walk up Konstantinos Street from here leads to the well-tended municipal gardens opposite the city stadium and, east of that, to the historical museum which boasts a collection of archives so large that it is second only to the General Archives in Athens.

Nea Chora is the nearest beach, a 20 minute walk west of the harbour, but is dirty and often packed. For better bathing, travel west on a blue city bus to Kalamaki beach or further on to Platanos or Agia Marina. Alternatively, go east to try a couple of lovely sandy and quieter beaches, at Kounoupidiana and Stavros, on the bubble-shaped peninsula of Akrotiri. This hems in the port of Souda on the north coast and the huge NATO base that is located beside it. Hania's airport is on the peninsula, 18km (11 miles) outside the city.

The road into the Akrotiri peninsula leads east out of Hania, passing the hill of Profitas Elias and the tomb of the greatest statesman Greece has known, Eleftherios Venizelos. The hill was bombarded by the ships of the Great Powers in April 1897 to subdue Cretan insurgents who were demanding union with Greece. There is a good sandy beach at Kounoupidiana and beyond that is Chorasfakion which is now being developed as a suburb of Hania. At the northern tip of the peninsula, the small fishing village of **Stavros** is pleasantly uncommercialised while still having a beautifully calm lagoon of a beach. Regular buses leave Hania for Stavros.

Akrotiri also has its attractions inland although these do not lie in the spartan and flat landscape; instead, they are man-made. Turn right at Chorasfakion and continue for 4km ($2^1/_2$ miles) before bearing left at a junction for the monastery of Agia Triada, first founded in 1606 and still very active today. Its Cretan monks, true to their tradition of hospitality, offer all visitors a glass of *raki* and a chunk of *lougoumi* (this is similar to Turkish Delight) after their guests have viewed the chapel with its huge, bright frescoes and lovely altar screen. A particularly pleasing feature of its domed roof are the stained-glass windows through which the sun reflects a myriad of colours onto the walls and floor. Another 4km ($2^1/_2$ miles) on, is the abandoned monastery of Gouvernetou, its church housing a gold-painted altar screen fronted by two ornate candlesticks. Built in 1548, Venetian engravings and sculptures can be seen on the exterior walls. Every 7 October pilgrims congregate at Gouvernetou in honour of its saint, Agios Ioannis or St John the Hermit.

A path to the north of the monastery leads down a series of steps carved into the rock to the Arkoudospilia (Bear Cave), a huge natural cavern with a few stalactites inside and the remains of a church crumbling to dust outside. A steep 20 minute downhill walk from the cave leads to the magnificent ruins of the Katholiko, a Catholic monastery built by the Venetians and dedicated to St John the Hermit. Some of the buildings are very well-preserved and the monastery dramatically spans a rocky ravine. Just prior to reaching the ruins, another cave can be seen cut into the cliff face. Allegedly where the Hermit lived, the cave and its stalactites can only be viewed with a flashlight; look out for the deep drop into a lower cave, beside the figure '8' carved into the floor on the left as one enters.

Scrambling down the rocks from the Katholiko to the basin of the ravine, a 15 minute walk leads to the north coast, a walk made under the imperious gaze of watchful mountain goats. At the coast the ravine opens up and it is possible to swim off the rocks. It should also be technically possible to walk west from here (although there is no path) around the steep and jagged coastline to Stavros — you will need good boots and plenty of water to try this.

The lush surrounds of Hania support many a small, agriculturally based village and a tour of the area not only reveals these but also offers more than a few sights of interest. The nearest village of note is 3km (2 miles) south at Mournies; quiet, leafy and unremarkable were it not for the fact that Venizelos was born here. The small stone house where he was born is open to visitors. There is not much besides this, though, so travelling east 11km (7 miles) along the northern coastal road, one can reach the ruins of ancient **Aptera**, one of the most important towns of the region from the Minoan age to its eventual sacking by the Saracens in the ninth century.

Aptera's name is Greek for 'without feathers' and arises from the mythological tale of how the Muses and the Sirens once held a singing competition here. The Muses sang more sweetly, and the Sirens, hardly gracious in defeat, pulled out their feathers and threw themselves off a nearby cliff. The actual remains are not too exciting but the old theatre, the water cisterns and parts of the walls can still be made out. Easier to identify are the very much intact stone walls and turrets of Idzeddin, a Turkish fortress that once guarded the mouth of Souda Bay. North-east of Aptera, **Kalives** is a coastal resort which is not as developed as much as one would expect, given its pleasant, sandy beach.

Kalives stands on the edge of a triangular peninsula that lies between the bays of Souda and Almiros, an area that boasts its own attractions. The town of **Almiros** is the next resort along from Kalives and, like its neighbour, does not suffer from over-development. Here one can view the recently excavated ruins of a sixth-century basilica with a delicately decorated mosaic floor.

Gavolohori, to the south, is a small and gently traditional village that takes its culture seriously. A whole range of events — music, dancing etc — take place during its folklore week at the end of July and beginning of August. During this week, on 29 July, ceremonies are held at the village church in honour of St Peter and St Paul. **Georgiopolis** is another resort with a long beach; it lies at the southern end of the peninsula and is linked by the Almiros river to Kournas, on the edge of some barren mountains and with a large and gleaming lake on its shores.

The Byzantine church of Agios Georgios in **Kournas** has frescoes dating from the twelfth and thirteenth centuries. **Assi Gonia**, a village high in the mountains, is the scene of great celebrations on the second day of Easter in memory of St George. An old ritual is re-enacted, gathering the animals of the village together in the square and dedicating their milk to the saint. In true Cretan fashion, a boisterous festival is then held, with feasting and dancing.

Heading back towards Hania, one can visit the largest town of the region, **Vamos**, positioned halfway between Kalives and Georgiopolis and a good place to be during the first week of August when its cultural week takes place. Further west, **Stilos** is a lush village near Aptera on the banks of the river Kyliaris, and **Malaxa**, 16km (10 miles) from Hania, is located high in the hills, with good views over Souda Bay.

Travelling south of Hania, it is not long before the road begins to ascend into the foothills of the Lefka Ori (White Mountains) and some lovely scenery is unfolded below, with panoramas north over Hania and the coast and south over the mountains themselves. Sixteen kilometres (10 miles) south of the city, and reachable from there on foot through a ravine, is **Therissos**, a charmingly ramshackle and welcoming village on the edge of the Lefka Ori.

The nearby village of **Meskla** is in a similarly lovely location and is one with a long past, emphasised by its fourteenth-century chapel, built on the remains of a fifth century basilica, next to the main church. Another church, the Metamorphosis, has frescoes originally painted in the fourteenth century although the building dates from some time before. **Lakki**, at the head of a verdant valley further south, sheltered many a member of the Cretan resistance during the German occupation. The tiny, orange-growing village of **Fournes** lies on the route from Meskla to Alikianos. It is a quiet village with an eleventh-century Byzantine church that hosts the solemn religious festival of the Raising of the Holy Cross annually on 14 September. If the foothills of the Lefka Ori have given you a taste for the mountains, then it is an easy matter to return to Hania to prepare for a hike through their very heart, along the path of the Samaria Gorge.

The Gorges

To experience some of the real natural beauty of Crete, coupled with a warm glow of self-achievement, hike through the **Samaria Gorge**. Beginning high in the Lefki Ori and ending down on the south coast of the island, its 16km (10 mile) length makes it the longest gorge in Europe and certainly one of the most spectacular. Formed over

Samaria — the longest gorge in Europe

millions of years by a river that still gushes down its rocky bed in winter, the cliffs at its flanks tower up to heights of 500m (1,640ft), their size being best-appreciated at the famous 'Iron Gates' where the gorge narrows to a width of only 3m (10ft).

The river keeps the valley splendidly lush and flowers are dotted all along the path, adding splashes of colour. Some of the plant species are unique to the gorge. High above, birds circle near their nests in the cliff faces. This region, and its surrounds, was declared a national park in 1962, to protect its beauty and to ensure the survival of the kri-kri, a Cretan mountain goat that has inhabited the island since Minoan times and that was, until recently, under threat of extinction. The Samaria Gorge is one of the few areas where they flourish in their natural habitat. They are shy creatures, though, and despite what the tourist brochures say, hikers are unlikely to see a kri-kri.

Given its appeal, it is only understandable that hundreds of tourists should descend daily into the gorge. Although the hike is rarely a solitary experience and the gorge is somewhat on the beaten track, it would be a pity to miss out on this opportunity while you are in the area. The hike is over a route that is well-marked, has plenty of amenities such as water facilities and toilets and is kept in immaculate condition. Beginning from the northern end, the hike should take between 4 and 7 hours to complete. The gorge is open daily from 6am to 4pm between 1 May and 31 October; visitors are allowed in after 4pm from either the northern or southern entrances but only for a 2km (1 mile) walk to ensure that the gorge is cleared by dusk. The hike is best made from north to south; not only are the public transport connections better by this route but it is also all downhill. Coming from south to north is a gruelling, sweaty slog. To enter the gorge one has to pay a modest admission fee that goes towards its upkeep.

Public buses make the glorious, mountainous journey from Hania and Rethimnon to **Omalos**, the main trailhead of the gorge and tour buses come from as far afield as Agios Nikolaos in eastern Crete, so getting to the gorge should not be a problem.

Although the Samaria Gorge is the main attraction of the Lefka Ori, it is by no means the only one and those who wish to see a little bit more of the region can always use the Kallergi refuge hut, an hour's walk from Omalos, as a base (see the Further Information section for the telephone number). From here several of the range's peaks can be climbed — Gingilos, Melidaou or Pahnes — before making the trek down Samaria. The descent is via the *xiloskalo* ('wooden staircase'), a long and steep set of steps that lead down past forests to the bed of the gorge. It is a rocky route most of the way — good, solid shoes are vital — and one cannot waver off the path without prior permission from the Hania forestry commission. Just before the gorge narrows to pass through the 'Iron Gates', you pass the ruined, frescoed church of Osia Maria, from which the word Samaria is derived.

Coming out of the gorge, it is another 20 minutes to **Agia Roumeli** and the welcome sight of restaurants, snack bars and rooms to let. This is a village that exists solely for and because of the hikers from the Samaria Gorge. In winter, when the gorge is closed, it becomes a veritable ghost town, with just a tiny handful of residents left. The ruins of a castle stand above it and there is a small and pebbly beach. From Agia Roumeli's small harbour, regular boats leave for Chorasfakion via Loutra. The caiques have a monopoly here and, as the only other way to Chorasfakion is a 10 hour hike, their owners feel free to charge rates way above the norm. Be sure to bring enough money. However, one does not have to go direct to Chorasfakion and then back to Hania. Those able to stay in the south for an extra day or two, and who are prepared to do a little extra hiking, can enjoy sleepy coastal villages, fine beaches and a gorge equal in prettiness,

The 'Iron Gates', Samaria
Gorge

The kri-kri, a mountain
goat which is a protected
species on Crete

if not in drama, to Samaria. The alternative begins at Loutra, 40 minutes east of Agia Roumeli by caique.

Loutra is a whitewashed little coastal village beautifully located in its own tiny cove; perfect picture-postcard material. It is very peaceful and quiet and a wonderful place to wind down and relax. There are a couple of rooms to let in the houses on the slight hill behind a harbourfront which is lined with small tavernas, most with tables and chairs right on the water's edge. The village exists for its visitors alone — only five families stay here in the winter, each with their own boat. Like Agia Roumeli, Loutra has no roads and is therefore blissfully free of cars. The hilly headland to the west of Loutra is fun to wander around, viewing what remains of two churches and a few walls; you may also see some of the bemused-looking mountain goats. Another church is cunningly hidden inside a large cave. The only drawback of Loutra is that it has no beach, although it is quite possible to swim off the rocks of the headland.

Although it is easy enough to take the caique from Loutra to Chorasfakion, the moderately easy $2^1/_2$ hour walk along the coastline will delight those who like solitary strolls, probably with only a few mountain goats for company, along a rugged coastline looking out over an endless sea. The path is barely visible from the bay at Loutra but, by walking out of town through the narrow streets behind the harbour, it is quite simple to locate. As you walk away, the views back to Loutra are lovely.

Around the headland, two fine swimming coves are reached, both hemmed in by steeply vertical cliffs and, as the path passes above them, accessible only by parachute. Further on, however, one can swim off the rocks at two shallow little coves, although better bathing is to be had within 20 minutes' walking of these coves. The path begins to ascend slightly, then curves round a headland and reveals the huge and spectacular bay that is Sweetwater beach. Its name is drawn from the freshwater springs that bubble beneath its rocky surface and support a mini-colony of campers who have built surprisingly sturdy-looking homes out of the rocks at the back of the beach. Note that Sweetwater is a nudist beach. To continue towards Chorasfakion from here it is necessary to clamber over some large misplaced boulders and the path alarmingly disappears. Some thoughtful soul, though, has piled up stones on the rocks, thus marking out the easiest route. The path is soon reached again and ascends to an asphalt road. A 30 minute walk down along this road leads to Chorasfakion.

Chorasfakion is a bright and breezy little town with a couple of

The picturesque village of Loutra

beaches and plenty of tourist facilities, mostly used by those who fancy a day or two's rest and relaxation after hiking the Samaria Gorge. With bus connections to Hania and Rethimnon and a boat service along the west coast to Paleohora, it is the nearest thing to a transportation hub on the southern coast of western Crete. Only 21km (13 miles) east is the historic and attractive coastal town of Frangokastello.

The first thing to catch the eye in **Frangokastello** is its wonderfully preserved, square-plan Venetian fortress. This was built in 1371 in the hope that its presence would subdue pirates, rebels and all others who were turning the region into an anarchic one. It stands on the edge of a long and clean sandy beach, lined at the back with fish tavernas. In recent times, developers have been trying to get their hands on Frangokastello but for the time-being it remains a bright and relatively uncommercialised town. A significant date for Frangokastello is 17 May. This is the anniversary of a terrible massacre in 1829 of Cretan rebels who had seized control of the fortress, by an overwhelmingly superior Turkish army. Ever since then, on this day, those slaughtered (the *drossolites* or 'dewy ones') are said to appear at either dawn or dusk and silently march across the shore to vanish into the sea by the fortress.

Back in Chorasfakion, there are two ways to return to Hania. The quickest and easiest way is by the bus service but more pleasing is the route that passes through another ravine, the beautiful and rarely-visited **Imbros Gorge**. One does not have to go far to reach the gorge. The hike begins at the tiny and untouched village of Kalimedes, about 1 hour by foot from Chorasfakion; those with hand luggage only can take the Hania bus to the Kalimedes junction, only a 10 minute walk away from the village. Go through Kalimedes and you will see a sign that points to the gorge, which is entered along its rocky bed. A fence will probably have to be climbed over — do not worry about this, it is there to keep goats in, not hikers out — and move into its gorgeously lush interior. It is a lovely gorge, not as spectacular as Samaria but one where it is possible to walk its entire $2^1/_2$ hour length and not see another soul. At some points its rocky cliffs narrow to less than 1m (3ft) in width.

The climb out of the gorge is very gradual — not at all strenuous — and ends at the village of Imbros with its very welcome café. It is only now that a problem may present itself; although Imbros lies on the Hania-Chorasfakion bus route, the buses that pass may well be full. A taxi may pass by, or one could consider hitching or calling for a taxi from the large and leafy village of Vrisses, 24km (15 miles) to the north. The journey up to Vrisses is superb; rollercoasting through the untamed Cretan countryside and passing tiny hamlets which are seemingly untouched by the twentieth century. At Vrisses one can pick up the northern coastal road back to Hania.

West of Hania

Although on the map it may look as though the coastal road west of Hania is one long string of glossy resorts, do not be put off. The resorts are there but they dwindle the further west one goes, coming to a virtual end at Kolimbari at the base of the middle of western Crete's three peninsulas, Rodopos. For those without their own transport, there is a bus that trundles fourteen times a day between Hania and the last major town on the west coast, Kastelli, so getting off the bus to explore the attractions en-route before picking the bus up again is no problem.

The best beach resort nearest to Hania is at **Agia Marina**, opposite the rocky, oddly-shaped islet of Agios Theodoros. It is claimed that the islet was once a whale intent on gobbling up Crete until Zeus came to the rescue and turned the hungry creature into a rock. Once called *Akoitos* (uninhabitable), it is populated today but only by the mountain goat, the endangered kri-kri. Further along the coast is Platanias with another good beach. The hill behind the resort was once the site of the ancient town's acropolis and offers great views.

Six kilometres (4 miles) west is **Maleme** which, because of its military airfield, was a prime objective for the German paratroopers in 1941 and some fearful battles were fought here. The Germans suffered terrible losses throughout Crete and their dead — all 6,580 of them — are buried at the war cemetery in Maleme. The cemetery is beautifully tended, a tribute to the Cretan spirit of forgiveness. Maleme, which has been inhabited since Mycenaean times, is now a beach resort.

Kolimbari is a small and pretty village with its own traditional pottery school and a pebble beach. It stands very near the famous monastery of Gonias. This was constructed in 1662 and is rich in icons and other ecclesiastical treasures, many of them are displayed in its small museum. The monks are understandably proud of the four iron cannonballs lodged in the walls, irrevocable proof of their resistance to the Turks. The monastery is closed between lunchtime and late afternoon and dress regulations are strictly enforced — arms and legs must be covered.

Kolimbari is positioned at the base of the barren and rocky Rodopos peninsula and, in season, caiques regularly ferry passengers from here up the peninsula's eastern coastline to Menias, with its small rocky beach and the remains of an ancient port. This was the port for ancient Diktyna, home of an important shrine to Artemis, goddess of hunting; the remains of the shrine, dating from the second century AD, can be seen. It is possible to walk to Diktyna from Rodopos, a village on the peninsula, but it is a hard 5 hour slog.

An easier walk from Rodopos is to the isolated church of Agios Ioannis, 2 hours away. The church holds a service every 29 August, in honour of St John the Hermit, that draws scores of pilgrims. Seven kilometres (4 miles) north of Kolimbari, and accessible by car, is **Afrata**, near the Hellinospilia, a massive cave with stalactites. Southwest of Kolimbari is Kato (Lower) Episkopi, with the interesting circular Byzantine church of the Archangel Michael in its centre. Its frescoes date back to the twelfth century.

Kastelli, after Hania the largest town of western Crete, has a definite charm although, initially at least, one may have to dig deep to find it. A scruffy yet appealing town, it is pleasantly hemmed in by hills and mountains to the south and by the Rodopos and Gramvoussa peninsulas east and west. It has a welcoming atmosphere which is particularly noticeable in some of the excellent tavernas along its quiet shores. The town is also known as Kissamos, its name during the days of the Roman occupation when it was an important commercial centre. A few traces of Roman rule lie around the town — the aqueduct, a cemetery and two second-century AD houses — but these are all fenced in and overgrown.

It was the Venetians who gave it the name of Kastelli; a name that has stuck even though its official name today is Kastelli Kissamos. Even more confusingly, Kastelli's port, which has connections to Pireaus via the island of Kythera, is usually referred to as Kissamos. With a good bus service around the region and a couple of car and moped rental agencies, the town is an excellent base from which to explore the western coast of Crete. Indeed, to stay a few nights, to try to get to know some of the friendly locals and to bathe off its rocky beach, is to gain a sense of Kastelli's elusive charm.

Kastelli's beach can only be described as adequate but this should give no cause for concern as some of Crete's finest beaches are within easy range. The best of these, and also the least-visited, is at the north-western tip of the Gramvoussa peninsula. One has to work hard to get there but it is worth it. Those who have a car, or who are ready to pay for a taxi up the dirt road that leads half-way up the peninsula, will find it much easier. For most people, the small village of **Kaliviani**, 12km (7 miles) west of Kastelli, will be the jumping-off point. One can take a taxi there or walk from the port of Kissamos along the coastline to the foot of the peninsula. It is far better to take a taxi because the 90 minute walk is not particularly pleasant; it crosses a filthy beach with the rusting wreck of a Lebanese tramp-steamer on its shores.

The gradual and fairly easy climb up the peninsula's dirt road offers some fine views as one heads north. The barren and completely infertile landscape provides a stunning contrast to the deep blue of the sea below. The impression one gets is of walking off the edge of the world. It is, however, totally unshaded; make sure that you bring a sun hat and as much water as possible.

After 2 hours the dirt road comes to an abrupt end and the only way on is via the overgrown but easily visible goat path. Keep heading north until the northern end of the peninsula is reached; this is a magnificent sight. Then follow the goat path back down the western coast and, a little more than 1 hour after the dirt road has been left, **Balou** beach comes into view and the effort is all made worthwhile. It is a large lagoon made gloriously spectacular by the sun reflecting off the water, turning it a multitude of blues offset against the golden sand. The lagoon's water is very shallow — chest-high at the deepest point — but it is lovely to splash around in after the hike. Freelance camping here is no problem, and the only drawback is the tar washed in from the fishing boats. Two small and rocky islets stand to the north, Agria (Wild) and Imeri (Tame) Gramvoussa. Agria Gramvoussa has the remains of a Venetian fortress, a popular base for Greek pirates following the War of Independence. Hence, Balou beach is sometimes referred to as Pirate beach.

Another marvellous beach lies to the west of Kastelli at **Falassarna**, a great stretch of sand and rocks that suffers from tarring but most definitely not from over-development. It is surprising that while this wonderful beach remains almost completely undeveloped, some miserable strips of sand and pebble elsewhere in the island are crammed to the hilt with holiday villas. Two buses a day travel from Kastelli to Falassarna, more go to Platanos, a 5km (3 mile) walk away. Falassarna was a port in ancient times and the ruins of a 'stone throne' to Poseidon, some walls, and the foundations of houses can still be seen.

More remnants of Crete's past can be seen at **Polirenia**, 7km (4 miles) south of Kastelli. Founded in the tenth century BC, this continued to be an important, agriculturally-based town up until the Turkish occupation but today it is only a small village. The ruins reflect its long history. Above the village is the ancient acropolis; the walls are Roman, added to by the Turks, and the arches Venetian. The church of the ninety-nine Holy Fathers was probably built from the stones of an ancient pagan temple. Only three buses a week make the uphill journey here from Kastelli but it is an enjoyable, if tiring, walk through field upon field of olive groves. At Grigoria, a hamlet just before Polirenia, there is a pleasant café with nice views over the hills where you can stop for refreshment.

Ten kilometres (6 miles) south of Kastelli, in the very heart of olive-farming country, is the lovely and untouched little village of **Topolia**, a fine base for walks or drives around the surrounding hills and valleys. The deep and atmospheric Cave of Agia Sophia is only a 20 minute walk away, along a road that passes above the steep and lush gorge of Koutsomatades. Pass through a tunnel hollowed out of the steep rock face to the right and only a short climb to the right is the cave. The dank and clammy interior, with bats flapping around at its rear, is best explored by flashlight so that you can see the stalactites and stalagmites. At the mouth of the cave there is a small chapel.

According to legend, many years ago a shepherd saw a beam of light shining across the gorge from the church of Agios Dimitrios opposite. The shepherd followed the beam into the cave and found an icon of Agia Sophia. He took the icon to Agios Dimitrios church but, in the fields the following day, he saw the same beam of light into the cave. Bemused, he followed it again and found the same icon embedded firmly into a rock, impossible to move. The chapel was built in honour of this miracle. Another, more macabre story is associated with the cave. During the Turkish occupation the local bishop and his brother inspired an insurrection. The enraged Turks began fearful reprisals against the local population in their search for the two men, who were hiding in the cave. To spare the villagers more persecution, the bishop and his brother asked their cousin to behead them and take their heads to the Turks to appease them; this he did. In later years, this eerie tale gained added credibility with the discovery of two headless skeletons in the cave.

From Agia Sophia walkers can continue to the hamlet of Koutsomatades. This has a population of thirty and is located off the asphalt on the left of the main road. Passing through the olive trees, climb a dirt track which is unsuitable for cars. It is an unshaded walk so bring a hat and water. With the view over the hills and the gorge getting better as one ascends steeply, climb to the top of the hill. Then bear left for the hilltop village of Mouri and from there descend to Voulgaro, 10km (6 miles) from Kastelli. While in Voulgaro, take a look at the Byzantine church of Agia Varvara with its fine eleventh-century frescoes. Do not take the left turn just before the peak of the hill; it winds its way down back to Koutsomatades, passing the tiny church of Agios Dimitrios with its twelve icons over the altar depicting the life of Christ.

Past Topolia the same road leads south to **Elos** which is part of the 'Ennia Horia', nine villages set among chestnut-tree covered mountains. Like the rest of the nine, it is beautifully located, high up and almost hidden against the green landscape. The villagers organise a chestnut festival every third Sunday in October that includes traditional Cretan songs and dancing. West of Elos is **Vathi**, another charming chestnut-growing settlement just off the asphalt road to the south. Staying on the asphalt road, one begins to bear north back to Kastelli, via the mountainous and well-watered village of Kambos, before arriving in **Sfinari**. It is possible to find a room to let here and stay for a while at this quiet and isolated little farming village and to swim off its narrow and rocky beach. The village is linked by daily bus to Kastelli.

The poor but easily negotiable road south of Vathi holds a couple of splendid sights in store. The first is 11km (7 miles) from Vathi at the gleaming white and ornately decorated Hrissoskalitissa monastery, built on a sparsely vegetated hill overlooking the Libyan Sea.

According to folklore, one of the ninety steps leading up to the entrance is made of gold, hence its name, which translates as 'Lady of the Golden Stair'. Pilgrims flock to the monastery on 15 August for its service of the Assumption of the Virgin Mary. Another 5km (3 miles) south is the tiny islet of **Elafonissi**, just offshore over a sea so shallow that at times it is possible to wade across to its beautiful lagoon of a beach. Despite its location, 73km (45 miles) from Hania, and its almost total lack of facilities, it is becoming quite popular but has so much sand that it is easy to find your own secluded spot. Both Hrissoskalitissa and Elafonissi are linked by direct bus to Kastelli.

Also linked by bus to Kastelli, and to Hania, is **Paleohora** on the southern coast of Crete. In the 1960s this was 'the' place to go among the hippy community, and although its image has now been changed and more tourist development has taken place, it is still young people that are mostly attracted to Paleohora. There are plenty of tavernas and hotels and a free and easy night life, not to mention the broad sands of its beach. Near the beach stands the ruins of a Venetian castle, built in 1279 but destroyed in 1539 by the Turk Barbarossa. Ten kilometres (6 miles) north-east of the town is **Azogyres** village, known for its monastery of Agion Pateron (Holy Fathers) which dates from the thirteenth century. A 45 minute caique journey east of Paleohora leads to the ruins of ancient **Lissos**, an important town up to its destruction by the Saracens in the ninth century. The remains of the baths, the water system and a temple can be seen, mostly dating from around 300BC.

Although a little bit too far off the beaten track for most, the small island of **Gavdos** is where to go if you are looking for almost complete isolation. The southernmost point in Europe, its population is tiny and consists mainly of shepherds — what accommodation the island has is in short supply. Gavdos is a little too rocky to be beautiful but its seclusion makes up for that and the beaches are good. Some claim it to be the true island of Kalypso, the beautiful nymph who held Odysseus captive on his way home from the Trojan War. The island is linked twice-weekly to Paleohora and occasionally to Chorasfakion, east along the coast.

Also connected to Paleohora by sea is **Sougia**, 10km (6 miles) to the east. Despite having a long and attractive pebble beach, this draws far less visitors than its western neighbour while still providing more than adequately for its tourists. One can also visit ancient Lissos from here, a 90 minute walk west. Nearer are the ruins of ancient Sysis; this mingles the remnants of its ancient past — tombs, walls, water cistern — with a sixth-century Byzantine basilica which has a fine mosaic floor. Near Rodovani are the remains of ancient Elyros, a Doric city also laid to waste by the Saracens. North of Sougia, on the Kastelli-Paleohora road, is another sad example of Cretan history in the modern village of Kandanos. Inhabited since Roman times, the old village was bulldozed and blown up by the Germans during World War II as a reprisal for the villagers sheltering members of the Cretan resistance.

Central Crete

All roads in central Crete eventually lead to Iraklion, the crowded capital of the island that lies 5km (3 miles) north of the reconstructed ruins of the Minoan city of Knossos, the seat of the great King Minos. This was the greatest city of ancient Crete and the site, predictably, is well on the beaten track. Yet also important were the finds made at three other cities — Agia Triada, Festos and Gortys — whose ruins lie west of Iraklion near the rapidly developing central southern coast. Sandwiched between these cities and Iraklion is Mount Ida (or Psiloritis), at 1,456m (8,056ft) the highest peak in Crete; its surrounds contain some of the loveliest and least-visited spots on the island. There are no beaches in this region — the nearest are at the resort of Matala, accessible from Festos or Gortys — but it does open up a part of Crete rarely seen by visitors.

After Knossos, **Festos**, 63km (39 miles) south-west of Iraklion and 78kms (48 miles) south-east of Rethimnon, was the most important city of Minoan Crete and maybe even before. Evidence suggests that it was inhabited in the Neolithic Age, approximately 6,000 years ago. The site is beautifully positioned with Mount Ida to the north and sweeping plains to the east, and the Italian archaeologists who ex-cavated it at the turn of the century unearthed the remains of two palaces. One was destroyed in around 1650BC, the other devastated about 1450BC by the same calamity that befell Knossos.

The palace was laid out in a similar fashion to that at Knossos; all ancillary buildings built around a central court from where the king ruled. The scattered and barely identifiable ruins around the site are the remains of the houses of those that lived around the palace, a population believed to be as strong as 50,000 at one time. The sheer age of the site makes it interesting in itself but the ruins are such that one has to let the imagination work overtime to build up a mental picture of how it once was. However, it is possible to recognise the court, an adjacent staircase, the kings' and queens' bedrooms and the water cisterns; the finds from the site can be seen at Iraklion's ar-chaeological museum. Interestingly enough, the kings who ruled

Festos — an important city of Minoan Crete

Festos seemed to be less concerned with grandeur, at least at this palace, than their counterparts at Knossos. The frescoes unearthed here were not of good quality.

By contrast, some of the choicest artefacts on display at the archaeological museum in Iraklion — such as frescoes and the Vase of the Harvesters — were found at **Agia Triada**, only a 45 minute walk away. Also beautifully located, this seems to have been a summer palace for the rulers of Festos. Its importance grew after the second destruction of Festos, whose inhabitants are believed to have fled here. Again, the ruins are a little confusing but one can take time off from exploring Minoan history to visit the site's church of Agios Georgios, built in the fourteenth century with its original frescoes in place. At the edge of the site stands the Byzantine church of Agia Triada, which gave the site its name.

From Festos and Agia Triada the road eastward heads 17km (10 miles) across the Messara Plain to Gortys. It passes through Mires, a small but busy town with a bank, some tavernas and a few rooms to let. Near the site of Gortys is the small but pleasant village of **Agii Deka** (Ten Saints), named after the ten early Christians who were put to death here by the Romans because of their faith. Their tombs lie in the crypt of the village church.

Although **Gortys** has been inhabited since Minoan times — the discovery of a sixteenth-century BC farmhouse here proves this — it cannot strictly be classified as a Minoan city, at least not by the evidence that excavations have revealed so far. Its impressive remains date mostly from the second and third centuries AD, during the Roman occupation when it was the capital and administrative centre of Crete and much of the North African coast. It is a very large site and some important finds were made here, none less so than the Laws of Gortys, inscribed on huge slabs of stone. Originally formulated in the sixth century BC, the Laws indicate a well-ordered society and one strictly divided between freemen and slaves. However, it was one liberal enough to accord slaves a number of rights, such as those to own property and to sue free men. The Laws were spoken well of by men as eminent as Plato, and the Romans are believed to have incorporated them into their rule. The city continued to flourish until its destruction in the ninth century by invading Saracens.

The sites boast a number of relatively well-preserved structures that include the Roman Praetorium, from where the governor ruled, and the Nymphaion, where the worship of the nymphs was conducted. Other temples include one to Apollo and another to the Egyptian divinities. The Odeon still stands, the place where the Laws of Gortys were discovered, as do a number of Roman statues. The first sight to greet the visitor, though, is not Roman but the Byzantine basilica of Agios Titus. Titus, who died at the end of the first century, was the first Bishop of Gortys and, therefore, probably the first bishop in Crete. His basilica, now in ruins, dates from the seventh century and was built to house his tomb. The basilica is among the oldest surviving Christian structures on Crete. From Gortys it is only 12km (7 miles) to Zaros, the base for some excellent off-the-beaten-track walks around the region of Mount Ida.

Zaros is a wonderfully scruffy little village, consisting only of one main street, and has a very special, welcoming atmosphere for visitors. The village is another world, away from the towns and coastal resorts. It is very much a farming community — the farmhands drive by each morning and evening on vehicles that resemble a cross between a lawnmower and a motorised tricycle. Many of the men still wear traditional costume but not for the benefit of tourists, of which there are very few. Traditional crafts are still practised here and there is an icon painter's workshop. However, best of all is a workshop at the top of the village where a craftsman makes those popular Cretan instruments, the lyre and bouzouki, by hand. Beautifully finished, they are real works of art.

Zaros is still one of these villages where visitors — but not tour

Monastery of Agios Nikolaos with the towering Ida Mountains in the background (ch1)

Whitewashed houses on the seafront at Chorasfakion (ch1)

The Byzantine basilica of
Agios Titus at the ancient
site of Gortys (ch1)

A horse is sometimes
more useful than a car
when negotiating the
rough terrain of Crete
(ch1)

Statues from the impressive ruins at Gortys

groups — are beckoned in off the street to sample some traditional Cretan hospitality, usually in the form of homemade *raki*, that bitterly strong drink made from the skin of grapes. Zaros is gradually becoming known to tour groups — mainly because of the presence of the fine Hotel Idi, 1km ($^1/_2$ mile) up the road which holds regular 'Cretan dance evenings' — but still remains untouched by tourism. There are no hotels apart from the Idi, but ask at one of the cafés for help and the owner will point out a house at the top of the village that rents out basic but acceptable rooms at reasonable prices. There are no tavernas either; one must either buy provisions at the village shop or eat at the Hotel Idi or its adjacent taverna, which has a large trout farm attached to it. The area around Zaros offers some wonderful walks.

A rewarding and not particularly tiring walk from Zaros is to negotiate the Zaros (or Rouves) Gorge; steep, quiet and incredibly spectacular in parts. Take the road up to the Hotel Idi and bear left along the asphalt until an attractive artificial lake is reached and a sign points out the path to the monasteries of Agios Nikolaos and Agios Ioannis. Follow the signs up a shady goat path until, after 15 minutes, Agios Nikolaos is reached at the head of the gorge. The friendly monks are happy to show those appropriately dressed — with arms and legs covered — around the small and atmospheric chapel. Notice the crutches and spectacles hanging from the icon of Agios Nikolaos; these were placed there by those faithful enough to discard them after praying to the saint to be cured. After the visit to the chapel it is usual for guests to be served *paximathi* (a rusky type of molar-shattering bread, peculiar to Crete) and a glass of the monks' excellent homemade red wine.

Go through the monastery to pick up a signposted path leading steadily uphill. As you climb, wooden handrails provide assistance. Soon you are in the heart of the gorge; this is green and lush, dominated by rocky cliffs at its flanks and with huge misplaced boulders lying on its bed. After $1^1/_2$ hours some stone picnic tables are reached. Eventually the walk ends at the dry river bed; continue along the path of the river to the monastery of Agios Ioannis before returning to Zaros. In total, the round-trip from Zaros to Agios Ioannis and back again takes roughly 6 hours.

Another two fine, old monasteries can be visited from Zaros, either by car or by another easy walk, along the base of Mount Ida to the north. Head west out of Zaros on the Kamares road, bear right after 3km (2 miles) and one more kilometre ($^1/_2$ mile) leads to the monastery of Vrondissi. This is beautifully located among green hills and

Beautifully hand-crafted instruments at a workshop in Zaros

has a fifteenth-century water fountain at its entrance. The monastery contains fine frescoes, which are claimed to be the work of the great El Greco.

Back on the Kamares road, continue 4km ($2^1/_2$ miles) to **Vorizia**, a small greystone village where you must ask for the key (try the village café) to the now abandoned monastery of Varsamonerou. Its church, Agios Fanourios, retains its original fifteenth-century frescoes. **Kamares** village is another 3km (2 miles) from Vorizia and a steep 4 hour climb from the village up the flanks of Mount Ida leads to the Kamares Cave, a sacred site during the Minoan era. The Kamares vases, now displayed in the archaeological museum in Iraklion, were discovered here.

It is possible to continue past the Kamares Cave and up to the peak of Mount Ida, at the top of Crete, but it is another 6 hours trekking and should only really be attempted by the serious hiker. An easier route is from Anogia on the other side of the mountain, 41km (25 miles) from Iraklion. A 3 hour walk leads to the foot of the mountain and another 5 hours, tough in parts, takes you to the summit. Near the foot of the mountains you can visit the Ideon Cave, with the Dikteon Cave on the Lassithi Plain to the east, one of the contenders for the birthplace of Zeus. Once used as an ancient place of worship, the finds from the cave are on show at Iraklion's archaeological museum.

Anogia itself is a sad but busy village — it draws tour buses, which stop to allow tourists to view the woollen handicraft shops for which it is known. There are more women than men in Anogia; in 1943 the Germans sacked the town and murdered much of its male population in revenge for the Allied kidnapping of the German commander on Crete, General Von Kreipe. The town has been bravely rebuilt in its traditional style. Thirteen kilometres (8 miles) west of Anogia, near Zoniana, is the Cave of Sentoni. Huge and beautiful sheets of stalactites and stalagmites can be seen here.

Further Information
— Western and Central Crete —

Agia Triada
Site open: Monday to Saturday 9am-3pm.
☎ 081 226092

Festos
Site open: 8am-5pm.
Closed Sundays.
☎ 0892 22615

Gortys
Site open: Monday to Saturday 9am-3pm, Sunday 9.30am-2.30pm.
☎ 081 226092

Hania
Archaeological Museum
Open: daily 8am-7pm. Monday 12.30-5pm, weekends 8.30am-3pm.
☎ 0821 20334

Historical Museum
Open: Monday to Friday 9.30am-1.30pm, 3-5.30pm.

Naval Museum
Open: daily 10am-2pm.
Closed Mondays.

Tourist/Information Office
The harbour
Open: March to October, Monday to Saturday 8.30am-8.30pm.
☎ 0821 43300

Tourist Office
40 Kriari Street
'Pantheo' building
☎ 0821 26426

Samaria Gorge
Kallergi Refuge Hut
☎ (0821) 24647

2 • Southern Peloponnese

Introduction

For a holiday that combines absolutely everything — wonderful beaches, fascinating ancient and medieval archaeological sites, outstanding landscapes and a fine, warm climate — look no further than the southern Peloponnese. This area is packed with attractions and there is something delightful to see, whether natural or man-made, almost everywhere the visitor goes.

Those who wish to just stretch out and relax have a wide choice before them; tiny mountain villages and pretty coastal towns; beach resorts with all the necessary facilities and quiet, secluded little coves which are rarely visited. The southern Peloponnese still belongs very much to the Greeks and what tourist development there is is very discreet. This beautiful region is certainly well off the beaten track.

All roads in the southern Peloponnese lead to its large, sprawling and earthquake-ruined capital Kalamata which, if one first arrives in the region at its airport or railway station, is a rather poor introduction to the area. Yet west of Kalamata are the fine medieval castles at the towns of Methoni, Koroni and Pylos, all of which have long sandy beaches in the town or nearby, and just north of these are the remains of the palace of the great King Nestor who features so heavily in the works of Homer. Further north again is the attractive little beach resort of Kiparissia, also with a medieval castle. Beyond that, moving north and then south again back to Kalamata, the lovely mountain villages of Andritsena and Karitena and the archaeological sites of ancient Bassae, Megalopolis and Messini are reached. East of Kalamata is Sparta, home of the fearsome Spartans of old, and with the remarkable ruins of Mystra — a Byzantine city, excavated in its entirety — only 6km (4 miles) away.

South of Sparta is the charming, attractive port of Gythion and that arid, barren area known as the Mani, which occupies the central prong of the southern Peloponnese's three peninsulas, and which could lay a good claim to being the most eerie and forbidding area in

Greece. A visit there makes for a marvellous day-trip. Further east is another medieval town — Monemvassia, built on a huge rock off-shore and cunningly hidden from the mainland. Finally there is the island of Kythera, visited by only a handful of people and with some fine, quiet beaches.

It is not recognised as such, but the Peloponnese is actually an island and has been so since the 1890s when Greek engineers finally completed the cutting of the Corinth Canal and brought to a close a project started by the Roman Emperor Nero. The new canal shortens the sea route to Pireaus from Europe considerably. Bridged by rail and road, it is a remarkable sight as one crosses it, particularly if a ship is squeezing its way through the 30m (100ft) gap. Across the canal, the land is mountainous and beautifully lush, criss-crossed by rivers and streams and is the perfect breeding ground for thousands of varieties of wild flowers such as orchids and crocuses. The southern Peloponnese is particularly beautiful, dominated by the towering, dramatic peak of Mount Taigetos, which is flanked by plains filled with trees full of citrus fruits, one of the main sources of income in the area. The coastline of the south is immediately distinctive, marked out by three large peninsulas thrusting south out of the main body of the region. Two of the peninsulas are fertile and green; the middle one — the Mani — is a virtual desert. In terms of administrative districts, two counties cover the southern Peloponnese; Messinia, which is the area west of Kalamata; and the much larger Laconia to the east.

The quickest way into the southern Peloponnese is on one of the daily flights from Athens to Kalamata, flight-time being a blink-and-you-miss-it 20 minutes. For most people, though, it is a case of crossing the Corinth Canal either by road, where one can be in Sparta 6 hours after leaving Athens, or by the slow trains which link Athens to Kalamata via Corinth, Mycenae, Argos and Tripoli.

There are several points of entry from the sea. From Pireaus a twice-weekly sailing goes to Kastelli on western Crete via the southern Peloponnesian ports of Monemvassia, Neapolis, the island of Kythera, Gythion, Kythera again and Antikythera. Hydrofoils from Pireaus put in at several of the Saronic Gulf islands before docking at Leonidio. Those arriving at Patras, the major port of the Peloponnese and at its north-western tip, can reach the south by either direct train to Kiparissia or by road. Anyone entering the Peloponnese from Epirus and the west of Greece can circumvent the long trip around the Gulf of Corinth by taking the very regular ferry from Antirrio across the Gulf of Patras to Rio, just north of Patras.

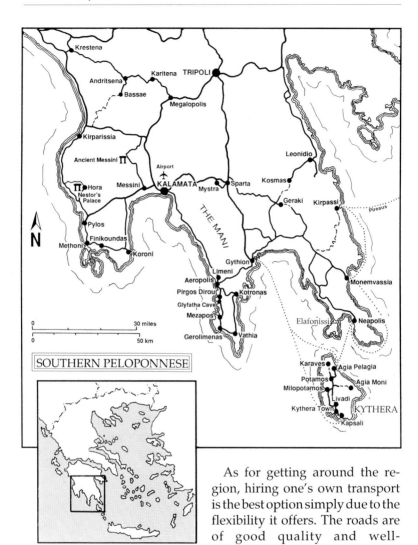

SOUTHERN PELOPONNESE

As for getting around the region, hiring one's own transport is the best option simply due to the flexibility it offers. The roads are of good quality and well-signposted. Yet those unwilling or unable to hire a car or powerful motorbike should have few difficulties seeing the southern Peloponnese. The rail service is far less extensive here than in the north but one can still travel between Kiparissia and Megalopolis via Kalamata. The really easy way to travel, though, is by bus. All of the major towns are connected with services of reasonable frequency and local buses seem to take in most places even if their services are limited to one or two a day. Hitchhiking, as with elsewhere in Greece, is poor between towns but excellent in the quiet, rural areas.

While travelling in the southern Peloponnese you may want to consider a few excursions to the north of the region to some of the finest archaeological sites in Greece, sites which are on the beaten track but still marvellous to see while you are in the area. In the north-west there are the ruins of ancient Olympia, the home of the Olympic Games and with an excellent museum. Clustered together in the north-east are three of the country's best-known sites. The superbly-preserved third-century BC theatre at Epidavros is so acoustically perfect that one can hear a whisper fifty-five rows back. Then there are the fascinating remains of the great city-state of Corinth, crowned by the medieval ruins on top of the Acrocorinth, which gazes out over the gulf. Finally, one can explore the remains of Mycenae, the capital of that great empire of around 1400 BC. This is where Schliemann discovered the gold death-mask then believed to be that of the great King Agamemnon. It is now one of the great prizes of the national archaeological museum in Athens. Known as the 'Mask of Agamemnon' it actually pre-dates this twelfth-century BC Mycenaean ruler by several centuries.

These four great archaeological sites — and there are many more scattered across the region — show the Peloponnese to be the birth-place of Ancient Greece, a period recorded from the ninth century BC onwards. The two greatest city-states of the day were at Corinth, a prosperous and hedonistic city and thus rebuked by the Apostle Paul in his Letter to the Corinthians; and Sparta, the terror of the area. It was the Spartans who lived under a self-imposed and extremely harsh regime of denial and discipline. They eventually gained dominance over Ancient Greece by defeating their rivals the Athenians in 404BC, a victory which brought the 27 year Peloponnesian Wars to a close. Within 60 years, however, the Macedonians of Philip the Second had over-run the region.

The Byzantines were slow to establish themselves in the Peloponnese and did not really assume control of the area until the ninth century AD; the preceding centuries had been anarchic, and marked by raid after raid from the Goths and others. The Venetians also showed an interest in the area, particularly because of the trade routes that its ports opened up, and founded Monemvassia and Pylos.

Then the Franks arrived. For the most part these were Crusaders en-route to the Holy Land who, after the sacking of Constantinople in 1204, conveniently forgot their holy pledge to liberate the holy sites from the infidel and decided to settle down in Greece. Within a very short period of time the Teutonic Knights had captured great chunks of the Peloponnese and divided it up amongst themselves. Thus the Peloponnese become as medieval as any part of northern Europe; full of knights clinking goblets in their grand turreted castles and taking part in jousting competitions in the surrounding fields. However, the Byzantines returned, defeating many of the Frankish princes and re-establishing themselves at centres such as Mystra. By 1460, though, the Turks had occupied the region and the Peloponnese fell into a decline that was only reversed in 1821 when the Greek War of Independence was declared here.

During the war the Egyptian vassal of the Turkish Sultan, Ibrahim Pasha, held most of the land and committed the most terrible atrocities, including genocide and slavery. Yet the war was won in the Peloponnese as the ships of the Great Powers turned their cannons on a combined Turkish-Egyptian fleet in Navarino Bay near Pylos in 1827 and effectively brought Ottoman sea-power to an end.

During World War II the Germans razed whole villages to the ground as part of reprisals for assisting the Greek resistance. In more recent years the Peloponnese has been the victim of earthquakes — at Corinth and at Kalamata in 1986.

The Messinia

Kalamata is the capital of the prefecture of Messinia. In 1986, a large earthquake shattered the city, killing 20, leaving over 10,000 homeless and turning many of its buildings into rubble. Kalamata is only just beginning its recovery.

The city is centred around the main square of Platia Georgios, home to most of the tourist amenities, and connected to the sea by the very long and straight Aristomenous Street that leads up to the busy port and a dirty beach. It is possible to swim here but, with so many better beaches along the Peloponnesian coastline, it is advisable to leave the swimsuit in the suitcase for the time being. Adjacent to the port, one block back, is a factory belonging to the American jeans company Levi's and its outlet store sells jeans and jackets at discount prices. It is around this area that accommodation is easiest found, but expect it to be of the basic variety. Many of the hotels around the town centre are still closed.

Back in the main town, visit the church of Agii Apostoli; a Byzantine structure of the thirteenth century, and scene of perhaps Kalamata's proudest moment. On 23 March, 1821, the Greek War of Liberation against their Turkish occupiers was formally announced here. Three blocks south of the church was once the site of the city's excellent Benaki museum. Since the earthquake, the exhibits have been moved to Sparta for safety's sake. No information is available on when it will re-open.

Like so many other towns in this region of Greece, Kalamata is dominated by the remains of a medieval castle, open to the public and fun to stroll around enjoying the ruins and the view. Originally the site of the acropolis of *Phara*, as the city was known in ancient times, the castle was completed in 1208 by the Frankish Crusader, Geoffrey de Villehardouin. It lasted until its demolition by first the Turks, then the Venetians in the late seventeenth century. A theatre has recently been built within the castle walls, to host concerts and plays. They mainly take place during the summer months of July and August.

From Kalamata is an excursion to the fine archaeological site of ancient **Messini** — not to be confused with new Messini, 5km (3 miles) west of Kalamata. The ancient city is only a 44km (27 miles) round-trip away. Without your own transport, though, getting there can be a problem. Only two buses daily make the journey from Kalamata to the nearby town of Mavromati and both turn around and come straight back again. Nevertheless, a visit is a worthwhile experience to see a tremendous example of an ancient city built with defence almost solely in mind as protection from the powerful and marauding Spartans. It was constructed on Mount Ithomi in 376BC. Parts of the city wall — which excavations have shown to be a full 9km (5 miles) in circumference — are still wonderfully intact, as is the Arcadia Gate, through which invaders would attempt to batter their way into the city. A footpath leading down from the site arrives at a sanctuary to Asclepius, god of healing. A tough uphill climb from Arcadia Gate leads to the peak of Mount Ithomi and the convent of Vourkano, built in the sixteenth century. Nuns are happy to show visitors around the chapel where they can view its colourful frescoes.

The road south to the tip of the Messinian peninsula is 51km (31 miles) long and passes beach after beach; all of them sandy, many of them secluded and most patronised solely by Greeks. The village of **Petalidi** claims to have the best and also has a few campsites where one can stay overnight. It is only a matter of time before developers begin to snap up the land around the coastline but, for now, it is easy to find your own strip of sand.

Koroni, on the eastern end of the peninsula, is a little more developed while easily avoiding the excesses of tourism. Its beach, Zanga, is seemingly endless and the attractively laid-out town is one of the prettiest in the region. In medieval times it was also one of the most important. For Koroni, along with Methoni on the western side of the peninsula, formed one of the 'twin eyes of Venice', thanks to the huge Venetian castles that crown both towns' entrances from the sea. Koroni castle is open to visitors but now its role seems to be more spiritual than militaristic. The convent of Prodromos lies inside and on its slopes stands the church of Panagia Elestria. Flowers and shrubs sprout everywhere, giving the definite impression that it is a castle with a difference. As is to be expected, the views from the ramparts are superb.

To reach the other 'eye of Venice', at Methoni, travel due west for 34km (21 miles) across a landscape filled with olive trees and via the village of **Finikoundas**. Unfortunately, getting there by public transport is a real nuisance. There is no bus service to cover the 18km (11 miles) journey between Koroni and Finikoundas and you have to make the expensive trip back up to Kalamata from where you can catch a connection to Methoni, via Pylos. You can avoid this by taking a taxi from Koroni to Finikoundas and picking up the Methoni bus from there. The service is limited to only two or three a day but those who miss the connection should not worry. Finikoundas has plenty of rooms to let (but no hotels) and is an utterly charming little fishing village, sited on a slight hill that descends to a gorgeous, half-moon beach. There is not much to do here; it is just the perfect place to relax.

Methoni and Koroni certainly have their similarities. Both are small and attractive towns with a small degree of tourist development (Methoni a little more); both are surrounded by large fields full of twisted olive trees; both have lovely sandy beaches; and both have medieval castles. While Koroni may have the better beach, **Methoni** undoubtedly has the more impressive castle. It stands almost on the beach itself but on its own little island, separated from the town by a huge moat. Entry is via a bridge, rebuilt in 1828, that leads through three gateways into the heart of the castle. In this large, empty area, an entire town once bustled. Parts of the Turkish baths remain, as does a Venetian church, and the Venetian symbol — the Lion of St Mark — can be seen engraved in many places.

Once called *Modon*, Methoni fell to the Venetians in 1125 who used it as a resting point for ships en-route to the sites and trading centres of the Holy Land. In 1500 it was conquered by the Ottomans and the last Venetian soldiers were slaughtered on the small islet at the end of a causeway to the south. There is plenty of accommodation in Methoni, with a few hotels, (mostly 'C' and 'D' grade), rooms to let and a campsite.

Pylos 9km (5 miles) north of Methoni and serviced by regular buses, is arguably one of the most beautiful towns in the southern Peloponnese. Its houses are built steeply on a hill that overlooks a quaint harbour filled with small, bobbing boats and hemmed in by the long and thin islet of Sfakteria, just offshore. The town is centred around a large and leafy *platia* next to the harbour and is sandwiched between two medieval castles. There is no beach although swimming is possible off the rocks (note that the water is very deep and totally unsuitable for children) but only 6km (4 miles) away are the marvellous sands of Navarino beach, to the north of the town.

Pylos' past goes back a long way. First mentioned by Homer in *The Odyssey*, this was the 'sandy Pylos' to which Telemachus travelled to seek out the wise King Nestor who would possibly know of his father's whereabouts. The first known battle fought here was in 425 BC when the Athenians defeated the Spartans after having trapped them between the shore and Sfakteria islet. As sea power became more important for nations, so did Pylos whose very deep, natural harbour proved irresistible for the Venetians. They defended the port by building two castles either side of it.

Just off the coast of Pylos, at Navarino Bay in October 1827, one of the most important battles of the Greek War of Liberation was fought and won, without the Greeks themselves even firing a shot. The superpowers of Britain, France and Russia were tired of the 6 year long war in Greece and outraged by the dreadful atrocities being committed in the Peloponnese by Ibrahim Pasha, an Egyptian vassal of the Turkish Sultan. Their ships sailed into Navarino Bay in the hope that this show of strength would force the Turks to grant autonomy to Greece in accordance with the Treaty of London, signed in July of that year by the three powers. Twenty-six warships lined up against the ninety-strong Turkish/Egyptian fleet. The superpowers sent over a small boat to negotiate, an Egyptian ship unleashed its cannon upon it and, by the morning, the Turkish/Egyptian fleet was no more. Greece gained independence within 12 months of the battle. A monument to the battle, in the form of two great cannons, stands proudly in the main square of Pylos.

The Venetian castles of Pylos serve as the town's main tourist attraction. The Paleokastro is a fairly dilapidated affair, 6km (4 miles) away at the end of the bay and is rarely visited. The other, Neokastro, is mostly intact and is only a 5 minute walk away from the main square. It cannot be seen from the town as it is totally concealed by towering pine trees. It is in excellent condition; within its fortified walls one can see a well-preserved mosque that was once a Venetian church, a citadel and a courtyard full of dungeons, each divided into

Boats in the harbour at Pylos

individual cells. The castle actually served as a prison up to the twentieth century. A museum is being planned which will be situated just inside the main square and will house a small selection of archaeological finds from the area.

When Telemachus, son of Odysseus, landed at Pylos in search of King Nestor, he had only to travel 13km (8 miles) north before reaching the great king's palace. The remains of the palace were only discovered in 1939, positioned on a lush hill overlooking the sea, and are believed to date from 1200BC. The ruins are sheltered from the elements under a rather inappropriate plastic roof and although they seem a little disappointing at first glance, they improve upon closer inspection. Each room is clearly labelled, from the throne room to the bathroom, allowing one to build up a good mental picture of its former size and grandeur. In the palace bathroom the thirty-two centuries-old bath tub has been left in place. Behind the palace stands a large Mycenaean tholos tomb, shaped like a giant, inverted beehive.

If possible, try to visit the museum in the town of **Hora**, 3km (2 miles) north of Nestor's Palace, before visiting the palace itself. Located at the far end of town, the museum displays finds from the site as well as a model reconstruction of the palace, giving an even better picture of how it once was. The artefacts on display include mosaics; beautifully handcrafted gold cups and some massive sarcophagi. However, pride of place goes to the Linear 'B' tablets (a script pre-dating Greek). These were the first ever discovered on the Greek mainland and thus show the site's linkage with the other great civilisations of the age — the Minoans and the Mycenaeans.

Like so many routes in this region, the 67km (41 miles) road from Pylos to Kiparissia is a lovely one with tiny coastal villages to the left and green fields and orange trees to the right. It is just as pleasant a journey from Hora from where its length is shortened to 42km (26 miles). There are plenty of places to break the journey, the most attractive being the small town of **Filiatra**, crammed with palm trees and with an ornate fountain in its main square. At the southern end of the town there is even a miniature Eiffel Tower. **Christiano**, 13km (8 miles) inland, is worth a detour should you wish to see an eleventh-century Byzantine church; and **Marathopolis**, 27km (17 miles) from Pylos, is a pleasant little town with little tourist development and a splendid rocky beach.

Kiparissia may not seem much at first glance but a stroll around will reveal a charming little town with a great deal going for it. In season, its main attraction is a 10 minute walk down from the town at the beach, an endless series of sandy coves that spread their way enticingly around the bay. Yet, despite this, the town makes few concessions to tourism. The shops cater solely for the locals and there are only a couple of pensions and a few rooms to let.

A very pleasant way to pass an hour here is to wander through the narrow streets of the residential area, climbing steadily past small houses with gardens full of flowers, and the gaily-frescoed church of Agios Antonio, to the Byzantine-Frankish castle that overlooks the bay. Be careful not to trip while wandering the ruins of this structure; the huge cacti below have a distinctly menacing look. Note that the rail tracks that circuit the Peloponnese begin at Kiparissia and services operate to the major Peloponnesian centres of Tripoli, Pirgos, Patras, Corinth and, of course, Athens.

North-east of Kiparissia, standing grandly alone on Mount Paliavlakitsa, are the ruins of ancient Bassae, a vastly under-rated archaeological site and one largely ignored by the majority of tourists, most of whom are intent on making the rush north to ancient Olympia. Getting there from Kiparissia, however, does involve some effort, particularly if using public transport. You can take a train or bus to Megalopolis and from there pick up one of the twice daily buses to Andritsena, a lovely town near Bassae; this is a 102km (63 mile) journey. Alternatively, make the train/bus journey due north to Krestena where you can pick up the Pirgos bus to Andritsena; a 93km (58 mile) trip. As the latter route continues down through Megalopolis, it is the better option and there is the added bonus of a detour to ancient Olympia, only 12km (7 miles) from Krestena. Drivers have the choice of a rough and unsurfaced road that travels the 56km (35 miles) to Bassae via the sorry remains of ancient Figalia, or a better road, 60km (37 miles) long, that runs north up the coastline to Tholo and bears right there.

To reach Bassae from Andritsena take the signposted road south out of the city and climb steadily along a precarious mountain ridge for 14km (9 miles). Note that no buses make the journey, visitors without a car will have to take a taxi. As the road ascends, the panorama reveals a remote, mountainous wilderness that becomes even more apparent when Bassae is finally reached. This is over 1,100m (3,600ft) above sea-level, and the ruins of the town can be seen spread out across the plateau. What immediately catches the eye, though, is the temple. Dedicated to Apollo Epicurus, this is the largest and one of the best-preserved ancient temples ever found in Greece. It was built as a mark of gratitude to the god Apollo by the people of nearby Figalia in return for their being saved from a dreadful plague that swept the region around 425BC. Although its current encasement in scaffolding for restoration purposes does tend to detract from its grandeur, it is still an impressive sight. It is believed that the architect was Iktinos, who went on to build a similar, smaller structure in Athens — the Parthenon.

Andritsena itself is a jumbled but very attractive mountain town with stone houses flanking the twisted streets and a stream that runs down to its plane-tree dominated, main square. It is a pleasant place to wander around, possibly visiting the small folk museum, and if you want to stay the night, there are two hotels and plenty of restaurants in the square. However, for a real treat of a town, head 28km (17 miles) south-east on the Megalopolis road for **Karitena**, now just a small town but in medieval times the most important in the region. Its medieval aura is still tangible today.

Strategically, Karitena was the ideal capital for Hugh de Bruyeres when he made the region his barony in 1209. It stands high on its own hill dominating the area. The new baron's first act was to construct a castle at the summit of a huge rock above the town. The castle took 45 years to complete and its remains testify to its sturdiness. The path leading up to it begins in the town centre. Down in the town, two Byzantine churches can be visited; the eleventh-century Panagia and the thirteenth-century Agios Nikolaos — if the latter is locked, ask in the nearby café for the key. From Agios Nikolaos follow the path down to the Frankish bridge that spans the river Lousios — it is this bridge that is depicted on a 5,000 drachma note.

Megalopolis, 16km (10 miles) from Karitena, has little to offer apart from good bus and train connections and a huge power station. However, it dates back 24 centuries and its original site, 2km (1 mile) out of the city on the Andritsena road, is a good place to visit. Its builder, the Theban leader Epaminondas, had ambitious plans for Megalopolis (its name means great city) and it became the capital of Arcadia, although continual Spartan attacks led to its abandonment only 2 centuries later. The prize of the ruins is the ancient theatre, one of the largest ever discovered in Greece, and originally built to seat 20,000 spectators. One of the reasons for visiting the site is that you will probably enjoy it alone.

There is a choice of routes out of Megalopolis, including a rather slow but direct route to Sparta through a series of small villages. The route outlined here, though, leads 56km (35 miles) due south along the E92 back to Kalamata, thus opening up the way to Sparta or the barren wilderness of the second peninsula of the Peloponnese — the Mani.

Laconia

Sparta is the capital of Laconia and the 2 hour, 60km (37 mile) journey there from Kalamata is exhilarating, cutting through the great barrier of Mount Taigetos via the Langada Pass and twisting under great clumps of overhanging rock. Twice-daily buses make the trip from Kalamata; at the half-way point of Artemissa the long bus is swapped for a shorter one for easier manoeuvrability. Mount Taigetos, which marks the end of the E4 walking trail that begins in the Spanish Pyrenees, is climbable — but only by experienced hikers with good maps, correct provisions and equipment, and a few days to spare. It is certainly not for the casual stroller.

One would expect the city of **Sparta**, the terror of the democratic city-states of ancient times, to be brimming over with the remains of great buildings that denote its past glory. Unfortunately, this is not the case. The culture of the dour and austere Spartans dismissed grand structures as mere frippery and led them instead to concentrate their efforts on producing a race of almost superhuman warriors, indifferent to pain and suffering and capable of withstanding all hardships. This was the city that 'exposed' sickly babies (left them outside to die) and the city that thrashed their young men mercilessly so that they could prove their courage in public as they came into

*Monemvassia with its forti-
fied sea wall, as seen from
the castle (ch2)*

*A ruined tower, epitomising the
starkness of the Mani (ch2)*

At anchor in Zante town's bay (ch3)

Fishing boats moored in the harbour at Sami, Cephalonia (ch3)

*Statue of the fearsome
Leonidas, Sparta*

manhood. No great philosophers came out of Sparta, just great warriors. Nevertheless, they were successful. Their eventual defeat of mighty Athens in the 27 year Peloponnesian War gave them the control of the entire region, although factional infighting eventually led them to withdraw. Sparta fell in the third century BC to Phillip the Second's Macedonians and the city never regained its former infamous glory, becoming rather as it is today — a pleasant little town with nothing particularly distinctive about it.

The new town of Sparta was constructed in 1834 and lies in the centre of a large citrus-fruit growing region; indeed, orange trees sprout colourfully all around the town. The archaeological museum is small but interesting and provides a good insight into the Spartan way of life. The fiercely imposing statue of Leonidas, complete with plumed helmet and shield, stands at the end of the road where the bus station is located. A short walk up the road to Tripoli leads to the sanctuary of Artemis Orthia, where young men underwent their ritual flogging. Behind the statue of Leonidas, excavations on what is believed to be the site of ancient Sparta are taking place. Although discoveries to date number only parts of an ancient theatre and a Byzantine wall, one of the archaeologists claims that it 'may be something special in 30 years'. However, what is something special today, is Mystra, 5km (3 miles) away and the reason most people visit Sparta.

Mystra is simply the excavated remains of an entire Byzantine city. Many claim that it is one of the finest sights in the entire Peloponnese as, unlike the ruins of the cities of Ancient Greece, the visitor has no need to build up an imaginary mental picture to visualise the city as it was. Its churches, mansions, palace and castle stand pretty much as they did centuries ago. Mystra is only 5km (3 miles) west of Sparta and it is a simple matter to get there — take a taxi or one of the regular buses that leave Sparta from the bus stop two blocks past the central square towards the Mystra road, not from the bus station. The buses go past the village of Nea (new) Mystra — there is nothing here except for a couple of cafés and a few tourist shops — and continues for another 1km ($^1/_2$ mile) up to the main entrance. Be sure to bring a good supply of water, the heat here can be blistering.

The founder of Mystra was not a Byzantine prince or emperor but a Frankish Crusader, William de Villehardouin, whose predecessor, Geoffrey, had carved out a principality for himself in Laconia and needed strongholds to defend it. The hill of Mystra was the perfect spot for such a fortification, separated from Mount Taigetos but still in a high, commanding position. Work began on a castle at the summit and was completed in 1249. The hill was named 'Myzethra' — after its resemblance to a popular cheese of that name. Unfortunately for William, though, he was only to hold Mystra for 10 years. In the furious battle of Pelagonia (in modern-day Yugoslavia), his Frankish forces were defeated by a Byzantine army under Emperor Michael Palailogos and William himself was taken captive; his ransom price was his castles — including Mystra — and the hapless Crusader had no choice but to acquiesce. Mystra became a Byzantine city. William did manage to rally his forces after his release and scored a few notable victories over the Byzantines but Mystra eluded him. During this time, many of the residents of *Lacedaemonia* (Sparta) began to move on to the hill below the castle for added protection. Mystra grew into a city, Frankish power died with William in 1278 and the city began to flourish.

Mystra was quick to put itself on the map. Fine churches were erected at lightning speed, attracting prominent theologians and, in

The well preserved remains of the Byzantine city of Mystra

due course, philosophers such as Plethon whose work put Plato into the fore of modern philosophy. It became a despotate, capital of its own principality, in 1348 and more churches and buildings were added to the city in accordance with its new status. Several of the despots of Mystra went on to become Byzantine Emperors, including possibly one of the greatest, Constantine XI. Its grandeur and culture soon led the city to be known as the 'Florence of the East', but the Turkish capture of Constantinople in 1453 sealed the Byzantine Mystra's fate. The Turkish occupation of the city began 7 years later.

Nevertheless, Mystra prospered under the Turks and its population apparently grew. It did even better between 1685 and 1715 when the Venetians occupied the city and the surrounding area. In 1715 the Turks reoccupied Mystra, only to lose it again (albeit briefly) to a combined Russo-Greek force. The citizens of Mystra rose in the rebellion of 1821, but were massacred in 1825 by the man who ravaged the entire southern Pelopennese — Ibrahim Pasha. Pasha sacked and burned Mystra and it was never to be occupied to any significant degree again, particularly after new Sparta was founded in 1834.

Spread out across the entire hill, the ruins of Mystra are extensive. Unfortunately, they are not very clearly marked and there can be confusion as to what building you are actually looking at, a confusion added to by the twisting, steep network of paths and alleyways that make it all too easy to lose track of where you are. So just stroll around at leisure without any specific route in mind; by regular reference to the map on sale at the site, all the buildings can be seen. It is the churches of Mystra that immediately catch the eye. Many are surprisingly intact and their sandy stone walls and multi-domed, tiled roofs appear in almost every section of the city. Most display wonderful frescoes on their walls but none more so than the monastery of Perivleptos where the fourteenth-century wall-paintings plaster almost every inch of its interior. They were cleaned in 1962 and so are particularly bright. Christ (Pantocrator) gazes down from the dome upon such illustrations as those of the Descent into Hell, the Incredulity of Thomas, and the Entry into Jerusalem.

Other fine frescoes can be seen at the convent of Pantanassa, constructed in 1428 and still in operation today. The portrayal of the Rising of Lazarus deserves particular attention. The Mitropolis (cathedral) of Agios Dimitrios dates from 1309 and, complete with belfry, is a very impressive structure. When you enter the narthex, take a look at its representations of the Second Coming. A small museum is attached to the building. Those who are thirsty should make a bee-line for Agios Dimitrios as there is a refreshing drinking fountain in the courtyard.

As you climb through the city towards the castle, you will almost certainly come to a huge empty shell of a building; this was the Palace of the Despots. The centre of the pomp and ceremony as well as the administration of Mystra, its former splendour can still be easily envisaged. The nearby church of Agia Sophia served as the palace chapel; the remains of a mosque at the foot of the hill performed a similar function for the Turks. Try to take a look at some of the mansions owned by the former worthies of Mystra — the Lascaris and the Frangopoulos abodes are the most noteworthy — yet these, like most of the mansions, are in a sorry state. The most visible sight in Mystra, though, is the castle built by William de Villehardouin. It is a tough climb up there — one best attempted in the early morning — but there are sensational views to be had; Mystra down below, Mount Taigetos and the plain of Sparta covered in olive and citrus trees and with the river Eurotes flowing across it. It is a peaceful panorama. Mystra as a whole is a site that can be viewed in peace; one of the nicest things about it is that it is large enough to be able to escape from tourist guides and their groups.

Gythion, 46km (28 miles) south of Sparta, is a bright and breezy port that merits a stopover at the very least. In ancient times it was the base for the Spartan fleet. Its houses are built around a maze of

Part of the old fortifications in Gythion

narrow alleyways. They descend sharply to a long and colourful waterfront which stretches from the town hall to the concrete causeway that links the offshore islet of Marathonissi to the mainland. At the busy harbour, women gut fish on the stone steps and fishermen mend their nets. The mountains of Sparta loom to the north. It is a very pleasant setting.

The waterfront has several hotels and signs for 'rooms to let', as well as a host of tavernas specialising in fish dishes. Find time to take a peek at the old antiques shop near the harbour, a real great-grandfather's attic of relics. As for other attractions, one can begin by wandering over to the town hall where Gythion's brand new archaeological museum is to be found. Its exhibits, all found in the area, look very impressive but, to date, are infuriatingly unmarked. A 5 minute walk through the town from here leads to a very well-preserved Roman theatre. Now next to an army barracks, it stands at the end of the appropriately but unimaginatively named 'Ancient Theatre' street.

Marathonissi, or *Cranae* as it was known in ancient times, is also worth visiting; it is possible to swim off the rocks from the end of the islet. In the centre is the Tzanetakos tower, built in the eighteenth century by the Turks as a look-out post against raiders from the Mani. The tower has been renovated by the Greek Tourist Office and houses a free museum. Marathonissi is featured in Greek mythology; Paris spent his first night with Helen here before whisking her off to Troy in an act that heralded the start of the 10 year Trojan War. Be aware that Gythion is also the major passenger ferry port of the Southern Peloponnese with twice-weekly connections to Pireaus via Kythera, Neapolis, Monemvassia and Kirparissi, and to Kastelli on western Crete via Kythera and Antikythera.

Gythion serves as one of the gateways to the Mani, and the largest town of this moody, forbidding yet exciting region is only 26km (16 miles) to the south-west, at Areopolis, on a route that passes the ruined thirteenth-century Frankish castle of Passava. It is from Aeropolis that the loop around the Mani peninsula is best begun. The town can also be reached from Kalamata along 82km (51 miles) of fantastic coastal and mountain road with superb panoramas. Initially running down the western side of Mount Taigetos, it passes the beach at the village of Almiro before climbing up into the mountains and then descending again to Kardamili whose long pebble beach has made it something of a small coastal resort.

Stoupa, just down the coast, has sandy beaches and caters well for visitors. Another good beach can be found at the next village, Agios Nikolaos. From here the road once again cuts inland over mountains before heading back to the coast and passing Kelefa castle, built by the Turks almost adjacent to the Passava castle on the other side of the peninsula. **Itilo**, once capital of the Mani, is the large village reached after the castle. Five kilometres (3 miles) north of Aeropolis is **Limeni**, a small fishing village built in a huge natural bay beneath the high rocky hills. It is a very quiet and secluded place where one can swim off the rocks. At the far end of the headland is a tiny, white fisherman's chapel with fading frescoes that depict the last days of Christ.

The Mani

'Pretty' and 'charming' are not adjectives that could be used in any description of the Mani. In fact, this is the starkest region in the entire Peloponnese. Bare, treeless mountains loom everywhere on this arid peninsula and its sheer cliffs plunge headlong down into the sea. There are no leafy parks or welcoming sandy beaches here but the gloss of mass tourism is also absent. Until comparatively recently, hardly any outsiders ventured into the Mani — there was no reason to go there. However, one who did was the soldier, author and Hellenophile Patrick Leigh-Fermor whose book *Mani* is a good companion for any prolonged tour of the region. There are certainly good reasons for making the trip here. The Mani's beauty lies in its barren nature. The infertile hills stretch peacefully and endlessly into the distance, forgotten villages and the famous Maniot towers are everywhere. The scenery, particularly on the tip of the peninsula at Cape Tenaro, is spectacular. As for the history of the region and its inhabitants, it is like the Mani's appearance — stark.

Some claim that the Maniots are direct descendants of the Spartans. If this were true it would explain a great deal. The Maniots are historically known as a fierce, strong people, intent on preserving their autonomy and their own way of life. The Romans never made any real attempt to impose their rule here; neither did the Byzantines who ignored this pagan outpost in the south — Christianity was not accepted here until the ninth century. They were an almost continual thorn in the Turkish flesh, never more so than in 1821 when Petrobey Mavromihalis, a local clan leader whom the Turks had charged with ruling the Mani on their behalf, rose up in rebellion and carried the entire Mani with him. Predictably, this happened one week before the War of Liberation was launched in the rest of Greece.

The Maniots gained their independence with the rest of Greece in 1827. Having regained their independence, though, the Maniots were not keen on subjugating themselves to rule from Athens. Mavromihalis was imprisoned by the first Greek President, Capodistrias, an act for which he paid with his life. The brothers of Mavromihalis assassinated him as he made his way to church. The Greek army was sent in force to the Mani in retaliation but the soldiers were sent back with their tails between their legs. Eventually the Maniots were persuaded to unite with the rest of Greece in 1834 after having been promised their own division within the army.

It was not only outsiders that the Mani clashed with. The 'hillbilly' image of the Maniots is only added to by the fact that blood feuds were a regular feature of life in the region from the Middle Ages onward. The problems arose when families from the north of the Mani began to move into the area, usually to flee fighting, and there was not enough fertile land to go round. The feuds could go on for years. They gave rise to a very distinctive feature of the Mani — great tower-houses that were the main strongholds of families in feud. Most still remain in place today, some crumbling and some in good repair, but a constant reminder of the Mani's tumultuous past.

Although **Areopolis** takes its name from Ares (Mars), god of war, the town is a gentle introduction to the Mani. It is the most developed Maniot town in terms of tourism and one can easily find a room to let in its old grey stone houses by wandering down the cobbled street that leads off the main square. Lined on two sides by restaurants, this square is dominated by a large statue of Petrobey Mavromihalis, standing proudly with a curved sword in hand. It was here that he declared the uprising against the Turks.

Areopolis is essentially a very quiet town and, on a hot afternoon when the streets are deserted, it takes on the atmosphere of a small Catalan village in siesta. It is the ideal base from which to explore the rest of the Mani and those seeking to taste the full flavour of the region can stay overnight in the Kapetanakos tower — an old family stronghold converted by the tourist office into a very pleasant guest house.

One of the main attractions in the Mani is the **Glyfatha Cave**, a huge underground lake on the coast which is reached from the village of Pirgos Dirou, 8km (5 miles) south of Aeropolis. Only discovered in 1985, this cave is the finest in the Peloponnese and not even the expensive admission fee by Greek standards (£5, $8 at the time of writing) should deter you from visiting it. The cave is quite remarkable. It can be explored only by boats that skim slowly over the calm waters past wonderful rock formations mirrored in the water and stalactites and stalagmites said to be 400 million years old. The boat trip lasts 30 minutes after which you can leisurely wander through to the exit, examining more formations in your own time. Be warned that the time between buying tickets and receiving an admission number and actually getting into the cave could, in season, be hours — the boats can only seat eight at a time. However, at least there is a pebble beach next to the main entrance where you can swim the time away while waiting for your number to be called.

South of Pirgos Dirou, the wild and windswept heart of 'Deep Mani' is entered. Harouda is passed, with its attractive Byzantine church, then Kafonia and Tsopokas before heading down to the rocky beach at the village of **Mezapos**. This village, once vital to the

Gerolimenas epitomises the ports on the Mani peninsula — quiet,
secluded and backed by an arid, barren landscape

region for its deep natural harbour, boasts several towers and, 4km
(2^1/$_2$ miles) away, are the ruins of the Frankish castle of the Maina.
This was built by William de Villehardouin in 1248 on a bare and
isolated rock just offshore.

Past Mezapos the towers are everywhere, blending into the sand-
coloured mountains. They are most notable at Kitta, another once
important town but, like the rest of the Mani, suffering badly from
the effects of depopulation as its young people leave for the cities.
Finally, 28km (17 miles) from Aeropolis, **Gerolimenas** is reached, on
the south-western tip of the peninsula. Picturesquely set within a
large harbour, it is a very quiet port with a couple of tavernas and a
few rooms to let.

The road cuts west behind Gerolimenas, passes tiny Alika and
arrives at **Vathia** which, despite having a population already down
to single figures, manages to retain an other-worldly atmosphere
that is heightened by the spectacular views over the mountains
down to the southern coast. Many of the closely-packed stone houses
are now dilapidated, as are most of the towers although one has been
restored by the Greek Tourist Office to serve as a guest house. A road
leads south from Vathia down to Cape Tenaro, the southernmost
point of mainland Greece. A small cave at Asomati Bay is said to be

Ruins at the Maniot village of Vathia

the entrance through which the dead passed into Hades, the Under-world. This area was once inhabited by the Ancient Greeks; a temple to Poseidon was discovered here, its stones being used in later years to build the low chapel at Asomati.

The western coastal road from Aeropolis to Gerolimenas is barren, but positively lush in comparison to the eastern coastal road from Vathia to Aeropolis. It seems incredible that the villages that dot the coastline manage to survive at all. Only scrub, prickly pears and the odd twisted olive tree take root here. Of the villages themselves, some are inhabited, some in ruins and the rest a curious mixture of the two, with whitewashed bricks tacked onto the grey slate. Of course, there are the inevitable towers, particularly at Lagia, just north of Vathia. The two largest villages on this side are **Kokola**, with two very small pebble beaches and a few rooms to let, and **Kotronas**, the last village on the eastern side of the Mani. There is a pebble beach here too, and the landscape is noticeably more fertile although a long way from being lush. In spring, wild gladioli grow along the sides of the road. It is another 16km (10 miles) from Kotronas back to Aeropolis. Note that to explore the Mani in depth, one ought to hire a car or a relatively powerful moped. No buses make the full circuit of the Mani and only two buses leave for Gerolimenas from Aeropolis daily.

Returning to Sparta, one has three further destinations to choose from in the southern Peloponnese. South across the sea on the thrice-weekly ferry to the island of Kythera; east to Monemvassia and eastern Laconia; and north-east to Geraki and Leonidio, the latter just over the county line in the prefecture of Arcadia.

Eastern Laconia

Modern **Geraki**, on the slopes of Mount Parnon, is 40km (25 miles) from Gythion and 38km (23 miles) from Sparta, and linked to the latter by a regular bus service. It is a pleasant, steeply built town which earns its money by harvesting the olive and citrus trees that surround it but contains nothing of real interest. However, old Geraki is quite different. It was the town that guarded the Mystra-Monemvassia road and its Byzantine remains are extensive, although one has to walk north for an hour to reach them. Its castle, built in 1256, is pleasingly preserved, as is the church of Agios Georgios within its thick walls. Below the castle there are more churches — ask the site's caretaker to open the doors of Agios Athanassios and Agios Ioannis — the Byzantine frescoes inside are well worth seeing.

Leonidio is 47km (29 miles) from Geraki, reached via a road that cuts its way through the fertile and thickly-forested slopes of Mount Parnon via the pretty mountain village of Kosmas and the fortress-like Eloni convent which is open to visitors. A very traditional town, only 4km (2$^1/_2$ miles) from the sea and lying on the river Dafno, its houses are suitably noteworthy, with their decorated, overhanging balconies. Easter week is a good time to be here. On Easter Saturday, effigies of Judas Iscariot are burned in the streets and Easter Sunday is the cue for street parties, with plenty of food and drink available for all.

Leonidio's port, **Plaka**, has a pebble beach, a few tavernas and a large choice of rooms to let. More good beaches can be found 9km (5 miles) south at Poulithra, which is where the asphalt ends. A long coastal highway begins from Leonidio and stretches up to Argos and the E92 from where one can return to Athens via the marvellous archaeological sites of ancient Mycenae and Corinth. In season there are hydrofoil connections to Monemvassia and to the Argo-Saronic islands of Spetses and Poros while en-route to Pireaus.

Monemvassia, another of the real treasures of the Peloponnese, can be reached by either passenger ferry (from Gythion, Kythera, Neapolis, Kastelli on Crete and Pireaus — also hydrofoils from Leonidio in season); or by 64km (40 miles) of road from Gythion. The latter is a lovely journey, passing small villages — set against fields

The church of Agia Sofia, perched high above the town of Monemvassia

of oranges and lemons — whose whitewashed houses have gardens full of a wide variety of roses. If travelling by public transport from Gythion, start the journey early in the day; several connections have to be made and to leave it too late is to risk having to walk or hitch the last 11km (7 miles) to Gefira, Monemvassia's sister town.

Those entering **Monemvassia** by road could be forgiven for initially wondering what all the fuss is about. The road slopes gently down to Gefira, a rapidly developing little port with a cheery atmosphere and little else, and all that can be seen is a gigantic rock standing just offshore and connected to the mainland by an asphalt road over a bridge. Monemvassia stands on the other side of that rock, facing out to sea. Known as the 'Gibraltar of Greece', it is a fortified medieval town, wonderfully atmospheric, full of history and crowned by the extensive ruins of a castle at the rock's summit. Although Monemvassia is now on the itinerary of several tour boats, it is mostly Greeks that visit this unique town.

Originally built by the Byzantines, it withstood 3 years of Frankish siege before falling to the Crusaders in 1249. Thirteen years later it reverted back to the Byzantines who gained the city as part of the ransom for the Frankish leader, William de Villehardouin. The town became wealthy and renowned, famous for the wines produced just inland, well-populated and strong enough to determine its own fate when the Ottomans arrived in the mid-fifteenth century.

Monemvassia subjugated itself to the more benign rule of the Venetians — most of the buildings seen today date from this period — but eventually fell under Turkish rule in 1540 during the reign of Sultan Suleiman the Magnificent. From this point on, Monemvassia fell into a decline and even when it was reclaimed for Greece, in a bloody battle just after the War of Liberation began in 1821, it never regained its former glory. Like all of the major southern Peloponnesian ports that serviced ships on their journeys around the coast to Pireaus, the opening of the Corinth Canal in the 1890s signalled the end of its importance.

Monemvassia means 'only entrance', a rather apt name as the town has only one entrance point; a small, wooden but iron-fronted gate that is a 10 minute walk from the restaurant at the far end of the causeway. Go through the gate to the main street — a mercifully brief row of boutiques and over-priced restaurants not repeated elsewhere on the rock. The rest of the town is a mass of ruined and renovated medieval houses and churches built along tiny crooked alleyways and constantly conjuring up visions of the past. There is a main square at the end of the main street, originally built around the town's water supply, a long sealed-up well. The cathedral of Monemvassia stands at its far side, a huge structure dating from the thirteenth century and usually open to visitors. By walking down to the sea wall from here, one can spend a pleasant hour scrambling around the rock itself. It is possible to swim off the rocks in a couple of places; otherwise try the small and rather dirty pebble beach at Gefira.

Although the Frankish castle above the town seems an almost impossible climb away, it actually takes only 15 minutes to ascend the easily defined path in a fairly easy walk that begins at the main square. It is certainly well worth the effort. The castle is a wonderful place to wander around, poking around the old look-out posts and store houses and other crumbling ruins. The views over Monemvassia are excellent, offering a totally different perspective of the town, and the smells of wild lavender and herbs fill the air. They grow everywhere and include a herb used in making Greek mountain tea. Those with small children should keep a good eye on them; some of the drops are sheer down to the jagged rocks below. The best-preserved structure by far is the thirteenth-century church of Agia Sophia, built on the edge of a precipice and with mysteriously fading frescoes.

The road south from Monemvassia is unremarkable, winding its way along the west coast of the Eastern Laconia peninsula before arriving in 61km (38 miles) at **Neapolis**, a pleasant coastal resort with sandy beaches and plenty of hotels and rooms to let. Once the southernmost port of the ancient Spartans, this is also the base from which to visit the islet of Elafonissi, easily visible from the shore. Another great place to get away from it all, there is nothing here but a couple of pensions, some tavernas and two of the best beaches in the region. The port at Neapolis is used by passenger ferries en-route to Gythion, Monemvassia, Kirparissi, Pireaus and to the island of Kythera, 2 hours to the south.

Kythera

Although Kythera gets very few tourists, it gets plenty of visitors. These are mostly Greek-Australians on holiday, seeing the family on their home island. There are very few islands that have been hit harder by the waves of Greek emigration to Australia. An estimated three-quarters of the populace have made the long journey south, thus giving Australia the local title of 'Big Kythera'. Nevertheless, the remittances sent home by the ex-patriots do keep Kythera wealthy, and this is important for an island that has suffered economically since the opening of the Corinth Canal, when its role as a stop-over point for ships en-route to Pireaus was taken away.

Kythera is unlikely ever to earn a great deal from tourism. It is a pretty, peaceful and quiet island, but one which is not exactly brimming over with attractions, and few people make the short but expensive daily flight from Athens or the ponderous 12 hour journey by ferry from Pireaus. Yet for those touring the southern Peloponnese, it is no great distance away and a good opportunity to view a small, off-the-beaten-track Greek island.

Kythera's most famous daughter is Aphrodite, goddess of love, who rose gracefully out of the sea just off its coastline and thus earned the island a place in Greek mythology. Historically, though, Kythera's past is a reflection of the entire southern Peloponnese — a succession of Byzantine, Venetian and Turkish overlords. However, there is one difference; astonishingly, Kythera is considered one of the Ionian Islands, despite them being hundreds of nautical miles away, and so came under British rule in 1815. Consequently, it had to wait a little longer than the rest of the Peloponnese for liberation. The British ceded Kythera to the new Greek state in 1864.

Boats arriving from Pireaus and Gythion usually dock at both of the island's ports, Agia Pelagia in the north and Kapsali in the south. Boats from Crete dock at Kapsali alone while Neapolis boats are served only by Agia Pelagia. It is a convenient situation as, ferry schedules permitting, one can explore the island from one end to the other without having to backtrack to leave.

Of the two ports, **Kapsali** is the better introduction to Kythera, a photogenic little village nestled in between two peninsulas and with a couple of pebbly beaches to swim off. It is towered over, though, by **Kythera town** (Chora), capital of Kythera and built high on the hill that stands behind and to the west of Kapsali. Built steeply, this small town still retains a few vestiges of the Venetian occupation, most noticeably in the castle which is still reasonably intact, dates from the early sixteenth century and is engraved in several places with the Lion of St Mark, the Venetian symbol. The lion can also be seen on several of the old Venetian mansions still standing in Kythera town. Just outside the town, on the road north, is the island's archaeological museum which houses a collection of finds ranging from the Mycenaean era to the British occupation.

Apart from the beaches at Kapsali, the nearest swimming spots are at Vroulia, 10km (6 miles) east of Kapsali past barren fields, where a taverna services the pebble beach. Accommodation is available in both Kapsali and Kythera town but in July and August, when most of the Kytheran-Australians come home, it is notoriously hard to find. There is a campsite near Kapsali.

With only one bus per day from Kythera town to Agia Pelagia, stopping at the villages in between, Kythera's public transport service is limited and so to explore the island properly, hire a moped in Kythera town. Travelling north out of the town, the first village reached is Livadi. From here an asphalt road leads to Drimon and on to the monastery of the Panagia Mirtidion, looking out over the west coast of Kythera in a region covered in cypress trees, and open to visitors. It is attractively imposing and draws hundreds of pilgrims to the festivities of 15 August, the Assumption of the Virgin Mary, which is celebrated here with zest.

Accessible from either Drimon or Livadia, lying in a valley several kilometres west of Kokana, is **Milopotamos** — a lush and attractive village with tiny streams running everywhere. From the town, a path leads down to a gushing waterfall, passing an old wooden watermill on the way. The ruins of a 400 year-old Venetian fortress stand just below the town. Only 30 minutes walk to the west is one of Kythera's main attractions — the Caves of Agia Sofia. There are several caves, with stalactites and stalagmites, and inside one there is a display of frescoes. This cave was once used as a church of Agia Sofia. Open only during summer months, the caves are best-visited with a guide who can be found by asking at the tavernas in Milopotamos.

Continuing north on the road to Agia Pelagia, **Potamos** is reached — the largest village of northern Kythera and one that draws Kytherans from far and wide to its weekly Sunday market. The road forks here; take the left road for the small village of Karaves and the pleasant beach at Platia Ammos. The right fork leads to Agia Pelagia, the island's northern port that doubles as a small resort with a pebble beach and a few rooms to let. The road passes the ruins of Palio Choras, the old capital of Kythera, but you have to look hard to spot them. Built high amongst huge rocks, Palio Choras presence remained unknown to many of the raiders that landed on the island. However, Barbarossa — the terrible Turkish admiral/pirate — discovered the town when he landed on Kythera in 1537 and its inhabitants were brutally massacred in the ensuing, one-sided battle. The town never really recovered.

Robinson Crusoe types may care to head south of Kythera for its small sister island of **Antikythera**. This is desolate and rocky; there are only two villages, about fifty inhabitants and a brand-new electricity system. The ferry from Kastelli (Crete) to Kythera stops here only twice a week, so be warned — if you go, you are committed to at least 3 days!

Further Information

— Southern Peloponnese —

Places of Interest

KYTHERA
Kythera town
Archaeological Museum
Open: 8.45am-3pm.
Closed Mondays.

Milopotamos
Caves of Agia Sofia
Open: July and August, 4-7pm.

THE MAINLAND

Gythion
Archaeological Museum
46km (28 miles) south of Sparta
Open: 8.45am-1.30pm Monday to Friday.

Hora
Archaeological Museum
3km (2 miles) north of Nestor's Palace
Open: 8.30am-3pm.
Closed Mondays.

Megalopolis
Ancient Theatre
16km (10 miles) from Karitena
Open: 9am-6pm daily.

Messini
Sanctuary to Asclepius
Open: 8.45am-3pm daily, 9.30am-2.30pm Sunday.

Methoni
Venetian Castle
Open: 8.30am-3pm daily.
Closed Mondays.
☎ 0731 25363

Mystra
5km (3 miles) east of Sparta
Open: 8am-6pm weekdays, 8am-3pm weekends.
☎ 0731 93377

Nestor's Palace
3km (2 miles) south of Hora
Open: 8.45am-3pm daily.
☎ 0763 31358

Pirgos Dirou
Glyfatha Cave
Open: 8am-6pm June to September; 8am-3pm October to May.
☎ 0733 62222/3

Pylos town
Medieval Castle (Neokastro)
9km (5 miles) north of Methoni
Open: 8.30am-3pm daily.
Closed Mondays.

Archaeological Museum
Open: 8.30am-3pm daily.
Closed Mondays.
☎ 0723 22448

Sparta
Archaeological Museum
Open: 8.45am-3pm. Sunday 9am-2.30pm.
☎ 0731 25363

Tourist Information Offices

Kalamata
☎ 0721 22059/21959

Sparta
Town hall
Vassileos Georgios Square
☎ 0731 26517

Traditional Guest Houses

Aeropolis
Kapetanakos Tower
☎ 0733 51233

Vathia
☎ 0733 54229

3 • The Ionian Islands and the North-West Peloponnese

Introduction

Forming a long string through the Adriatic Sea down the west coast of mainland Greece, the Ionian Islands are in many ways very different from any other Greek island chain. The differences show in their climate, history, culture and often in their landscape. They provide a completely new perspective on the country for the visitor. The chain is composed of seven islands in total but only three are covered here, the southern islands of Zakynthos, Cephalonia and Ithaca. Of the others, Paxos and Lefkada are covered elsewhere in this book as is Kythera, totally divorced geographically from the rest of the group and lying off the coast of the south-east Peloponnese. The largest island of the chain, Corfu (Kerkira) is annually submerged by wave upon wave of tourists and is about as on the beaten track as any Greek island can be. Some argue that Zakynthos, with its gorgeous beaches, is rapidly following in the wake of Corfu but, as yet, with all the holidaymakers clustered together in the south of the island, this is not the case. Cephalonia and Ithaca remain beautiful, quiet and draw only a handful of visitors. The three islands are very different but they are all very attractive.

The dissimilarities between the Ionian Islands and the rest of Greece stem as a direct result of their history; for the chain, with the exceptions of Lefkada and Kythera, never had to endure the stagnant, repressive and suffocating rule of the Turks. Instead, they remained in the hands of the Venetians, rulers who were often no less harsh than the Turks but who at least pushed the islands forward culturally and economically, so much so that they were fiercely squabbled over at the end of the eighteenth century when Venetian power collapsed. Yet the Ionian Islands, particularly Ithaca, were put well on the map long before the Venetians, by Homer. Ithaca was the homeland of the great King Odysseus, whose 10 year struggle to return to his palace and family after the Trojan War is recorded in one of the great classics of Homer, *The Odyssey*. Moreover, it made Ithaca the spiritual, if not the actual destination of many Victorian travellers.

The exploits of Odysseus took place around the twelfth century BC and, around 500 years later, the Corinthians captured the islands for the purpose of trade. The Roman rule here was perfunctory, but little is known of this era or indeed of the rule of the Corinthians, for, following the fall of Rome, northern raiders descended upon the islands and ransacked them, destroying cities and carrying off anything of value. It was not long, however, before the Byzantines arrived, building castles and cities; their rule lasted until the Knights of the Second Crusade forced them out. After the Crusaders, in 1386, came the Venetians.

It was the rule of the Venetians that shaped the Ionian Islands culturally and their influence is still obvious today. The islands' capitals, notably Corfu town and Zante town (Zakynthos) were made beautiful by tall and grand Renaissance structures; indeed, when Zante town was demolished by earthquake in 1953, the town was completely rebuilt on the old Venetian model. The islands' music carries a definite Italian influence and one is more likely to see a guitar than a lyre or santouri at live performances. Embroidery, the main recreation of the women of the Greek Islands, never caught on here; the Venetian art of lace-making was practised instead.

Painters flourished here, often fleeing to the islands from the Turks whose Islamic faith forbade the representation of the human form. Examples of the work of the Ionian School can be seen across the islands, in the icons of the churches. Yet despite this dilution of their culture, the Greeks maintained their own identity here and produced their own greats. Solomos, the national poet, was a native of these islands, as were Capodistria, the first prime minister of Greece, and Metaxas, the prime minister who took Greece into World War II.

After Napoleon conquered the Venetians in 1796 the Ionian Islands came under French jurisdiction yet the French only held them for 3 years before being evicted by a combined Russo-Turkish fleet. They reverted back to Napoleon in 1807 but, after the French defeat at Waterloo in 1815, came under the rule of the British. The British held the islands under a military protectorate and for the most part governed the islands well, laying their commercial infrastructure before ceding them to the 36 year-old Greek state in 1864. The people of Zakynthos, Cephalonia and Ithaca needed the help of their countrymen dearly in 1953. This was the year of the earthquake that shook the islands, killing hundreds and turning much of the remnants of their Venetian past into rubble.

To get to these three islands one can either go by air or sea, or by train or bus from Athens. Both Zakynthos (Zante) and Cephalonia (Argostoli) have airports, the latter being the quieter with daily flights to Athens and links in season with Corfu and Zakynthos. Zakynthos airport has the same connections but also handles hundreds of charter flights from Europe in the summer.

By sea from the mainland, Zakynthos is linked only with Killini; Cephalonia with Killini and Patras; and Ithaca with Patras and Astakos. All three islands are linked by ferry but bear in mind that, if travelling without your own transport, bus connections with the ferries are very limited and one may have to wait a few hours at the port before getting away.

Both Patras and Killini can be reached by train from Athens and all three islands operate a bus service to and from Athens where the price of the ferry is included in the bus ticket. The bad bus service on the islands can make getting around a frustrating and time-consuming experience. If at all possible, you should hire your own transport. Except in high season on Zakynthos, finding a room to let should rarely pose a problem.

Although the Ionian Islands have fine and hot summers, anyone who visits them between late September and mid-April stands a good chance of getting thoroughly drenched, for these are the wettest of all the Greek Islands. However, the rain also serves to make them the lushest and greenest; Zakynthos, in particular, is covered in forest, vegetation and, in spring, lovely wild flowers from end to end. Cephalonia is not short on lovely landscapes either and, being the most mountainous of the Ionian chain, offers some dramatic panoramas. However, perhaps the most dramatic of all is Ithaca, small, arid and very rocky but with a sheer and jagged coastline that contrasts with the blue sea. The best time of year to visit the islands is either June or early September; avoiding the rains and the holidaymakers who flock to Zakynthos in July and August.

Zakynthos is also a popular stopping-off point for migratory birds although their numbers are rapidly dwindling due to the Zakynthian fondness for hunting. Another species gradually being scared away from Zakynthos is the Carreta Carreta — giant loggerhead sea turtles that have laid their eggs on the soft sands of the south of the island since time began. As humans are also attracted to the soft sands, inadvertently destroying the turtles' eggs, these huge and wonderful creatures are being forced elsewhere.

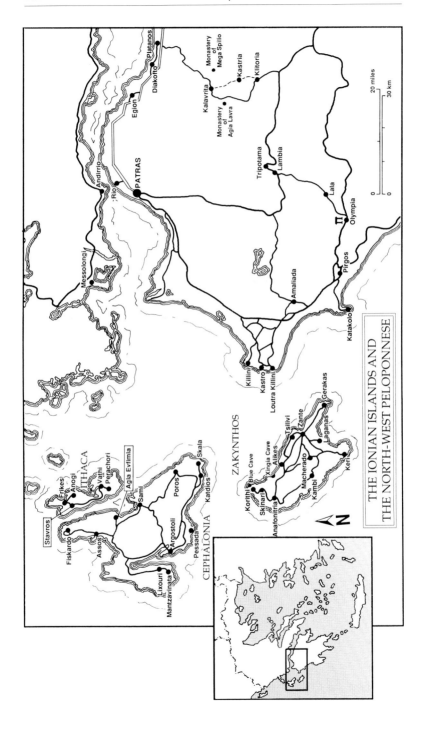

THE IONIAN ISLANDS AND
THE NORTH-WEST PELOPONNESE

Also included in this chapter is the north-west of the Peloponnese, a district known as the Eleia; a tour of this area makes a fine comparison to any tour of the Ionian Islands. In general, the region draws very few visitors, most people preferring to make a bee-line directly for Patras to take a ferry to the Ionian Islands or beyond. Yet this is a lovely region with a lot more to offer than just connections elsewhere. It is a lush and mountainous area but has fine beaches, medieval castles and the astounding remains of ancient Olympia, home of the Olympic Games. For information concerning the history and other aspects of the Peloponnese, see the introduction to the 'Southern Peloponnese' chapter.

The capital of this region is Patras, the number two port of Greece after Pireaus and the country's third largest city. From here one can travel south-east, past long beaches, to the beautiful sands and the medieval castle on the Killini peninsula. Then the route moves south to the town of Pirgos, which has some good beaches nearby, before heading inland to the ruins of ancient Olympia. One can now travel north-east, climbing high into the mountains, twisting along the ridges with ravines and rivers down below, and up to the mountainous village of Kalavrita. It is from here that one can take the old Italian train down through the hills and valleys to the coastal resort of Diakofto, on a rail journey that is said to be one of the most beautiful in Europe. Apart from this train line, travelling by public transport in the interior can be a slow and wearisome affair. However, the buses along the main coastal road are fast and frequent and the train often provides a cheaper alternative.

The Ionian Islands

Zakynthos

The green, colourful and mountainous island of Zakynthos (or Zante) is the southernmost of the Ionian chain and is, for many, the most beautiful, eclipsing even Corfu. It is so beautiful that its long-time occupiers, the Venetians, themselves great lovers of style and grace, would refer to the island as the 'Venice of the East'. The comparison was hardly geographically accurate — Zakynthos does not even possess a river, let alone a network of canals. However, its buildings, particularly those in the capital of Zante town, were fine and grand, its cultural reputation second-to-none.

The island's grandeur served only to compound the tragedy of the 1953 earthquake. Zakynthos was the hardest hit island of all, with over 300 casualties and only three buildings left standing in Zante

A panorama of Zante town

town — the church of Agios Dionysios, a nearby school and the National Bank of Greece. Yet Zakynthos has bounced back quickly and with style, making full use of its finest asset; a coastline endowed with excellent, soft and sandy beaches. This has inevitably led to tourists outnumbering islanders during the months of July and August but the island is still far from selling its soul completely to tourism. Most visitors cluster around the beaches of the south, leaving the rest of the coast and the interior to the islanders and the relatively few tourists that make their way there.

The island's name derives from two possible sources, the most likely being a reflection of its undulating landscape; *za* is town in ancient Greek and *kynthos* means hill. The other suggests that it is named after Zakynthos, a son of a king of Troy. The island can certainly trace its history back to the Trojan War and beyond. Homer wrote that a dozen ships were sent from here to the war; he also mentions the island in a more ignominious fashion, for supplying 20 of the unruly suitors of Penelope, wife of Odysseus.

The islanders participated in the Peloponnesian Wars and actively resisted the Romans. Indeed, history shows Zakynthos to be a proudly independent island, stubbornly intolerant of would-be occupiers until the Roman general Fulvius sacked the island in 150BC and finally cowed the Zantiots into submission. For the next two millennia, the island became the property of whichever power

was strongest in the region at any one time. The Venetians dominated from the twelfth century onward and loved Zakynthos, so
much so that when they lost the island to the Turks in 1479, they
bought it back 5 years later for 500 gold ducats. The British were the
last foreign occupiers and it was they who ceded Zakynthos to the
new Greek state in 1864.

Zakynthos can be reached by air — there are daily services to
Athens and charters from northern Europe; by hydrofoil from Patras
or by the twice daily ferry that shuttles across from Killini in the
Peloponnese. Buses from Athens to Killini are timed to connect with
the boat. There is no better introduction to the island than where the
boats dock, at **Zante town**. It is hard to believe that in August 1953 it
was nothing but a pile of rubble as today it is a very attractive town
indeed. Sandwiched between the sea and a high hill covered in trees
with an old Venetian castle standing on top, it curves splendidly
around its bay to the large and tree-lined main square, kept in
immaculate condition.

Following the earthquake, Zante was rebuilt in its old style over
the objections of those who wanted to rebuild with functionalism
rather than aesthetics in mind. Consequently, the town has
'Venetian' stamped all over it; in the spacious squares, the statues
and busts, and most noticeably, the buildings — often elaborate and
spired affairs. It could never have hoped to recapture the grandeur
of its past but it made a good effort, particularly as the builders were
limited by the necessity to use earthquake-proof, reinforced concrete. However, this was a wise move; a series of tremors that struck
Zakynthos in 1981 caused no damage. There is plenty of accommodation available in the town, in hotels and private rooms (owners
greet all boats that dock), a restaurant is never far away and the same
applies to car and moped rental establishments.

As with so many cultures suppressed by foreign occupation,
Zakynthos often found release in the arts and the town's sights are
a reflection of this. The island has produced writers, artists and
musicians in numbers totally disproportionate to its population
count and one can learn more about them in the museum of
Dionysios Solomos and Famous Zakynthians. Solomos is a favourite
son of Zakynthos. A poet of the Greek War of Independence, the first
verse of his 'Hymn to Liberty' has been adopted as the Greek National Anthem. Zante's main square, dominated by a statue of the
great man, is named after him.

The post-Byzantine museum boasts a large collection of icons,
mostly of the Ionian School yet with many painted by Cretans who

fled to Venetian Zakynthos after Crete was over-run by the Turks in the seventeenth century. This museum stands on the main square, near the fifteenth-century church of Agios Nikolaos, restored since 1953 and a lovely building. Zante's finest church, though, is the one dedicated to the island's patron saint, Agios Dionysios. A 5 minute walk south of the main square, this massive construction, set next to a very Venetian bell-tower, has a superbly decorated interior with stained-glass windows and a ceiling that has every inch covered in murals. A silver casket holds the remains of the saint. Men in shorts and women with arms and legs exposed will be denied entry.

For the best view of Zante, and one that includes the west coast of the Peloponnese, walk up to the Venetian castle. There are a few tavernas near the entrance where one can sip a drink and watch the sun go down. Just below the castle, the tiny chapel of Zoodohos Pigi epitomises Greek island charm.

The bus service on Zakynthos, while being acceptable by Greek island standards, is still irregular, thus keeping those who hire out cars and mopeds happy. The best way to see the island is under your own steam. A good starting point of any tour is the Gerakes peninsula, lush and fertile and with a coastline of sandy beaches, ideal for swimming and fishing. Offshore is the pit of Inoussae, at $4^1/_2$km (3 miles) the deepest trench in the Mediterranean basin. To get there, leave Zante on the south-easterly road, passing the resort of Argassi whose thin beach hardly justifies its overdevelopment. Further along is the old look-out post of Mount Skopus on which stands the fourteenth-century church of the Virgin Skopiotissa, built on the site of an ancient temple to Artemis. Its central icon of the Virgin once hung in a church in Constantinople (Istanbul) before its sacking by the Ottomans in 1453.

The peninsula proper consists of beaches all the way around, the best being at Vassiliki near the peninsula's tip. Other good options are Porto Zoro, Porto Roma, Agios Nikolaos and Gerakes itself; quiet and secluded little coves are easy to find. The villages near the beaches all have a few pensions and tavernas but development here is surprisingly scarce. It is the place to come for a quiet beach holiday.

Accessible by foot from Gerakes or by road from Zante, is the calm and sheltered bay of Laganas, hemmed in by the two peninsulas of Zakynthos and lined along its entire 9km (5 miles) length by sandy beaches. This is the tourist mecca of Zakynthos, drawing thousands of visitors in high season and, as such, it is not described in detail here. Holidaymakers are not the only species attracted to Laganas Bay. Female Carreta Carreta, the giant loggerhead sea turtles weighing up to 90kg (200lb), crawl up onto the soft sands between June and September to lay their eggs for that year before slipping back into the sea. Sadly, tourism is slowly killing them off. Thousands of the young die each year, the eggs and nests smashed by beach umbrellas, deck chairs and bikes.

Keri, the only village of any significance on the hilly southern peninsula, is chalk to the cheese of Laganas. One of the few villages not flattened by the earthquake, it is a quiet place surrounded by olive trees and unflustered by the activity of the headland. There are a few rooms to let for those who enjoy the peace. One can walk out to the lighthouse, perched gingerly on the edge of a sheer cliff, or down to the pebble beach. Its church of the Virgin of Keriotissa has a silver icon of the Virgin and a finely carved wooden altar screen.

The Zakynthos Plain stretches north of Zante along the eastern coastline and reveals yet more beaches. Four kilometres ($2^1/_2$ miles) from Zante is **Tsilivi**. This is a huge beach but it has been developed a little too much for its own good. The same applies to Alikes, further north. However, from Alikes (or Zante) one can board a caique bound for the Kianoun, or Blue Cave. When the sun hits this cave at a certain angle, it glows a deep and beautiful blue. Do ensure, though, that the caique to the cave will arrive at the time when the sun is in the correct position, otherwise there will be no blue sparkle. This time varies throughout the year but it is best to aim for between 8.30 and 10am. There is another cave that can be visited on the way back. This is the Xingia Cave where the sulphuric, and murky water that gushes from its mouth is said to contain healing properties.

Even without tourism, Zakynthos would be a relatively wealthy island, being renowned for its production of olive oil, currants and wines. Village life in the interior is, therefore, still very much alive and existing totally independently of tourism. Not many travel into the interior — most dash for the beaches instead — but those that do can discover a whole new Zakynthos.

Macherado, 10km (6 miles) east of Zante, is a village known primarily for its lively feast day of Agia Mavra, held on the first Sunday in June. The village church of the same name is particularly ornate, with its imposing bell-tower standing away from the main body, and contains a miraculous icon of the saint that drips with votive offerings. **Agia Marina**, north of Macherado on the edge of the Zakynthian hills, has a similarly lovely church that boasts a perfectly carved altar screen.

Up in the hills west of Macherado is the village of **Agios Nikolaos**, especially quaint and with a road that leads north-west to **Kambi**, a

Macherado's dominating bell-tower

small village on the west coast that offers outstanding views of the sunset. **Mariai**, north of Kambi and inland, is a hill village interesting for the lady it is named after — Mary Magdalene — who is said to have visited Zakynthos en-route to Rome. The village church is dedicated to her. As the road climbs north again, it reaches **Anafonitria**, home of Dionysios, patron saint of Zakynthos. A monastery stands near the site, now inhabited by nuns who will show visitors the cell where Dionysios allegedly prayed and studied.

The extreme north of Zakynthos is wild and rocky and supports only a few old and traditional settlements such as Skinari and Korithi. The monastery of Theotokas Spilaiotissa at the village of Orthonies is of interest; built in the sixteenth century, its library dates from its original construction and is priceless. Further south is **Katastari**, the second largest town of the island and positioned above Alikes beach. The region from here south to Zante is crammed with small villages and hamlets, none with any outstanding sights but each with their own appeal. Perhaps the prettiest are the three Geraki villages — upper, middle and lower.

Easter is a particularly good time to be on Zakynthos. On Easter Friday in Zante huge crowds congregate outside the church of Agios Nikolaos in a brief service that ends with hundreds of fireworks being shot into the sky. A 2 week carnival precedes Lent including the parade of the 'Funeral of the Masks' through Zante on the last Sunday prior to Lent. Agios Dionysios has two festivals in his honour — on 24 August and 17 December — these also end with fireworks in Zante. It is celebrated more reverently in the saint's home village of Anafonitria. Live theatre is the order of the day at the end of August and beginning of September when Zakynthos hosts the International Meeting of Medieval and Popular Theatre.

Cephalonia

The island of Cephalonia is the largest of the Ionian chain and is only now waking up to the possibilities of tourism. Previously it was considered (and considered itself) something of a backwater for visitors, its mountainous and often inaccessible terrain being unable to compete with the rolling hills and the beaches of Zakynthos to the south. Its architecture holds little of interest because, as with Zakynthos, Cephalonia's Venetian-style towns and villages, with the exception of Fiskardo in the north, had to be completely rebuilt after the 1953 earthquake. It was an island to go to escape the crowds; nothing more. However, one does not have to dig very deep to find real beauty and appeal in Cephalonia; there are gorgeous beaches, a delightfully unspoilt interior, fine caves to explore and an atmosphere of everyday Greek life, barely touched by tourism. Add this to the many mysteries and legends associated with Cephalonia, and one has an island at least equal in attraction to the others in its group.

Cephalonia's name is derived either from its masses of fir trees (*Abies cephalonica*) or from King Cephalos, a mythical figure who made the mistake of not responding to the goddess Hera's love for him. She consequently made his life a misery. The latter explanation is quite possible, given that Cephalonia can trace its history way back to the Mycenaean era and probably before. Tombs have been discovered dating from this age and the island is mentioned by Homer in *The Odyssey*.

In later years Cephalonia vigorously defended itself against Roman attacks; the town of Sami held out for 4 months against the legions. However, after its inevitable defeat, the island spent the next

2,000 years being handed around amongst the Byzantines, pirates, Normans, Venetians, French, Russians and British. Of all the Ionian Islanders, Cephalonians were the most active in resisting British rule and a series of revolts swept the island in 1848-49. Italy occupied the island during World War II although, remarkably, the Italian garrison stationed here joined forces with the Greek rebels in opposing a German takeover. The victorious Germans executed the Italians en-masse.

The prime minister of Greece who took the country into World War II was a Cephalonian, John Metaxas, the island's most famous (and, for some, most notorious) son. Although a dictator, his famous 'No' to Mussolini's ultimatum in October 1940 caused Greece to enter the war and exemplified the nation's pride and independence. 'Ochi' ('No') Day is a national holiday in Greece, held on 28 October.

Cephalonia has an airport, linked daily all-year round to Athens and with some in-season connections to Zakynthos and Corfu. However, most visitors arrive by boat and where the boat docks depends on where it has come from. Argostoli, the capital, is connected to Paxos, Corfu and Brindisi (Italy); Pessada to Skinari on Zakynthos; Poros to Killini in the Peloponnese; Sami to Patras and Vathi (Ithaca); Agios Evfimia to Astakos in southern Epirus; and Fiskardo to Vassiliki (Lefkada) and Frikes (Ithaca). Those without their own transport should be aware that Cephalonia's bus service is absolutely diabolical and that there could be a long wait at the port for a connection to wherever one wants to go. Try, therefore, to dock at Argostoli or Sami.

Capital of Cephalonia since 1757, **Argostoli** is unusually positioned between two peninsulas and is a sprawling and thriving town that has gamely tried to make up for its almost total destruction in 1953. Virtually every building in the town was levelled by the earthquake, including its fine old Venetian structures. However, with the help of donations from wealthy Cephalonian emigrés, it has been rebuilt as an earthquake-proof and attractive town where life seems to centre around the spacious main square, lined with hotels, some good restaurants and, to one side, the archaeological museum. This is a well-presented museum with a selection of coins, jars, jewellery etc; all found on Cephalonia and with many dating back 30 centuries to the Mycenaean era.

Those with time for only one museum in Argostoli may be better off walking two blocks away from the archaeological museum, parallel to the waterfront, to the Koryialenios library. Nicely rebuilt after 1953, the library itself houses a small collection of Byzantine icons but the main attraction is on its ground floor in the history and folklore museum. There are many such museums in Greece but this one is a real treat, a delightful hotch-potch of all the facets of Cephalonian life since the Venetian occupation. Particularly interesting are the pre- and post-earthquake photographs of Argostoli.

One of the geological oddities of Cephalonia lies a pleasant half-hour walk away from Argostoli at the Katavrothes (sink-holes). Here the sea mysteriously plunges down through two cracks in the rocks but does not reappear; geologists have discovered that it courses its route eastward across the island and rejoins the sea at Sami. Continuing around the peninsula from here (or by a more direct route from Argostoli) leads to two wonderfully sandy beaches backed by lines of fir trees, at Plati Gialos and Makri Gialos. Argostoli also has its very own man-made lagoon, created by a stone-arched British bridge completed in 1842 which links one side of Argostoli with the other on the main body of the island. Over the bridge one can see the ruins of ancient Krane, consisting mainly of walls first constructed up to 26 centuries ago.

Frequent boats leave Argostoli daily and cross the bay to **Lixouri**, the main town of the island's largest peninsula, the Palli, thus saving you the long journey north and then south again. There is nothing particularly special about Lixouri, it is just a very new, functional town. The statue in the central square is of a local poet and cynic Andreas Laskaratos. There are a few rooms to let and these are useful for those making the excursion south along the eastern coastline of the peninsula to a whole series of lovely and splendidly isolated beaches. The nearest is about a 30 minute walk from Lixouri but there are better ones further south at Michalitsata, Lepeda, Agios Georgios and Xi. You can take a taxi until the coastal road begins to turn inland and then walk from there. Be sure to bring provisions such as water as there are no facilities. Easily visible from Agios Georgios beach is the rock of Kounopetra which, before the 1953 earthquake, would give the strange illusion of slightly swaying from side to side.

As the road south out of Lixouri cuts inland, the landscape opens up into lush and green hills and fields with the sea deeply blue in the background. This is a sparsely populated region, most of the land is given over to agriculture. At Mantzavinata the asphalt ends and the unpaved road bounces high over the mountains out to the rocky west coast, bearing west at the attractive hill village of Havriata.

On the west coast are the two monasteries of Tafion and Kipoureon, with truly spectacular coastal views from the latter. To return to Lixouri double back to Havriata and bear north to Havdata, worth a stop for its pretty church of Agii Apostoli. Lixouri is only 8km (5 miles) east of here.

Travelling north-west from Lixouri, you come across a quiet and rural area with appealing little villages and hamlets dotted among the hills. Those who see organised folk-dancing at Kaminarata can consider themselves lucky; its folk-dance troupe has won awards across Greece and abroad. More beaches can be found on the coast north of Lixouri; the popular, shallow and safe Agios Spirodon which is nearest to Lixouri and beyond, the quieter Petani.

Three kilometres (2 miles) past the village of Livadion, a minor road cuts north inland up to the northern tip of the peninsula and another beach, that of Agios Spirodon, which rarely gets more than a handful of visitors. The main road from Livadion curves around the bay and back on to the main body of Cephalonia where it joins the Argostoli-Fiskardo road.

It is a lovely journey between Argostoli and Fiskardo. A coastal route for virtually its entire length, it darts through pretty little villages, skirts the eastern slopes of Mount Agia Dinati, and then climbs into the northern peninsula, more hills to the east and sheer cliffs to the west. Below these cliffs are some glorious beaches; one of these, Myrtos, is said to be the Ionian Islands' finest, its white sand hemmed steeply in by cliffs.

Before Myrtos, Agia Kiriaki beach can be reached from the village of Angonas and, 8km (5 miles) beyond Myrtos, Assos beach supplies more good swimming and bathing. Above its bay, on a headland, are the ruins of a grand old Venetian castle, built in the sixteenth century to guard against pirates raiding the north of the island. Frustratingly, though, only one bus per day makes the Argostoli-Fiskardo run, not returning from Fiskardo until the following morning.

Named after the Norman Crusader, Robert Guiscard, who died of fever in 1085 on a boat off its rocky shores, **Fiskardo** was the only town on Cephalonia to escape destruction in the 1953 earthquake. Consequently, it has managed to retain much of its eighteenth-century appeal. Its whitewashed houses, with their red-tiled roofs, squeeze cosily together along the attractive harbourside and although the trappings of tourism are everywhere, they do not detract too much from this charming village. A rocky beach is only a 10 minute walk away.

Retracing one's path back from Fiskardo, a junction is reached after 26km (16 miles); west leads to Argostoli, east to Sami (the ancient capital of Cephalonia), via the quiet little port of Agia Evfimia. With Argostoli, **Sami** is the major port of Cephalonia and is currently trying to establish itself as a summer resort as well. Its beach, a short walk to the north, is of fine sand and the harbour is attractive enough, despite being lined with a row of rather uniform buildings, mostly tourist boutiques. The people of Sami held out against the Roman invasion in 187BC for 4 months; the walls of the old city where they made their last stand can still be seen, on the two hills behind the town.

Nature provides the major attraction near Sami, though, in the form of two fascinating caves, of Drograti and Melissani. Drograti lies off the Sami-Argostoli road, 4km ($2^1/_2$ miles) out of town. You have to descend into the earth to reach its massive chamber, crammed with stalactites and stalagmites millions of years old. Acoustically it is so good that summer concerts are occasionally held in this chamber. The Melissani Cave is more unusual; you can only explore its two caverns in a boat rowed by a guide who points out the strange rock formations. Its subterranean lake is clear and very deep at points and, as the only light comes through a hole in the roof, the trip can be spooky and very atmospheric. The Melissani Cave is the closest to Sami, only a half-hour walk north of town and with signposts pointing the way as one nears the cave.

The next setttlement on the west coast south of Sami is Poros, the road there being a minor one but very attractive, cutting through mountains and passing the village of Agios Nikolaos near the full and blue Lake Avythos. This is extremely deep and its name means 'bottomless'.

From the lake it is only 11km (7 miles) across a lush and well-watered landscape to Poros. Sheltered prettily by mountains, **Poros** has a spacious waterfront, an attractive beach and plenty of facilities for visitors, as well as a connection three times a day with Killini on the mainland.

Skala, on the island's south-western tip, offers more of the same but is a little quieter. Skala was an important town of ancient Cephalonia; the remains of a temple to Apollo have been found in its vicinity, as has a Roman villa containing some dramatic mosaics now on display at the archaeological museum in Argostoli. **Katelios**, on the south coast, 6km (4 miles) east of Skala, has a good beach.

A few kilometres north of Katelios is **Markopoulo**, a run-of-the-mill village 364 days of the year but one of the most fascinating villages in all of Greece on 15 August, the day of the Assumption of the Virgin Mary. On this day, a unique and mysterious occurence takes place; small and harmless snakes, with a distinctive cross-mark on their heads, slither up the aisle of the church to its silver icon of the

Virgin. To the villagers these snakes are holy and are captured, only to be released after the service, when they promptly disappear to return again the following year. Scientists have concluded that the church lies on the snakes' migratory trail and that, as the villagers never harm them, they have no reason to change their route. However, if that is the case, it seems strange that the snakes did not appear in times of great trauma for Cephalonia — during the German occupation and in 1953, the earthquake year.

From Markopoulo the road leads north-west back to Argostoli, passing to the south of Cephalonia's highest peak, the 1,600m (5,250ft) high Mount Enos. The mountain has been declared a national park to ensure the survival of a unique species of black pine trees that grow here. Just before Peratata one can bear north for the monastery dedicated to Agios Gerosimos, patron saint of the island, and a building dominated by an almost Teutonic bell-tower. Great festivities take place at the monastery on 16 August (the day of the saint's death) and 20 October, when his relics are taken out of the chapel and laid beside a well Gerosimos is said to have dug himself. The chapel's interior is colourfully and gaily decorated.

South of the main Argostoli road is the convent of Agios Andreas, with seventeenth-century frescoes and a casket that contains what is alleged to be the sole of the saint's foot. Above this pleasantly restored building is the castle of Agios Georgios, built in the sixteenth century and surrounded by formidable stone fortifications. The ruins that lie on the hill around the castle are the remains of what was the capital of Cephalonia until 1757. The castle can be visited, the impressive walls remain intact but it has few buildings left standing inside. Most noticeable of these is the crumbling Catholic church of Agios Nikolaos. It is only 9km (5 miles) from the castle to Argostoli through the region known as Livatho.

Ithaca

With a jagged and indented coastline and a wild and dramatically rocky interior, the small and splendidly unspoilt island of Ithaca holds a special place in the hearts of travellers, bibliophiles and lovers of Greek mythology alike. It was the home of Odysseus, the cunning and courageous king whose 10 year struggle to return to his homeland after the Trojan War is faithfully recorded in Homer's *The Odyssey*.

Ithaca is a peaceful island and one relatively unruffled by the twentieth century. There is no industry to speak of, great chunks of the island can only be explored by foot and few concessions have been made to the tourist industry. It is an island known to many but visited by few. With hardly any beaches and a practically non-existent nightlife outside of the capital Vathi, Ithaca is hardly the ideal package holiday destination. Yet it is a welcoming island, small enough to be easily manageable and with its own very special set of attractions. Most of its 'sights', though, are centred around the Homeric legend, so a reading of *The Odyssey* before setting foot on the island would be a good idea. Besides, the book gives Ithaca a whole new dimension.

The Ithaca of today is probably the Ithaca of Homer, despite the efforts of some archaeologists to prove that either Lefkada or Cephalonia was the actual home of Odysseus. Their arguments were helped by the scarcity of archaeological finds on Ithaca that can be undeniably linked to Homer. Nevertheless, Homer's descriptions of the island in question seems to clinch the argument; rocky, severe, no grassland, no tracks, unsuited for horses, and good for goats. Ithaca fits the bill for all of these and there is one find at least that cannot be refuted — a small triangle of slate discovered in a cave in the north of the island and inscribed, 'A Prayer to Odysseus'.

Few island capitals have a more beautiful location than **Vathi**. It is an enchanting sight upon arrival, as the boat glides around the headland into the deeply blue bay of Molos and the town comes into view, its whitewashed houses forming an amphitheatre around the harbour. The tiny and unusually wooded islet of Zazaretto centres the bay which is hemmed in by barren and infertile mountains. Vathi is a popular yacht station and, on most days, bright sails line part of the waterfront, adding a splash of colour.

The town itself is tiny, stretching only a few blocks back from the waterfront on Odysseus Street; it owes its quaint, nineteenth-century appeal to its rebuilding after the 1953 earthquake rocked most of Ithaca. Vathi was reconstructed in its original style. There is not a great deal of accommodation available and some of the hotels are certainly over-priced but there is an old and basic pension which has cheap rooms and plenty of character. It is sited in a small alley off Odysseus Street just before the town hall. At the town hall, on the ground floor, tourist information about Ithaca can be obtained.

As for sights, there is a small archaeology museum, whose exhibits date back up to 30 centuries and the town church, Taxiarchos, pleasantly but darkly decorated and with an icon that is claimed to be the work of the great El Greco. A 20 minute walk north of the town leads to a narrow strip of pebbles that could just about be described as a beach. As beaches go, it would not be worth a second glance anywhere else, but on Ithaca, where swimming spots are few and far between, it may as well be Miami. There are other beaches at the extreme east of Vathi but these are only accessible on foot; in season, occasional caiques from Vathi shuttle bathers to and fro.

Ithaca is a dumb-bell shaped island, its two halves linked by a narrow waist and an asphalt road along which the island's bus rumbles, although not too often. There is no bus service in winter and only a twice-daily service in season from Vathi to the village of Kioni in the north-east. Cars and mopeds can be rented in Vathi. Alternatively, one could try to see the island by a combination of walking and hitch-hiking — most car drivers are willing to stop.

The island's first Homeric sight is only 3km (2 miles) out of Vathi, on the northern road that leads past the harbour; the Cave of the Nymphs, where Odysseus allegedly hid the marvellous gifts given to him by the Phaecians. The dirt path to the cave is signposted off the main road and it is a charming stroll up to its mouth through olive trees overlooking the bay. To enter, clamber through the narrow opening and descend a ladder into its musty and cool interior. The only light comes from a hole in the roof high above so a flashlight is necessary to see the few stalactites inside.

South of Vathi, 90 minutes of uphill hiking brings you to the Fountain of Arethusa, its fresh water spurting out of a rock just above Perapigadia Bay and the place where the disguised Odysseus met and tested his loyal swineherd Eumaeus. A dirt path connects the fountain to Perachori, an eighteenth-century village and the only settlement of any size south of Vathi. The monastery of Taxiarches, built in the seventeenth century but now deserted, is a 60 minute and mostly uphill walk away to the south-west.

Past the Cave of the Nymphs, the road curves around the bay before ascending sharply and steeply over the mountain ridge that is the waist of Ithaca. Just prior to the climb, on top of the mountain ridge, are the ruins of ancient Alakomenes, mistakenly claimed by the great German archaeologist, Heinrich Schliemann, to be the site of the castle of Odysseus. Although a few walls and the remains of a temple dating from 800BC can be seen, it is a stiff climb up there and a hard job to find the site — really one for archaeology buffs only. Also, just before the ascent, there is is a road bearing left to the bay of Pisa Aetos, which has a pebble beach that is said to be the best on Ithaca.

Over the waist of the island a choice of routes is presented to Stavros, the major village of the north; one inland and one coastal. The coastal route is flatter and quicker and offers views across the channel to Ithaca's big sister, Cephalonia. Halfway to Stavros, **Agios Ioannis** is passed, and here you can stop for a swim off the small beach. However, the inland route is the more interesting, twisting and winding its way through the mountainous interior. The first notable sight reached is Laertes farm, set in a rocky and scrubby field used for grazing goats. Laertes was the father of Odysseus and it was here that he went to live in despair for his lost son.

Further on is the convent of Kathara, built in the seventeenth century and beautifully set high on a mountain top that allows some of the best views of Ithaca, gazing across the waist of the island and down to Vathi. To get even higher, you can climb the steps of its blue and white bell tower. Nearer to Stavros, over a landscape dominated by great table-tops of rock, is the small and quiet village of **Anogi**, capital of the island in the tenth century. Its fourteenth-century Byzantine church is now happily restored after being damaged in the 1953 earthquake and boasts beautiful, original frescoes. The doors are likely to be locked; ask in the village as to who has the key.

Stavros is set in one of the lusher regions of Ithaca and is a busy and friendly village with a few tavernas and rooms to let for those wishing to stay. It is apt that a bust of a stern-looking Odysseus should gaze out over the Bay of Pilos from the leafy main square as Stavros has more Homeric connections than any other village on the island. A 10 minute walk north of Stavros up to Pilikata Hill is the site where archaeologists, digging beneath the remains of a Venetian fortress, discovered the remains of a Mycenaean settlement that many believe to be the Palace of Odysseus. Their claims are backed up by the finds made in the Pilos Cave, just above the bay said to be ancient Ithaca's main port, where more Mycenaean artefacts were unearthed. Should this current school of thought be correct, the Pilos Cave would be the hottest contender for the actual site of the Cave of the Nymphs. Unfortunately, though, the cave is now closed forever — the excavation work, combined with the 1953 earthquake, caused its roof to collapse.

North of Stavros is the tiny hamlet of **Pilikata** and signs here point to the Odysseus museum, run by the village schoolmaster and his wife. This displays some of the finds from Pilikata Hill and from the Pilos Cave. Dating back up to 28 centuries, the finds include tripods used in worship, vases, mugs and the famous stone with the inscription, 'A Prayer to Odysseus'. Particularly interesting is a collection of jars with unusual bases that were able to slot into wooden planks while on board ship and thus prevent spillage. Ask at the museum for directions to Homer's stone, a huge rock overlooking the sea with stone steps cut into it that lead to the top. This was, in fact, an ancient look-out post but islanders claim it was here that Homer would sit and lecture his pupils. The asphalt road that bends north-east out of Stavros leads to a few small fishing villages, of which the prettiest is **Kioni**. Just before Kioni is **Frikes**, the port for the in-season daily ferries to Vathi and all-year round services to Fiskardo on Cephalonia and Vassiliki on Lefkada.

The North-West Peloponnese

Patras and the West Coast

The majority of visitors to the north-west Peloponnese will, at some stage or another, arrive in **Patras**, the transit point en-route to the Ionian Islands and beyond. Linked by main road and by train to Athens, the city is home to 200,000 and is the third largest city in Greece, as well as being a centre for heavy industry and the country's largest port, after Pireaus. It would be inconceivable that a city of this size, and one that can trace its roots back to ancient times, should not have some sights of interest and Patras is no exception; it is a city with a little more to offer than just connections elsewhere.

Eight blocks back from Trion Simahon Square, on the very long and busy waterfront, is a steep staircase that leads up to the Venetian castle, built during their brief occupation of 1687-1715. It is a tough climb but worth the struggle to see the well-preserved walls and keep and to enjoy a fine panorama of Patras and the narrow channel beyond. Unfortunately, nothing remains of the acropolis of ancient Patras, which originally occupied the site of the castle, but beneath the ruins stands a Roman Odeon, in a condition good enough to enable it to host performances during the Patras festival.

More portable remains of Patras' past can be seen at the archaeological museum, just off Olgas Square, one block east and two blocks back from Trion Simahon Square, where some of the artefacts date back nearly 30 centuries to the Mycenaean Age. Another building associated with the history of Patras stands at the western end of the waterfront; the large and magnificent multi-domed church of Agios Andreas, built in memory of the great disciple of Christ, Andrew, who lived and was crucified in Patras. Inside the vividly decorated church is a casket containing the head of the saint, a gift from the Vatican to Patras.

An excursion with a difference can be made 9km (5 miles) south of Patras to the Achaia Clauss Winery, where visitors get a free, guided tour of the factory as well as a glass of its finest wine to sample; a sweet but very dark wine named Mavrodaphne ('Black Daphne').

The waterfront at Patras

The wine is named after a Greek girl the company's founder (Baron Von Clauss) desired but could not marry.

Culturally, there is a great deal going on in Patras. Its lengthy pre-Lent Carnival begins on 17 January and is celebrated with street parties and dancing. An International Arts Festival is held annually between mid-June and mid-August, marked by a series of musical and theatrical performances, some at the old Roman Odeon. Inquire at the tourist office for details (see the Further Information section at the end of this chapter).

There is little of interest between Patras and Killini, 71km (44 miles) to the west, apart from an 8km (5 miles) stretch of sandy beach at Kalogria, 22km (13 miles) out of Patras. Despite its size, it still gets packed with Patrasians at weekends. However, the beaches at **Killini** are longer and quieter, on the headland of a small promontory jutting out into the sea on the west coast. The sands start at the town of Killini and continue south for 11km (7 miles) to the spa at Loutra Killini. The most appealing aspect of the small town of Killini is its regular ferry connections with Zakynthos and Cephalonia.

Loutra Killini, however, is a large tourist complex and its famous hot spas have facilities that are claimed to be the best in Greece. There are two hotels ('A' and 'C' class), a campsite and entertainment that includes horse-riding, nightclubs and tennis, as well as watersports off the wonderful beach on which it stands.

In between Killini and Loutra Killini, in a region rich with citrus fruits, is the small and pleasing village of **Kastro**, built on a hill looking out to sea. Above the village is Chlemoutsi castle, built in the thirteenth century by the Crusader who dominated much of the Peloponnese, Geoffrey de Villehardouin. Partly restored, it is in fine condition and offers superb views across the water to Zakynthos from its solid turrets and ramparts. The charming little church just below the castle also dates from the thirteenth century.

To head south from Killini, double back 13km (8 miles) to rejoin the main coastal road. After 5km (3 miles) you can bear east through fields of twisted olive trees to the new town of **Amaliada**, from where you can make the 8km (5 mile) detour to ancient Elis. This was the predecessor of today's Olympic village, a place where athletes would rest and train before participating in the Olympic Games. The ruins, standing near to the huge Pinios dam, are not particularly outstanding but you can view its ancient theatre and a couple of temples to Aphrodite. South of Amaliada, on the coastal road, you can easily reach a few pleasant little seaside villages — Dounekia, Skafidia, Agios Andreas — before arriving at Pirgos. This is the capital of Eleia, the district that covers most of the north-western Peloponnese.

With good bus and train connections, **Pirgos** is a busy and not especially attractive town. It has a population of 20,000 and is an important commercial centre, particularly for the currant industry. The town had to be rebuilt after World War II, following an horrific street battle between the Greek resistance and Greek Nazis, who had retained control of the town after the German retreat. Its only sights of note are two large neo-Classical buildings, the municipal theatre and the municipal market.

On the tip of the peninsula, to the west, is **Katakolo**, 13km (8 miles) away and an old but atmospheric port with a long beach that provides shallow and safe bathing. Around the bay, at another good beach, is Agios Andreas, a Frankish castle that continues to crumble on top of a hill. Offshore, but visible only to those wearing flippers and with an aqualung strapped to their back, are the submerged ruins of Fia. However, the most rewarding excursion from Pirgos is to the outstanding ruins of ancient Olympia, 19km (12 miles) to the east and possibly the most durable symbol of Ancient Greece.

Olympia and Inland

The archaeological sites of the Peloponnese are known for their lovely settings and **Olympia** is no exception; tucked away in a lush valley bordered by the Alfios river and the Hill of Kronos, smothered in pine trees. It would be a fine location for a city but Olympia never became that; its only buildings were there for the administration of the Games, held on this site every 4 years from approximately 1000 BC to the end of the fourth century AD. Originally held in honour of the marriage of a local king's daughter to the god Pelops, the Games began to grow quickly in popularity until 776BC, when they were dedicated to Zeus and began to attract athletes from all of the Greek city-states. They all competed for the honour of wearing the sole prize, the *kallistefano* — the olive crown, made of a branch always cut from the same tree. The Games became so popular that all warring city-states would declare and adhere to a truce, 3 months prior to and during the competitions.

The first Games featured track events only but, in time, expanded to include the pentathlon, discus and javelin throwing, the high-jump and others still practised today. The two most popular events of the past are not competed for today; the *pantakrion*, a brutal combination of all-in wrestling and kick-boxing and the chariot race, which resulted in many a death under wheels and hooves. Art and literature contests were also held. It was a strictly all-male event — women were allegedly thrown from clifftops if they entered the stadium — and also a religious festival. Athletes would dedicate themselves to the gods before participating and the site's Temple to Zeus once contained one of the Seven Wonders of the Ancient World; a 13m (43ft) high statue of Zeus, built in gold and ivory.

The Romans enjoyed the Games but trivialised them somewhat, to the extent that the obese and insane Emperor Nero managed to win (not entirely legitimately, one suspects!) the singing and lyre-playing competitions as well as the chariot race, in the 69AD Olympiad. Yet, in 393AD, the Emperor Theodosius banned the Games due to their association with paganism and, 33 years later, the site was destroyed. The statue of Zeus was taken to Constantinople (Istanbul) only to be tragically destroyed by fire in the fifth century.

Thankfully, the Byzantine engineers who stripped Olympia and the earthquakes that subsequently rocked the site, did not do as much damage as could be expected and much can still be seen today, extensively spread out with some of its old columns majestically re-erected. As in the past, the Temple to Zeus remains the centrepiece; some indication of its size is given by the gigantic columns strewn

Olympia: part of the ruined stadium

beneath its stage. It is hemmed in by the walls of the Altis Grove where the contests were originally held before a new stadium was constructed to the east, beneath the Hill of Kronos.

Entering through a stone arch, one can see the start and finish lines of the running track, nearly 200m (180 yards) in length, and the stone seats where the judges sat. South of the stadium is the Hippodrome, where the chariots would thunder around its track and beyond that, the ruins of the house built for the Emperor Nero during his 'victorious' stay at the Games. Nearby stands a monument marking the spot where the heart of Pierre de Coubertin, the man who revived the Olympic Games in Athens in 1896, is buried.

As one enters the site, the Gymnasium is to the right and the Prytaneion (the administrative building) to the left. Beside this is the seventh-century BC Temple of Hera (wife and sister of Zeus) and the best-preserved of all the Olympian structures with many of its columns still standing. It was here that the marvellous statue of Hermes, the work of the sculptor Praxiteles, was housed. Races were held in honour of Hera in front of the temple although only virgins from Eleia were allowed to compete. The second-century fountain house is next to the temple, then comes the fourth-century BC Metroon — another temple. Behind that are the state treasuries, a kind of warehouse for the items used in sacrifice and rituals.

On the other side of the Altis, behind the Temple to Zeus, is the council house where competitors would swear their oath of honour before participating in the Games. Besides this is the Leonidaion, a once-grand hostel for visiting dignitaries and, moving back towards the entrance, the workshop of the great Pheidias, claimed to be the creator of the statue of Zeus. A few columns stand of the old Palaestra, next to the entrance, where competitors in the *pantakrion* would train before the event. Adjacent to the Palaestra are two monuments; the circular one was erected by Phillip the Second of Macedonia, in memory of his victories over the Greek city-states. The other is an altar dedicated to the god Pelops, whose marriage led to the first Olympic Games.

Aside from the buildings, the excavations at Olympia unearthed some stunning artefacts which are now displayed in the site's museum. Pride of place belongs to the beautiful finds from the Temple to Zeus, including a frieze depicting the Twelve Tasks of Hercules. Not far behind in importance is Praxiteles' graceful and relaxed statue of Hermes, dating from the fourth century BC. A beautifully sculpted Head of Hera can be seen, as well as numerous items pertaining to the Games themselves. A more modern history of the Games can be seen in the museum of the Olympic Games in the nearby village of new Olympia, housing memorabilia from the Games since their revival in 1896. The village is linked by train and by a very regular bus service to Pirgos.

The inland route that meanders its way over the hills back to Patras is another of those that offer a view of Greece that few get to see. Unfortunately, it is a route that can only really be enjoyed in its entirety by those with their own transport, due to the infrequency of the local bus services. Yet those dependent on public transport can still enjoy part of the route in a very special way, on the old rack and pinion railway that links the coastal town of Diakofto with the mountain town of Kalavrita.

After 15km (8 miles) of steady ascent north-east from Olympia through fields of chestnut trees you reach the village of **Lala**, on the edge of the forest of Finios, named after the kind centaur who sheltered the mighty Hercules. On the same road, 18km (11 miles) further on, is **Lambia**, set high in the mountains and more of a tiny district than a village, split as it is into seven separate neighbourhoods. The road then descends slightly, moving due east via small Tripotama to a junction 39km (24 miles) from Lambia. Here you can bear left through the old and atmospheric village of Klitoria and, just beyond the village, the road divides. Both routes lead to Kalavrita and both are equally appealing as they slice their way along mountainous slopes. On the northern road, signposted from Kastria village, is the Cave of the Lakes. A slender passage has to be negotiated before reaching a gigantic cavern with no less than fifteen tiny lakes covering its floor, their calm surface occasionally rippled by small waterfalls. The stalagmites and stalactites make intriguing rock formations. From the cave a minor road runs along the slopes of Mount Arsaneia (Helmos) to Kalavrita.

Despite its dramatic location between two mountains, **Kalavrita** is a sad little town and a monument in itself to the atrocities committed in war. In 1943 the occupying German forces massacred 1,436 people here — the entire male population of Kalavrita. The village clock is permanently set at 2.34; the time the massacre began. A plain white cross stands on a hill behind the town in memory of those who were murdered. There is not a great deal to see in Kalavrita beyond this but there is plenty of accommodation available as some very pleasant excursions can be made from the town.

The nearest excursion takes you 5km (3 miles) south of Kalavrita on the alternative road to Klitoria; to the monastery of Agia Lavra, overlooking the Vouraikos valley and now rebuilt after being burned down by the Germans in 1943. The magic number here seems to be 961; the monastery was originally constructed in AD961, it stands 961m (3,152ft) above sea-level and once housed 961 monks. It has been rebuilt majestically and inside the chapel one can see seventeenth-century frescoes and a delicately carved icon screen. A monument to the dead of the Greek War of Independence stands opposite the monastery; an apt site as this was where the Greeks declared their 6 year war of liberation.

The monastery of Mega Spileo ('Big Cave') has a good claim to being the oldest monastery in Greece. Situated 9km (5 miles) north-east of Kalavrita, it is a quite breathtaking sight — a massive building, part of which is wedged inside a huge cavern in the vertical cliff face it stands against; hence its name. The monastery was first built inside this cave in AD362; since then successive fires have damaged it to the degree that the structure's oldest buildings now date from the seventeenth century. The church itself is rich in decoration and

A narrow gorge and footbridge, Kalavrita

features an icon of the Panagia (Virgin Mary) alleged to be the work of the Apostle Luke. Mega Spileo is still an active monastery — it offers overnight facilities, but for men only. The nearest village is **Zahlorou**, a beautiful and shady little place and one of the stops on the funicular railway between Kalavrita and Diakofto.

Originally built by an Italian mining company in the nineteenth century, the railway makes for a super little 70 minute journey.

Admittedly, it is best-appreciated from Diakofto, so that you can watch the mountains rise spectacularly on either side of the narrow track. The train follows the path of the Vouraikos valley, slowly chugging over bridges and through windowed tunnels and twisting steeply from sea-level up to Kalavrita at an altitude of 750m (2,460ft). Two stops are made, at Treklia and Zahlorou and, as six trains a day make the journey, one can easily get off at Zahlorou to view the monastery of Mega Spileo before continuing the trip later in the day. It is certainly a journey worth arranging an itinerary around. Tickets for the journey can be bought at any of the stations.

By road it is 22km (13 miles) from Zahlorou to the main road on the north coast of the Peloponnese. To the east is the modern coastal village of **Astraka**, a good base for the journey up to the mountain village of Solos and the subsequent hike up Mount Arsaneia. This is a 6 hour climb, gruelling in parts but immensely rewarding and not only for the splendid panoramas it offers; it culminates at the 200m (650ft) high waterfall of Mavroneri. Back at Astraka it is an easy journey back to Patras, 65km (40 miles) west, passing a whole succession of coastal villages including the town of **Egion**, with its old district by the shore and the new town above it. Lungos and Lambiri both have nice beaches and Rio is the port from where the half hourly ferries to Andirrio, in central Greece, leave. From Rio it is another 8km (5 miles) to Patras.

Further Information
— Ionian Islands and North-West Peloponnese —
THE IONIAN ISLANDS

CEPHALONIA
Argostoli
Archaeological Museum
Open: 8am-2.30pm Monday to Friday, 8am-1pm Saturday and Sunday.
Closed Tuesdays.
☎ 0671 28300

History and Folklore Museum
Open: 8.30am-2pm Monday to Friday, 10am-12noon Saturday.
Closed Tuesdays.
☎ 0671 28835

Tourist Office
The waterfront
Open: April to October, 8am-2pm Monday to Saturday.
☎ 0671 22847

Sami
Drogati and Melissani Caves
Open: 9am-8pm daily.

ITHACA
Stavros
Odysseus Museum
Open: 9am-2pm daily.
Closed Mondays.

Vathi
Tourist information can be obtained from:
Town Hall, Odysseus Street
Open: 8am-2pm Monday to Friday.

ZAKYNTHOS
Zante
Post-Byzantine Museum
Open: 8.30am-3pm.
Closed Mondays and Saturdays.

Museum of Dionysios Solomos and Famous Zakynthians
Open: 9am-2pm daily

Venetian Castle
Open: 9am-3pm.
Closed Mondays.

The nearest tourist offices are at Cephalonia and Patras. For information, try the police in Zante:
☎ 0695 22550

THE NORTH-WEST PELOPONNESE

Killini
Chlemoutsi Castle
Village of Kastro
Open: 8.30am-3pm.
Closed Mondays.

Olympia
Archaeological Museum
Open: in-season 8am-7pm, 9am-5pm Sunday; off-season 9am-3pm.
☎ 0624 21529/22742

Museum of the Olympic Games
Village of New Olympia
Open: 8am-3.30pm daily, 9am-4.30pm Sunday.
☎ 0624 25572/22596

The Site
Open: in-season 8am-7pm, 9am-6pm Sunday; off-season 9am-3pm.
☎ 0624 22517

Olympia Information Office
☎ 0624 23100/23125

Patras
Achaia Clauss Winery
Guided tours: summer 9am-1pm, 4pm-6.30pm; winter 10am-4.30pm.

Archaeological Museum
Open: 8.30am-3pm.
Closed Saturdays and Mondays.

Tourist Office
The waterfront,
outside the Customs House.
Open: 7am-9.30pm, daily.
☎ 061 420304/5

4 • Mount Pelion
and the Sporades

Introduction

Although there are similarities between the three regions covered here — northern Evia, the islands of the Sporades and the Mount Pelion peninsula — each vary quite considerably and have very much their own appeal, history and traditional identity. All three are included together in this chapter because their geographical location and easy transportation links mean that the adventurous traveller can cover a large portion, if not all of the region, within a relatively short period of time and thus view a good cross-section of both island and mainland Greece. Visitors arriving in Athens can be in Halkida (also called Halkis), capital of the island of Evia, in less than 2 hours by either bus or train.

From Halkida, a good route would be to travel across Evia to visit the town of Kimi and to catch the ferry to Skyros, an island steeped in tradition. Return to Kimi and then to Halkida before exploring the forests, towns and beaches of northern Evia, ending at the spa resort of Edipsos where you can take one of twelve ferries daily to Arkitsa on the mainland, 50 minutes away.

Visit the beaches and ancient sites of the eastern mainland coast before arriving at the wealthy and industrialised city of Volos. From here you can easily loop around and take in the beauty of the Mount Pelion peninsula before returning to Volos where daily ferries leave for the Sporades and the two lovely but very different islands of Skopelos and Alonissos. Both have ferry services to either Volos or the port of Agios Konstantinos, further south. From either there are regular connections back to Athens.

Note that, in season, caiques leave from Platania in southern Pelion to Koukounaries beach on Skiathos, an island with daily connections to Skopelos. Skiathos houses the region's only airport since the temporary closure of the one at Volos. However, Skiathos is not included here; in recent years this island has become decidedly on the beaten track (possibly due to it having over sixty beaches). For the same reason, and because of the increasing industrialisation of the area, southern Evia is also not covered.

Although getting from 'A' to 'B' presents few problems, seeing the main attractions around some towns can sometimes prove a little more difficult. Those wishing to see as much as possible within a set period of time should be prepared to hire their own transport. Mopeds and scooters are ideal ways of getting around Skopelos, Skyros and Alonissos, and rental shops abound. Be warned that helmets are very rarely provided and that insurance is likely to be of the 'third-party' variety only. For the Mount Pelion peninsula, a car or more powerful motorbike are the better options as some of the roads in this hilly region may be a little too taxing for 50cc engines. Cars can be rented in Volos — there is a whole string of establishments on the first road back from the waterfront.

Bus services in the three regions vary. On Evia there are regular connections between Halkida and Kimi but only two or three daily from Halkida to the north. Buses from Volos travel to Makrinitsa, Agios Ioannis, Platania, Drakia, Portaria, Afissos, Horefto, Zagora and Hania, all villages on the Mount Pelion peninsula. Of the islands, Skopelos has a bus that ambles seven times a day up and down the inhabited eastern coast but the service on Skyros is limited to the road between Skyros town and the port Linaria, plus a few of the more popular beaches. There are no buses whatsoever on Alonissos. Throughout all the regions hitch-hiking is quite acceptable and often successful.

Each of the three regions features in some way in the Greek myths. Mount Pelion was the home of those wise, strong and semi-immortal creations — the half-man, half-horse Centaurs; Volos was the departure point for Jason and his Argonauts in their quest for the Golden Fleece; and Skyros was the hideout of the warrior Achilles, placed here by his mother to avoid being drafted into the Trojan War. The waters off Evia were said to contain the submerged home of the sea-god Poseidon and the island itself was where Pelops and Myrtilus fled to, together with the lovely daughter of King Oenomaus whose heart Pelops had won after a chariot race marked by skullduggery. By pre-arrangement, Myrtilus was to share the young princess with Pelops but the latter drowned the unfortunate Myrtilus in the sea just south of the Evian gulf — the Myrtoan Sea.

Aside from mythology, there is nothing distinctly remarkable about the more modern history of the region which is a reflection of

In many areas agriculture, rather than tourism, is still the primary source of income

*The attractive church of Zoodohos Pigi
with its Venetian bell-tower, Zante town (ch3)*

The serene beauty of the Blue Cave, Zakynthos (ch3)

A characteristically peaceful bay near Sknari, Zakynthos (ch3)

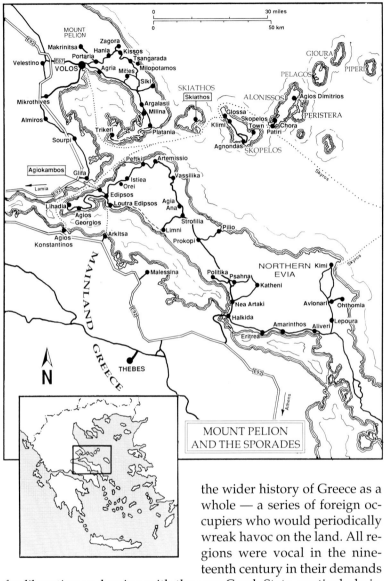

MOUNT PELION
AND THE SPORADES

the wider history of Greece as a
whole — a series of foreign occupiers who would periodically
wreak havoc on the land. All regions were vocal in the nineteenth century in their demands
for liberation and union with the new Greek State, particularly in
Mount Pelion, where fierce battles were fought between nationalists
and the Turkish forces in and around Makrinitsa in 1878. Evia and
the islands of the Sporades were added to the new Greek state in
1830; Pelion had to wait a little longer. Along with the rest of
Thessaly, it became part of Greece in 1881.

Mount Pelion, northern Evia and the Sporades are best-visited between the months of early May and mid September; May and September are only for the really tourist-shy. Climatically, it is very hot at this time of year although without the searing heat of the southern Dodecanese, for example. During the winter months, the region is one of the wettest spots in Greece. The Mount Pelion area is refreshingly cool all year round.

Summer is also the best time to try your hand at the various sports available in the region, most of which inevitably involve the sea. All of the popular resorts — Kala Nera in Mount Pelion, Edipsos on Evia, Marpounta on Alonissos, for example — have plenty of establishments hiring windsurfers, speedboats for waterskiers etc. At Halkida, capital of Evia, there is a waterskiing training centre. It is possible to ski on terra firma during the winter months at the Agriolefkes ski centre near Hania in Mount Pelion although this is dependent on snowfall, which has been sparse in recent years. Hikers ascending Mount Dirfis on Evia may stay at the mountain refuge hut there, just over half-way up. It is best to call and reserve a bed (see the Further Information section for the telephone number). The refuge is near the village of Liri where there are also ski lifts and slopes.

While in this part of Greece, sample a few of the local specialities. Although fish is the first item on most menus — served head, tail, fins and all — there is also *tyropsomi*, a type of cheesebread unique to the Pelion village of Milies. Also in Pelion, try *spetzofai*, a spicy concoction of sausages and peppers, and *vassoulada*, also served with peppers and a variant of the bean soup served everywhere in Greece. Local pickles and herbs can be bought almost anywhere in Pelion. This is a region that just brims with vegetation; in spring look out for the crocuses on the upper slopes of the mountain and, further down, cyclamens. On the island of Skopelos, tall irises grow freely. Those with an interest in flora may also care to visit Kato Lehonia and Ano Lehonia, two Pelion villages whose income is derived from the commercial cultivation of flowers.

Throughout the three regions accommodation is not difficult to find although you may have to look a little harder in the height of summer. The main towns all have hotels and even some of the smallest villages have a room or two to let. However, for a taste of the past, stay in some of the traditional guest houses in Mount Pelion; old mansions converted by the Greek National Tourist Office into rustic but smart and modern buildings. Such guest houses can be found at the Pelion villages of Makrinitsa, Milies and Vizitsa.

Volos

Any visitor to this part of Greece is likely, at some stage, to pass through the booming city of **Volos** which, while it may not be the place to linger for a few days, does provide an excellent insight into modern Greek city life. Capital of the prefecture of Magnesia and a major transportation hub, this is a city 70,000 strong, heavily industrialised with wide streets and large shopping precincts behind a lengthy waterfront. Its appearance is very new — the buildings of Volos were reconstructed in concrete, square, shake-proof blocks after an earthquake struck the city in 1955. Traffic moves ceaselessly down the grid-plan layout of streets and ships bellow as they leave the harbour usually en-route to the Sporades but often as far away as the Middle East. Yet Volos is an open and welcoming place with its own attractions, both in the city and in the surrounding area. If the pace and noise become too much, the cool and lush hills of the Mount Pelion peninsula are a 30 minute drive away.

Volos features in one of the most famous legends of Greek mythology as it was from here that Jason set sail on the *Argo* in his quest for the Golden Fleece. The city was then called *Iolkos* — the name Volos is believed to have derived from. Little now remains of this old Mycenaean city, save for a small site near the railway station, but those interested in discovering more of the history of the region can visit the archaeological museum, located at the far eastern end of the waterfront. The museum is well-presented, with the emphasis on education, and is marked in English. It displays the marvellous funeral steles (carved grave stones) from the cemetery of ancient Dimitrias, 4km ($2^1/_2$ miles) away and a host of finds from other sites such as Dimini and Sesklo, many dating back to the Bronze Age.

Just before the archaeological museum and unmarked on the literature handed out by the local tourist office, is a very different type of museum but one equally deserving of a visit. The museum of popular art is, in fact, a gallery featuring bright and colourful paintings and sculptures that fill the walls of several rooms. The remarkable thing about this display is that it is all the work of one man, Austides Laoudis, who began painting in 1981 at the ripe old age of 77. The museum is entered through the kitchen and there is no entrance fee. However, Mr Laoudis will ask you to sign his visitors' book. More modern examples of Greek art can be seen in the town hall which houses the municipal gallery. Several churches are worth popping into — particularly the huge Agios Konstantinos; this is sited on the waterfront, a 10 minute walk west of the archaeological museum.

Volos is an industrial city producing tobacco, textiles and iron-works so most tourists just pass through, heading for Mount Pelion peninsula or the Sporades. Those staying overnight have plenty of hotels to choose from, it is difficult to miss the more upmarket establishments but cheaper rooms can be found around the western end of the harbour. The tavernas in this area look a little down-at-heel but some surprisingly good and inexpensive fish dishes are there to be enjoyed. The waterfront is lined with cafés and restaurants and small *souvlaki* and *tost* fast-food joints are everywhere. The Greek National Tourist Office for the Thessaly region is based in Volos between the main town and the bus and railway stations (see the Further Information section at the end of the chapter).

Exploring the surrounds of Volos makes for a good day-trip as there are a number of archaeological sites and pleasant beaches in the area. Just out of town and reached by turning off the main road to Larissa, are the remains of the ancient Neolithic cities of Dimini and Sesklo, the latter is 14km (9 miles) from Volos. At **Dimini**, inhabited between 4000 and 1200BC, two *tholos* (bee-hive) tombs can be seen, believed to be those of kings of the settlement. At **Sesklo** the remains of the town's acropolis date back 8,000 years, making it the oldest in Greece. Back in Volos and taking the Lamia road south, the old Hellenic city of Dimitrias is arrived at after 4km ($2^1/_2$ miles). Its extensive ruins are set among pine trees and include a palace, temple and theatre. Nearby is the beach resort at Alikes and further down the coast are the beaches of Maratho and Chrysi Akti.

The road continues to Mikrothives where it forks south for Lamia and for Glifa, where you can make the ferry crossing to Edipsos in northern Evia. En-route is the town of **Almiros** which has a small archaeological museum and by cutting left, you reach the beaches of Amaliapoli. On the main road the large villages of Sourpi and Pteleos are passed before Glifa is reached, 75km (46 miles) from Volos.

Northern Evia

The largest Greek island after Crete, Evia runs down the eastern coast of central Greece, its soft contours seemingly able to fit like a jigsaw piece into the mainland it was once attached to. Its separation was supposedly the result of a furious blow from the trident of the sea-god Poseidon. A more plausible explanation is that it was caused by a terrible earthquake. Yet, despite its proximity to the mainland, Evia still manages to retain its own identity.

A green and fertile island, Evia's mountainous interior houses quiet villages and its coastline boasts both bustling resorts and peaceful sandy stretches so the fact that the island receives large numbers of visitors is no real surprise. However, the vast majority of tourists are Greeks and you can still savour the beauties of Evia without feeling like just another face in the crowd. For ease of access to Mount Pelion peninsula and the Sporades and because much of the south-western coast of Evia is rapidly becoming industrialised, only northern Evia is covered here. The dividing line between north and south is the Halkida-Kimi road, via Lepoura.

Evia is certainly one of the most accessible of the Greek Islands, with no fewer than six ferry crossing points. Northern Evia is entered from Glifa to Agiokambos (seven ferries daily), Arkitsa to Edipsos (twelve daily) and Oropos to Eritrea (sixteen daily); while in the south there are services from Rafina to Marmari (one daily), Rafina to Karistos (one daily) and Agia Marina to Nea Stira (seven daily).

There is no airport on the island and the most convenient route (particularly from Athens) into Evia is over the 70m (230ft) bridge that links the mainland with Halkida, the island's capital. The bridge crosses the Evripos Straits whose strange tidal currents have puzzled scientists for centuries, including Aristotle who was driven to despair by his inability to understand why the tide should inexplicably change direction several times a day. Once there, getting around the north of Evia will pose few problems for those with their own transport; Evia's bus service, while a great deal better than most Greek island services, is still whimsical. Cars, motorbikes and mopeds can be hired in Halkida and in the resort centres.

Despite its size, Evia as a whole never held any great importance during Classical times, with the exceptions of Halkida and Eritrea which were great trading and shipping centres respectively. The island's main role, though, was as a base for the city-states (particularly Athens, whose control Evia came under in 500BC) to graze their animals and grow their crops.

In 338BC Philip the Second, father of Alexander the Great, took control of the island for the Macedonians and, from this point on, Evia's history mirrors that of most of mainland Greece — rule by Macedonians, Romans, Byzantines, Franks, Venetians and the Turks, who settled on Evia in large numbers. In 1830 it became part of the original Greek kingdom. It is interesting to note that the word 'Greece' comes from the Graeci, an Eviot tribe in Roman times. The Romans used Graeci to refer to all Hellenes, a misnomer that continues today.

In ancient times **Halkida's** trading power was such that it dominated great portions of Greece to the extent that the three-pronged peninsula of Halikidiki in Macedonia drew its name from the city. Halkida itself either derives its name from the Greek *Halkos* meaning 'copper' (there was once a thriving copper-processing industry here) or from *Halki*, a shell used in dyeing fabrics.

Halkida's ancient heritage has now disappeared but remnants of its more modern history remain such as the ruins of a seventeenth-century Turkish castle built high above the city. Underneath this is the old Turkish quarter, far more atmospheric than the new town and host to a lively market at the end of July that lasts for 10 days. The old mosque here is now converted into a Byzantine museum. Next to it stands the curious basilica-cum-cathedral of Agia Paraskevi, the work of thirteenth-century crusaders. Back in the new town, the archaeological museum displays the best finds from the excavations at Eritrea. Should you wish to stay overnight in Halkida, there are several hotels, many near the bridge as you cross onto Evia.

South out of Halkida, on the road that cuts up to Kimi on the eastern coast, is **Eritrea**, once a major maritime centre and home to a great school of philosophy before the entire city was destroyed in 87BC. Today it is a bustling coastal resort, drawing sun-seekers to the nearby beach at Malakonta. As can be imagined, the beach is hardly secluded. Much of the old city is still in evidence, though, despite having had the new city built right on top of it, and the ruins of the agora, the temple of Apollo, the theatre and the gymnasium remain. Finds from the ancient city are housed in the small museum of Eritrea.

Further along the coast, **Amarinthos** is a far less developed resort with a good beach and a row of waterfront restaurants renowned for their fine fish dishes. Above the harbour are two Byzantine churches, Metamorfossis and Kimissis Theotokou. Continuing south to the Lepoura junction, the unremarkable town of Aliveri is passed, dominated by its power station.

The Lepoura to Kimi road winds its way peacefully through the green mountains, passing a series of small rural villages. Thirteen kilometres (8 miles) out of Lepoura the road forks right for a small detour to the village of **Ohthomia** which stands high above a string of sandy beaches. **Avlonari** lies on the same road to Ohthomia and has a fine twelfth-century basilica dedicated to Agios Demetrios.

Back on the main road, it is another 23km (14 miles) to **Kimi**. Dubbed the 'Balcony of the Aegean' and the 'Gateway to the Sporades', this town stands on a cliff a full 250m (820ft) above the water in a green, well-wooded region. This is the major town on the eastern coast and used to have a thriving fig industry up until the

The theatre in the ancient city of Eritrea

1950s when disease wiped out the crop. Although houses built in traditional, red-roofed style can still be seen, they are gradually being replaced by more modern dwellings.

Examples of Evian handicrafts can be seen in the folklore museum on the road leading 4km (2¹/₂ miles) down to the port of Paralia Kimi. As its name suggests, there is a sandy beach (*paralia* means beach) and boats leave from the port for the island of Skyros once a day off-season, twice-daily in season. A 20 minute walk north of Kimi town leads to the therapeutic mineral springs at Honeftiko and inland, reached by a 90 minute walk, is the convent of Sotiros, steeply built on the side of a hill. No good roads connect Kimi with the rest of northern Evia.

The northern road out of Halkida leads to quiet Nea Artaki where a fork in the road leads inland through the village of Katheni, before climbing steeply through forests to Seni. This is the starting point for the ascent of Mount Dirfi, over 1,700m (5,550ft) above sea level. There is a mountain refuge hut (☎ 0221 25230) at 1,150m (3,770ft) where hikers can rest or stay overnight before the hard 90 minute climb to the summit. Heading back to Nea Artaki, take the northern road to Prokopi. Detours can be made en-route to the villages of Psahna and Politika, the latter having a fifteenth-century Byzantine church.

Unlike great chunks of northern Evia, **Prokopi** has been unscarred by forest fire and is set at the end of a ravine in a green and well-forested area. A castle is perched precariously above the town. Prokopi's population of 1,200 is mainly composed of Greeks from Asia Minor who were forced to leave Turkey after the heavy Greek defeat in the 1922 war with Turkey resulted in a mass population exchange. The church of Agios Ioannis (St John of Russia) contains the saint's relics and his festival day on 27 May draws hordes of pilgrims.

From Prokopi, the northern road leads 16km (10 miles) to Strofilia where a left turn takes you to the whitewashed houses of the quiet coastal town of **Limni**. Mythology relates that Zeus married his sister Hera in this town and although one can no longer view their wedding temple (this was destroyed by earthquake many centuries ago), the convent of Galataki can be visited in a 1 hour climb south out of town. Limni possesses a row of shingle beaches and, with several rooms to let, the town is waking up to its potential as a coastal resort.

It is a poor road that leads up the north-western coast to Edipsos so, returning to Strofilia, take the road's northern route up to the tip of Evia. The first village passed is **Agia Ana**, charming and traditional with a long, sandy beach not far away. After Vassilika the road curves around Cape Artemissio, scene of a furious sea battle between the Hellenes and the invading Persians in 480BC. It was on this cape, in 1928, that two of the great treasures of the National Archaeological Museum in Athens were dredged out of a shipwreck; the bronze nude of Zeus (or Poseidon) and the Little Jockey, frantically urging on his horse.

Just beyond the village of Artemissio is the beach resort of Peftki, which is popular among the Greeks. **Istiea**, the next large town along, nestles among fields and orchards. This was said to be the town where Hera, wife of Zeus, would graze her bulls. **Irei**, 6km (4 miles) further on, has a marble bull standing in the village square. The bull was found off the coast in the 1960s and dates back to 400BC. Orei has an excellent strategic location dominating the Evoikos channel it stands on. The Franks were quick to realise this and built a large fortress which bisects today's town. Down the coast before Edipsos is the coastal resort of Agiokambos.

Edipsos and its sister town of Loutra Edipsos have over eighty-five hotels of class 'C' and above. There are beaches, tavernas, night-

A view over the town of Edipsos

clubs, cinemas and a tourist pavilion but these are not the town's main attractions. The attraction is that Loutra Edipsos has a hot spa and the largest hydrotherapy-physiotherapy centre in Greece. Its sulphurous waters were mentioned by Aristotle and Plutarch, and Roman and Byzantine emperors are said to have bathed in them to soothe their ailments. The warrior Hercules apparently gained his strength here. Muscular and gynaecological complaints reportedly benefit from treatment at the spa. Driving west out of Edipsos, on the peninsula that stretches into the Gulf of Evia, you reach the wooded town of Lihadia. The beach and coastal resort of Agios Georgios is nearby.

Mount Pelion

Named after the mountain that runs down the spine of this 'Italian-boot' shaped peninsula, the area of Mount Pelion remains unknown to and unvisited by the vast majority of overseas visitors to Greece. This is surprising when one considers the claim of many that the peninsula is the most beautiful region in Greece. Lush and richly green, its altitude and close proximity to the sea combine to keep

Mount Pelion cool during even the sweltering summer months, making for wonderful hikes over the hills and between the deeply traditional villages. Both coastlines are dotted with splendid beaches, mostly sandy and ideal for bathing. Plenty of Greeks are 'in-the-know' regarding Mount Pelion, the consequence of this being that several villages on the western coastline near Volos have been transformed into popular holiday spots with all the usual facilities. Yet the beaches on the east coast are equally good, less visited and with cleaner swimming; the east coast faces the wide expanse of the Aegean Sea while the west coast is hemmed in by mainland Greece.

As well as enjoying the beaches, you can always explore the Pelion villages, in themselves unique to the region. The peninsula has been settled since ancient times — its abundance of water providing for good agriculture — but it was only when Slavic invaders from the north arrived in the sixth century that the villages of today began to be founded. Their Slavic names are still retained — Markrinitsa, Zagora, Vizitsa etc.

During the Frankish period, which was ushered in by the sacking of Constantinople by Crusaders in 1204, the peninsula became a large commercial centre, trading with Franks, Byzantines, Genoans and Venetians alike. It continued this role into the Ottoman occupation, a time of prosperity for Pelion. Not only did agriculture and industries such as textiles thrive, but so did cultural and intellectual pursuits, embodied in the famous nineteenth-century schools in the large villages of Zagora and Milies. Whether they are large or small, the Pelion villages are something to be seen, either being split into four distinct neighbourhoods (as in Ano Volos and Tsangarada) or built around a cobbled *platia* (square) which is often shaded by a large plane tree. The houses themselves are steeply built, tall with plenty of windows, slate roofs and overhanging first (and sometimes second) stories. The beauty of the villages are often enhanced by the residents' gardens — in most cases they are immaculate and over-flowing with flowers.

East Pelion

The first town encountered on the north-western road out of Volos is the wealthy suburb of **Ano Volos**, split into four neighbourhoods and offering a tantalising glimpse of what Mount Pelion holds in store. Its size robs it of the sheer beauty of the inland villages but its slopes are green and fresh and many of the houses constructed in typical Pelion fashion. One of the neighbourhoods, Anakassia houses the Theophiles museum, which is dedicated to the rambling nineteenth-century folk artist and features many of his wall-paintings; other samples of his work can be seen in the Alli Meria district, in the old Velentza bakery.

From Ano Volos the main city stretches out beneath the steeply climbing road that leads to **Portaria**, a large and very attractive village that combines a deeply traditional appearance with an air of evening bustle, unusual in Greek villages. In the stone-paved main square a plane tree stands, a common feature in Pelion setttlements. Accommodation is available here, from the cheaper hotels on the main square to the excellent Despotiko, a converted Pelion mansion located in the mass of cobbled streets that lie to the right of the main road.

Ignoring the right fork on the asphalt road, head out of Portaria to **Makrinitsa**, the 'Balcony of Pelion' and architecturally one of the most striking villages in the region. The traditional houses clamber upwards on top of each other, built onto the green slopes by the ingenious method of having three levels at the front of the house and one at the back. So steep is Makrinitsa that there is a 300m (980ft) difference between the 'top' and the 'bottom' of the village. The cobbled, leafy *platia* is centred around an old, hollowed-out tree next to a tiny church; a nearby taverna features a wall painting by Theophiles.

The Ministry of Tourism has declared Makrinitsa a 'traditional settlement' — all new constructions must be of traditional style. From the main street you can make the 3 hour trek to the top of Pliasidi, one of the peaks of Pelion. May Day is a great day in Makrinitsa, marking the beginning of a traditional festival that lasts 3 days and is said to include elements of the ancient festival for Dionysus.

Retracing the road back to Portaria, passing a picturesque waterfall, a left fork leads over the spine of Mount Pelion and into the heart of the peninsula, leaving the view of Volos far behind. The first village is passed at 1,200m (4,000ft), the modern and tiny **Hania** ('old inns') near the winter ski resort of Agriolefkes which has a refuge, lifts and runs for the experienced and beginners.

From Hania the road twists down through chestnut trees towards the Aegean until a junction is reached. Turning left leads to **Zagora**, one of the largest villages of Pelion and a major fruit-growing centre which produces pears, plums, strawberries and Pelion apples, famous throughout Greece. Orchards and fields are everywhere. It has been a prosperous village for many years; in the eighteenth century Zagora housed a flourishing textile industry exporting its produce from Horefto, 8km (5 miles) downhill. Some fine churches can be seen in Zagora, notably Agios Georgios with its lovely carved altar screen. Behind this church is the library which was founded in 1762 and features sixteenth-century prints of the works of Homer and Plato. A map of the world dated 1715 is quite intriguing. **Horefto** still has a small anchorage but people visit the hamlet today for its long and sandy beach, hemmed in by trees. Accommodation is available both here and in Zagora. North of Zagora is the Byzantine monastery of Rasova and, beyond that, is **Pouri**, another steeply built village — even the *platia* here is on three different levels.

Heading back to and beyond the junction where you turned left for Zagora, a series of charming villages are passed — Makrirahi, Anilio and Kissos — the latter is home to the eighteenth century church of Agia Marina with its colourful frescoes. Not only are their settings lovely, but the gardens are immaculately maintained and brimming with flowers. There is little hint that 6km (4 miles) down to the coast from Kissos is the most developed region of eastern Pelion — the hotels, restaurants and gorgeous sandy beach of Agios Ioannis. In season, this will be packed with holidaymakers (mostly Greeks) but quieter bathing can be found by walking south for less than an hour. This is **Damouhari**; quiet with two white pebble beaches and the remains of a Venetian castle to explore.

From Damouhari the road leads up to Mouressi, with a stop for the icons that adorn its church of the Dormition of the Virgin and 5km (3 miles) further on **Tsangarada**, a large and sprawling village split into four distinct districts. Its name has Slavic origins and could mean either 'nice view' or 'royal village'. Either is equally applicable as the village offers splendid views of the ridge of Mount Pelion and its old mansions bear witness to the days when Tsangarada was a major silkworm-growing and wood-cutting centre. An enormous plane tree stands in the quaint, flag-stoned village *platia*. The tree is said to be over 1,000 years old and is an astonishing 18m (59ft) in diameter. Wooden blocks support its gnarled and sagging branches. With several rooms to let, Tsangarada makes a good base for exploring Mount Pelion. **Milopotamos**, 8km (5 miles) down to the coast, has another of Pelion's lovely sandy beaches; it is ideal for swimming.

South Pelion

South of Tsangarada, the area is less inhabited and those short of time may wish to head south past Lambinou before turning right to the village of Milies, from where the road runs along the western coast back to Volos. Alternatively, you can keep heading south — past

Neohori and the turn-off to Afetes there is a fork in the road — bear left for the small village of Siki with its nearby monastery of Agios Prodomos, built in 1875. Back on the main north-south road, it is 8km (5 miles) to what can be considered the capital of south Pelion, **Argalasti**. This is more of a town than a village and its amenities include a police station, a post office, a library and a branch of the OTE (the Greek telephone system). A number of ruined medieval Byzantine buildings were found in the region — many near the monastery of Agios Nikolaos — and stones from these buildings have been used in some of Argalasti's more modern constructions, although you will have to look hard to find them.

Several very pleasant villages and beaches are easily accessible from Argalasti. North-west of the town are the mountain hamlets of Kalithea and Xinovrisi, set beautifully on steep green slopes that overlook the Aegean. Returning from here to Argalasti, a right fork runs east to **Paltsi**, another small village with a road descending to a shore that is renowned for its good fishing. Twelve kilometres (8 miles) north of Argalasti, on the west coast, is **Lefokastro** which has a long, quiet sandy beach. A coastal road links it with **Kalamos** to the south; wooded slopes leading gently down to the sea give it a similar appeal and setting to Lefokastro.

You have to return to Argalasti to head south once more to the developed resort of **Horto**, built around the tiny bay of Valtoudi. There is a disco to entertain those staying overnight here. The small islet offshore is called Alatas. It is uninhabited but caiques make the 10 minute crossing in season to visit the monastery of Agia Saranda there. Caiques also cross from Milina, another resort 3km (2 miles) south and once a shipbuilding centre. Its roots go back to Mycenaean times when it was the town of *Olizon*.

Several small, pretty but unremarkable villages are clustered in-land from Milina in a dense, olive-growing region. A junction be-tween two of them, Lefkos and Promiri, travels down to the splendid beach at Platania, very popular among Greek holidaymakers, and a little further west, the beach at Mikro. **Platania** used to be as far as the road went on Mount Pelion, but a recently constructed road skirts Mount Tisseo, running along the coastline to **Trikeri**. Due to its previous isolation, this village has retained a good deal of its tradi-tional character. Its port, Agia Kirriaki, is a small and sleepy fishing hamlet. **Palio**, the tiny islet off the tip of the Pelion peninsula, is very rarely visited; its three small settlements make their living from the fishing industry.

West Pelion

The west coast of Mount Pelion is easily reached from Volos and is heavily commercialised, catering mainly for Greek tourists. Inland, however, the traditional character of the peninsula reasserts itself.

The road south-east from Volos arrives first at Agria whose proximity to the city makes it a little more popular than its long and thin beach justifies. Hotels and restaurants abound. Just up from the town, on the hill at Anemoutsa, stands a chapel housing a remarkable iconostatis; carved from wood by a local craftsman, it features daily events in the life of locals.

Beyond Agria on the main road, a left turn climbs Mount Pelion to **Drakia**. This is another charmingly located village, its wealthy past reflected in several mansions, all featuring a distinctive tower. One such mansion, Triandafylou, houses works by Ioannis Pagonis, the eighteenth-century folk painter who was born in the village. Traditional costumes and music mark Drakia's folk festival on 23 August. A secondary road links Drakia with Agios Lavrendis, architecturally one of the most charming villages of the area.

Back on the main road from Volos, the air becomes deliciously fragrant as Kato Lehonia and Ano Lehonia are passed. This is a major fruit and flower growing region and camellias, roses and other flowers bloom everywhere. At this point, one can turn right for a swim at a choice of seaside resorts — Platanidios, Malaki and Kato Gatzea — before reaching **Kala Nera**, the prime resort of the western Pelion coastline and still only 19km (12 miles) from Volos. Kala Nera can be translated as 'good waters' and is named after the freshwater springs that service the village, often in the form of attractive fountains. The town is cool and leafy, with poplar, plane and eucalyptus trees. At the beach, the trees just stretch along behind the sand.

Beyond Kala Nera the road forks, the left turn leading uphill to **Milies** through apple orchards — *milies* is Greek for apples. This is a large village, its buildings steeped in traditional Pelion architecture and centred around the shady *platia* that overlooks the gulf below. 'Little Smokey', a slow steam train, once linked the village to Volos but development of Pelion's road network rendered the small engine redundant. Plans to re-introduce the service as a tourist attraction are developing rapidly. In the meantime, the quaint old railway station itself is worth a look.

Milies has a strong intellectual and cultural heritage that began when the centaur Cheiron schooled his students in a cave (this can be found near the railway station). A famous school was founded here in the eighteenth century, patronised by intellectuals such as

Phillipidis, Gazis and Konstandas. Some of their works, as well as other artefacts from the region, are housed in Milies library which is open to visitors. All three men were instrumental in the liberation of Thessaly as a whole. In the *platia*, the church of the Taxiarches is festooned with frescoes. Milies has its own culinary speciality, *tyropsomi*, a tasty cheese-bread.

By taking the north-west road out of the village, you are beginning the journey back to Volos via Vizitsa, a quiet and restful village. Like Drakia, Vizitsa mansions are of the 'tower' variety and although some are tragically falling to rack and ruin, others are being restored by the Greek Tourist Office as 'traditional guesthouses'.

The Sporades

Skopelos

With Skiathos only a 90 minute ferry journey away, Skopelos can be expected to draw its fair share of summer sun-seekers; and draw them it does, although the number of visitors comes nowhere near approaching those of its neighbour. There are a few hotels, several tavernas and plenty of English-speaking locals but what tourist facilities there are on this island exist as much for the Skopoleans as they do for their summer itinerants. In the main, the 103km^2 (40sq miles) of Skopelos are as untouched by tourism as a Greek island of such beauty can expect to be.

Despite a name that means 'steep rock', Skopelos is not a rocky island. Like Skiathos it is well-watered, with firs, pines and wild flowers in abundance. During the spring, the fields and roadsides are covered in colour — look out for the wild irises in particular. Fields of olives, plums and pears can be seen, contributing to an island economy that rests more on fishing and agriculture than tourism.

As islanders have resisted all government blandishments to build an airport here, the only way onto the island is from the sea. Regular passenger ferries and the rapid but expensive 'Flying Dolphin' hydrofoils arrive from Volos, Agios Konstantinos, Skiathos and Alonissos at the rate of at least one per day from each port. Boats dock at Skopelos town, the island's capital, and at Loutraki, 3km (2 miles) below the second town of Glossa. Most dock at both ports, some at only one. There is a bus service between Loutraki and Skopelos town, a lovely hour long journey along a snaking asphalt road on the western coast that passes glorious beaches and forests of green.

Skopelos town stretches itself lazily along a great half-moon of a waterfront, its whitewashed and steeply packed houses providing a

Skopelos town with its houses rising steeply from the waterfront

sparkling contrast against the deep blue of the bay. The narrow and crazily-paved streets are enough to frustrate the finest cartographer but any student of architecture will delight in this town. The houses are a bizarre mix of architectural styles — Turkish, Macedonian Venetian — a reflection of the island's history. The ruins of a Venetian castle are incorporated in the top of the town and can be reached by climbing the stone steps at the end of the waterfront (adjacent to where the ferries dock), past a series of small churches.

The visitor will see a large number of churches and chapels in Skopelos. Despite its diminutive size, the island claims 360 in all, with 123 in Skopelos town itself. One of the churches, Zoodohos Pigi, has an icon reputedly painted by the Apostle Luke; another, Episkopi, is built on what is believed to be the spot where Reginus, the patron saint of Skopelos, was murdered in the fourth century.

Just outside Skopelos town, on the other side of the bay, are three monasteries; the sixteenth-century Metamorphosis and the eighteenth-century Evangelismos and Propramou. The latter is a convent. All three can be visited, either by organised tours arranged by the travel agents on the waterfront or by a long but pleasant morning stroll. The monasteries are open between 8am and 1pm, closing for a lengthy siesta before re-opening the gates between 5 and 7pm. Skirts and shawls are provided for those improperly dressed i.e. whose arms and/or legs are uncovered.

Those seeking to stretch the body instead of the mind can do so at two sandy beaches near the main town. To reach the first, the popular and crescent shaped Agios Konstantinos, take the donkey path that

Whitewashed walls and overhanging eaves help to deflect the strong heat of the sun. This house is at Makrihari, east Pelion (ch4)

A tree's roots growing into the folded strata of a cliff face on Alonissos (ch4)

Children in colourful traditional dress in Metsovo, Epirus (ch5)

begins at the back of the town near the Venetian castle. The second is Glysteri, reached by a 45 minute walk through olive groves and nestled in a quiet, sheltered cove. Serviced by a single taverna, this is an excellent spot for a beach party.

The rest of the island's towns and villages are settled on the western coast and linked by the asphalt Skopelos-Loutraki road. Many of the villages have beaches and where there are beaches there are usually a few rooms to let, ideal for those who want a few quiet days. The first village reached out of Skopelos town is **Staphylos**, with a long, sandy-shingly beach a short walk from the main road. An easy climb over a few rocks connects it to Velanio, which serves as the island's only official nudist beach. It was at Staphylos in 1927 that a great royal tomb was discovered, believed to be that of King Staphylos of Crete and confirming the historians' theory that Skopelos was once a Cretan colony. Artefacts from the tomb are displayed in the museum at Volos. Further up the coast is **Agnondas** where small boats leave regularly in season for the beach of Limenari, sandy and accessible only from the sea.

Halfway to Glossa are the twin beaches of Panormos and Milia, the latter said by some to be the island's finest and, a 10 minute drive further on, you reach the squat town of **Elios** with its tiny harbour and sandy beach. It was to Elios that the people of Klimi, 3km (2 miles) south of Glossa, came after the 1965 earthquake shattered their town. **Klimi** is now the island's 'ghost town' but like Chora on Alonissos, its renovatable properties are gradually being bought up as holiday retreats.

Despite its pleasing location among the trees, the steeply built town of **Glossa** is rather plain. It is, however, the place to start the 3 hour round trip walk to Agios Ioannis, a small church perched on top of a huge rock just off the coast. Heading out of Glossa in the direction of Skopelos town, bear left onto a dirt path upon reaching a disco. The walk is a beautifully tranquil one, graced with wild flowers and offering striking views of the eastern coastline; 111 steep and treacherous steps lead up to the church. The rocky cove below is ideal for a refreshing dip before beginning the 90 minute trek back to Glossa.

Alonissos

Situated thirty minutes east of Skopelos by ferry, what the rocky island of Alonissos lacks in public transportation, asphalt roads and tourist facilities more than makes up for through its friendly charm. With its isolated beaches, shady walks, submerged cities, eight small

Boats in the harbour at Loutraki on the island of Skopelos

satellite islands to visit and the chance to be an archaeologist for the day, the tourist industry is slowly waking up to its potential. This does not seem to thrill the 1,500 residents of the island — like the Skopoleans, they have recently scuppered plans to build an airport here — as Alonissos is already popular with holidaymakers from mid-July to the end of August. For the rest of the year, though, fishing retains its spot as the island's prime industry and the heady scent of wild flowers returns to replace that of Ambre Solaire. Yet, even in high season, Alonissos receives its guests in the manner that permeates the entire island — relaxed, calm and unobtrusive.

This easy-going air conceals the sad history of Alonissos which, in recent years, has suffered greviously at the hands of man and nature. No sooner had the island's profitable vineyards been totally wiped out by disease, when the earthquake of 1965 struck, ravaging the capital town of Chora. The Greek government of the day compounded this tragedy by decreeing that the tiny port of Patiri, next to the fishing hamlet of Vitsi on the south coast, be expanded to serve as the capital town rather than rebuilding Chora which is beautifully but inconveniently located on a tall hill overlooking the sea. Unable to obtain the funding to rebuild their homes, the residents of Chora were forced to move to the new town that was hastily being built and Chora fell to ruin as it became the island's 'ghost town'.

Patitiri itself is a friendly and welcoming place but has squat houses and rubble-strewn streets. There are a couple of hotels and plenty of rooms to let, advertised by owners who greet the boats arriving at the harbour. The town is linked to Chora by dirt road, or more pleasantly, by the old mule track, a 30 minute walk through meadows from the top of Patitiri. The old capital is now regaining some of its pre-1965 charm, the whitewashed houses gradually being bought up as holiday retreats. A taverna just before the town offers drinks, food and good views of the coastline. The small beach of Vrisitsa is only a 20 minute walk away.

The nearest beach to Patitiri is sandy-shingly Marpounta, hemmed in by jagged volcanic rock. Some say an ancient Hellenic water tower lies submerged offshore but few claim to have actually seen it. Nearby is the Marpounta Hotel which offers tennis, waterskiing, motor-boat hire and windsurfing among its services. The walk to Marpounta is a pleasant one, beginning at the hotel on top of the hill at the end of the waterfront and slowly descending past deciduous trees. Note the steel trays attached to the tree trunks; the sap collected in these is used in the making of the drink *retsina*, giving it the distinctive, woody taste.

Getting around Alonissos is not an easy afair as only the south of this long and thin island is in any way developed, the highlands of the north being a wild tangle of forests. Motorbikes may make some progress on the unpaved roads but the best way to see the north is by boat. Ikos Travel, on the waterfront at Patiri, runs caiques in the summer to the beaches in the north and a weekly boat circumnavigates the island for a price that includes lunch. The manager of Ikos Travel is a good source for any further information about Alonissos but don't smoke in his office — there's a 5,000 drachma fine!

The beaches north of Patitiri are mainly located on the eastern coast, the first ones reached being the lovely stretches of sand at Chrisimilia and the delightfully named **Kokkino Kastro**. It is the latter that stands as a monument to the mistake of an early Greek government who actually gave Alonissos the wrong name in the rush to restore ancient Greek names after the Turkish occupation. For Alonissos is not the site of ancient Alonissos — it is the site of ancient Ikos, a city now submerged off the beach at Kokkino Kastro. A wall at the northern end of the cove once belonged to the old acropolis and, by swimming about 30m (100ft) out, some of the submerged walls of the city can be made out among the waves.

Further up the coast are the quiet and atmospheric villages of Steni Vali and Kalamakia; both have beaches, pensions and tavernas where one can eat under the stars while gazing out to sea. Keep going north for the beach at Agios Dimitrious while, at the northern tip of the island, the coves at Gerakis and Kopelousako are rarely visited by bathers.

On the west coast, directly opposite Steni Vali on the map, is Tsoukalia beach. This was the old clay-pot making centre of Ikos and today, thousands of years on, fragments of pottery can still be found on the beach and on nearby hills. Lucky people may find fragments that are stamped IKION (Produce of Ikos). These fragments have no commercial value but those tempted to take them home should remember the strict laws in Greece that govern the export of antiquities. Antiquities are defined as objects that date from before 1830. To be in possession of any of these objects is a criminal offence. Unfortunately, the kilns once used to fire the pots are gradually being destroyed by roadworks in the area.

Alonissos has eight satellite islands, some of them reached by excursion boats from Patiri, the others accessible only by hiring a boat. Peristera is the nearest but, apart from some sandy beaches, has little to draw the visitor. The same applies to Skangoura whose monastery is tended by a single monk. **Kyra Panagia** (or Pelagos) is owned by the Megista Lavra monastery on Mount Athos although its two monasteries are now deserted. The hulk of a twelfth-century Byzantine ship can be seen offshore at Agios Petras bay. Recent excavations here by the University of London have unearthed what is believed to be one of the first prehistoric settlements in the Mediterranean. The island of Psathoura, which has ancient ruins extending into the sea, is the hottest contender for being the actual site of ancient Alonissos.

Pappou is populated only by hares, and tiny **Gioura** has recently been declared a national park to protect a very rare breed of goat that inhabits its rocks. It also has a beautiful stalactite- and stalagmite-filled cave, reputedly that of the fearsome Cyclops in Homer's *The Odyssey*. This can be visited but bring your own torch. Apart from Cyclops, the only inhabitants of the cave have been monks from Mount Athos who eked out a spartan existence here in the fourteenth and fifteenth centuries. Their oil lamps can still be seen, embedded in the rock. The island of **Piperi**, the furthest away from Alonissos, is a sanctuary and monitoring centre of the very rare monk seal. Humans unconnected with the project are prohibited from the island but anyone with a real urge to visit should try obtaining a permit from the Ministry of Tourism at 2 Amerikas Street, Athens (☎ [01] 322 3111).

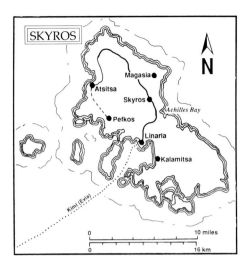

Skyros

The rugged, wooded island of Skyros is set apart from the rest of the Sporades and not only in a geographical sense. It certainly has some common denominators with its neighbours to the north-west; fine beaches, an undulating landscape and a fishing-based economy for example; but this is an island that is very individualistic. Poor connections with the mainland, the departure of much of the island's youth and, until very recently, only tiny numbers of tourists, have kept Skyros on a back-burner for years. Consequently, Skyrian dress, customs, folklore and festivals have survived more or less intact and, even if the number of visitors is now growing, it is this unique nature that keeps the island off the beaten track.

The sea-nymph Thetis, mother of the great warrior hero Achilles, certainly saw Skyros as an out-of-the-way place. It was here that she hid her beloved son, dressed in womens' clothing, in order that he would not be sent to fight at Troy. However, the cunning Odysseus tricked him into revealing his identity and Achilles joined the Greek forces only to die from an arrow wound in the heel. It was on Skyros that the great Athenian Theseus was murdered, pushed to his death from the town's acropolis by King Lykomedes of Skyroas. His death led to an Athenian invasion and the start of the long association between the city and the island. Even today, many young Skyrians choose to live in Athens where economic opportunities are rather more advanced than they are on Skyros.

There is no ferry service between Skyros and the other islands of the Sporades but in season the speedy 'Flying Dolphins' hydrofoils make the journey twice-weekly from Volos. The most common route onto the island is by the twice-daily ferry from Kimi on Evia. Out of season, the service may drop to one a day, leaving mid-afternoon. Kimi is easily reached from Athens by bus or train to Halkida, capital of Evia, and then a bus for Kimi. It is a 2 hour crossing, the boat always docking at **Linaria**, one of only two towns on the island and in itself little more than a quiet and pretty fishing village. It does have a beach and several rooms to let as well as a bus connection with the capital of the island, Skyros town (or Chora). There is an airport on Skyros with daily flights to Athens.

Skyros town rises steeply up from the waterfront and caters well for visitors with hotels, campsites and plenty of rooms to let. Staying in the latter will probably provide the opportunity to get inside a traditional Skyriot home, which tends to remind one of the house of an old hoarder who cannot bear to throw anything away. Decorative plates, icons, copperware, handicrafts and other such items fill the shelves and walls, often drawn from all over the world. The practice dates back from the days when large collections of bits and pieces were seen as status symbols by the wealthy. Ask to see any room offered before agreeing to stay. Those staying in hotels or in camp-sites need not miss out on the experience — the Faltaits museum, donated by a descendant of the once-powerful Skyrian family of the same name, contains model reconstructions of the houses' interiors as well as the usual displays of handicrafts and embroidery. Many of the items are handmade on the island and are for sale.

The town's archaeological museum houses local finds dating back three millennia and is located off a *platia* dedicated to the English poet Rupert Brooke. A nude bronze statue of the great man stands in the centre of the square. Brooke died of blood poisoning in 1915 on a French hospital ship just off the Skyrian coast. He was buried at the southern tip of the island near the bay of Tris Boukes and his well-maintained tomb can be visited by caique, taxi or on foot (2 hours) from Kalamitsa, just south of Linaria.

The Venetian fortress that dominates Skyros town is only the most recent of a series of structures that have stood on this excellent strategic point. The Byzantines built here before the Venetians and the remains of the Classical walls that can be seen are from the acropolis of ancient Skyros, from where King Lykomedes pushed the hapless Theseus to his death. Just below the castle is the now de-serted tenth-century monastery of Agios Georgios, dedicated to the patron saint of Skyros.

The carnival (the 3 week period before Lent) is a great time to be on

Skyros. The celebrations during this holy period are more than tinged with a touch of tradition. Every day for the 3 weeks, a strange procession makes its way up to the monastery of Agios Georgios. It includes the Old Man dressed in a goatskin and attached to dozens of bells; the Korela, a man dressed as a Skyrian woman; and the Frangos, a man dressed as a seventeenth-century European. Together they perform the Goat Dance. Some say the dance is a throwback to the days when islanders worshipped goats, others that it recalls a dispute between goatherds and landowers. Whatever the source, it is unique to Skyros. A strange Skyrian superstition is also enacted at this time. If a person sneezes during the final Sunday meal before Lent, their shirt is rent from top to bottom. Failure to do this will result in their death before the year is out.

Two small fishing hamlets, Magasia and Molos, lie a short walk north of Skyros town and both have sandy, long and very popular beaches; there are plenty of tavernas and rooms to let. Magasia is host in mid-June to another unique Skyrian festival, as local youths hold races on a breed of horses, similar to Shetland ponies, that are native to Skyros. These tiny ponies live mainly around the south of the island and although disease and starvation have caused the dwindling of their numbers, they can still be seen, usually in a domesticated environment. Due south of Skyros town there are fine beaches at Basales and around Achilles Bay. A 10 minute walk south of the bay leads to a quiet nudist beach.

The bus service on Skyros is limited, serving only the main towns and the most popular beaches. Getting around the island, therefore, is best achieved by hiring a moped or car; but take it easy — many of the roads are unpaved.

There is really very little to see in the north of Skyros. Great chunks of this dense and hilly region are inaccessible but the island's airport is based here, as are a number of military installations. Rather, take the road west out of Skyros town and head 15km (9 miles) to the relaxation/meditation/fitness centre at **Atsitsa.** This is positioned on the beach; pines provide a backdrop against the sand in an idyllic setting. Activities range from windsurfing, dance and aerobics to yoga, music and painting. For the address and telephone number see the Further Information section.

A very poor road links Atsitsa with Agios Fokas and, further down on the western coast, with Pefkos. The latter just has the edge in terms of looks and facilities. Those travelling on the asphalt Skyros town - Linaria road should fork right for both beaches before Linaria. There is another splendid beach at **Kalamitsa**, reached by turning left at the

Achilles Bay turn-off on the Linaria road. Kalamitsa is the nearest settlement to the grave of Rupert Brooke. Back in Skyros town, a 45 minute walk north-west leads to the monastery of Agios Dimitrios. To gain entrance to the chapel with its sixteenth-century frescoes, ask at Skyros Travel (see Further Information section) the day before.

Further Information
— Mount Pelion and the Sporades —

EVIA
Kimi
Folklore Museum
Open: 10am-1pm, 4.30-7.30pm daily.

Mountain Refuge Hut
Mount Dirfis
☎ 0288 51285 or 0221 25230

SKYROS
Atsitsa
The Skyros Centre
Information can be obtained at:
1 Fawley Road, London NW6 1SL
☎ 071 431 0867

Skyros Town
Archaeological Museum
Open: 8.45am-3pm.
Closed Mondays.

Faltaits Museum
Open: late morning/early evening daily.

Skyros Travel
North of the main square
☎ 0222 91123

VOLOS
Archaeological Museum
Open: 8.30am-3pm daily.
Closed Monday.
☎ 0421 25285

Dimini
Archaeological Site
Open: daily 8.30-3pm.
Closed Monday.
☎ 0421 25285

Museum of Popular Art
Open: 10am-1pm, 5-7pm daily.

Theophiles Museum
Anakassia (Ano Volos)
Open: 9am-6pm daily
☎ 0421 43088

Tourist Office
Riga Ferous Street
Open: 7.30am-2.30pm,
Monday to Friday.
☎ 0421 23500

SKOPELOS
Skopelos Town
Metamorphosis, Evangelismos and Propramou monasteries
Open: 8am-1pm, 5-7pm daily.

ALONISSOS
Patiri
Ikos Travel
The waterfront
☎ 0424 65320

HALKIDA
Waterskiing Training Centre
1 Dimitriou Street
☎ 0221 26456

5 • Epirus and Lefkada

Introduction

W edged into Greece by the Ionian Sea to the west and the Albanian border to the north-west, Epirus is the most mountainous region in Greece and offers some of the most beautifully striking panoramas in the country. Bare and arid on their upper slopes, green and well-forested at the lower levels, these mountains form part of the Pindos range and scythe down the east of the region, their snow-capped peaks providing a great natural barrier that seals Epirus off from the rest of the country. The mountains are the main attraction of the area, offering fine hiking opportunities, but Epirus has more to offer besides these; there are good beaches on the west coast and some truly ancient archaeological sites. Beyond these attractions, there is the chance to see a part of Greece that very few visitors are aware even exists.

Ioannina is the capital of Epirus, a bright and modern city yet with a fine old town and a fantastic location, sited on the shores of a lake in a bowl of mountains. With its own airport, which has daily flights to Athens, it is the ideal place to begin a tour of the region, offering easy access to the Zagorohoria. This is a mountainous region full of traditional villages and the jumping-off point for a number of hikes in their surrounds, up past the snowline to the peaks or through dramatic ravines.

One can visit Konitsa, the major town of northern Epirus and only a stone's throw from the still-disputed Albanian border before returning to Ioannina and heading for the coast. Possibilities include the beach resort of Parga or further south to the beaches around Preveza. Near Preveza are the ruins of the once great city of Nikopolis, built by the Roman Octavian as a thanksgiving to the gods for his victory over the ships of Antony and Cleopatra, in a sea-battle that took place off the Preveza coast. The lovely town of Arta is just east of here and from the town one can either head north back to Ioannina, following the route of the Arachtos river, or head south

121

past the Ambracian Gulf into southern Epirus. Most people will find that this region does not hold the great attractions of the north but one can visit Messolongi, the town of the great Hellenophile Lord Byron; and the island of Lefkada whose attractions are, as yet, known mainly to Greek holidaymakers only.

In ancient times the cities of Epirus never achieved the same power or status of the great city-states of Attica and the Peloponnese. Perpetually warring amongst themselves, they proved easy pickings for the Macedonians of Phillip the Second. In 295BC, though, King Pyrrus, head of the Molossian tribe, was granted control of the region, managed to achieve some unity of the cities, and even won several wars in Italy. Yet his death sent the region into decline and by 168BC the Roman legions had swept through Epirus, destroying many of its cities and enslaving thousands. Ancient Epirus, however, did hold two sites of great importance, both of which are still visitable today; the oak-tree oracle to Zeus at Dodoni and the Necromanteion of Efyra, where the souls of the dead would enter the Underworld of Hades. The Byzantine era saw Christianity establish itself in Epirus and many fine churches were built. However, the region suffered under constant attacks from Serbs, Goths and Slavs and stability was only achieved when Epirus was declared a despotate in 1204.

The fortunes of Epirus from then on seemed to depend on whoever ruled as despot. Some men were just and fair, others brutal and corrupt. When the Turks took Epirus in the 1430s, they maintained the despotate system of administration. In fact, Turkish rule began well for Epirus; cities such as Ioannina were granted economic and cultural privileges and the traditional Epirot industries of wood-carving, fabric-making and silver-smithing flourished. However, as the revolts against the Turks grew, so too did the repression, culminating in the arrival of Ali Pasha in 1778. The most feared despot of all, his duplicitous and cruel rule was finally brought to an end on the orders of the Turkish Sultan himself in 1822.

Shortly after Ali Pasha's death, the new Greek state was founded and Epirus gradually became incorporated into it; Arta in 1881, Ioannina in 1913; and its boundaries were finally drawn at the end of the Second Balkan War of 1913. Between 1945 and 1948 Epirus was the scene of some of the bitterest fighting of the Greek Civil War. The communists, operating from their bases in Yugoslavia and Albania, very nearly gained ascendancy but were finally defeated by the democratic forces, with the aid of Great Britain and the United States.

Architecturally, traces of Turkish rule are all over Epirus, their

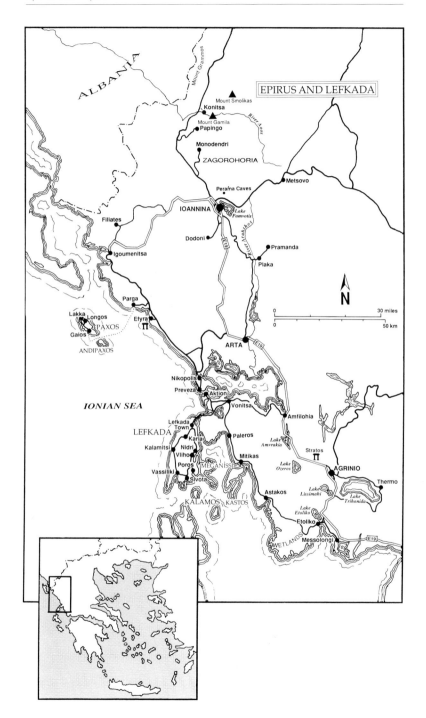

high balconied and wooden-framed houses often standing attractively beside more modern structures. Another architectural feature common in Epirus, but most noticeable in the Zagorohoria region, are the villages that seem to blend mysteriously in with the landscape. They are built out of the grey slate commonly found in the area, a substance easy to chisel and work and thus used in the making of courtyards and floors as well as houses, leaving the villages camouflaged against the terrain.

Epirus is not the greatest of places for nightlife — that can only be found around the major cities and in Parga — but it is an area that will delight the nature lover. The lower slopes of the Pindos mountains are plastered with dense vegetation, well-forested with black pines, oaks, beeches and the rombola, a type of pine unique to the Balkans. The array of wild flowers, particularly in the gorges in spring, is stunning; bellflowers, orchids and lilies, to name but a few.

There is a wide variety of animal life ranging from the brilliantly coloured butterflies, to the wild boars, wolves and bears that live high in the most inaccessible regions of the mountains. Red squirrels are sometimes seen in the woodlands and, up amongst the peaks, there are birds of prey and, occasionally, vultures. Waterbirds flock to the Messolongi Wetlands, just west of the town of Messolongi. Although this huge and swampy delta is slowly drying up, it is still the best place in Epirus to see herons, egrets and storks.

Getting to Epirus poses few problems. The quickest, easiest but most expensive way is by air from Athens, over the Pindos to either Ioannina and Vonitsa. It is also possible to arrive by sea — from Italy, Yugoslavia or Corfu — at the port of Igoumenitsa or from the Ionian islands of Cephalonia and Ithaca to Astakos in southern Epirus. Although the Pindos mountains have made it logistically impossible for Epirus to have a rail network, the region can be entered by road from north, south and east. Kastoria, in northern Macedonia, has a direct road link to Konitsa and from Thessaly and southern Macedonia in the east one can make the crossing of the Pindos in a spectacular fashion, through the 1,700m (5,580ft) high Katari Pass, continually being cleared of snow in winter.

If you are travelling from the Peloponnese, cross by ferry from Rio to Andirrio, near Messolongi. The Epirot public bus service is frequent and quick between major towns but can be slow and irregular to the less populous centres. As for its climate, Epirus is fine and warm in the summer but in winter months suffers from heavy snows that render parts of the region inaccessible; for this reason, the best time of year to visit is between spring and autumn.

Ioannina's medieval castle

Ioannina

The bright and pleasant city of **Ioannina** (pronounced Yaneena) is the capital of Epirus and the most logical point from which to begin any tour of the region. Its connections are good, being linked by daily flights to Athens and by roads to the east and to the west where Igoumenitsa is only 88km (54 miles) away.

To arrive from the east is to negotiate the hairpin-twisting of the Katari Pass which slices its way vertiginously through the Pindos mountains at an altitude of 1,700m (5,580ft) and passes the Vlach village of Metsovo (see Chapter 6) just over the border from Thessaly. It is a spectacular way to enter Ioannina; towards the end the road soars downward bringing the city, amphitheatrically built around Lake Pamvotis, closer and closer before touching down level with the water and rounding half of the lake into the city.

If the noise and bustle and high-rise buildings endemic to any modern city are immediately noticeable, so too are the green parks; the grey stone walls of the old city; Lake Pamvotis with the small island of Nissi rising from its centre; and the ruined medieval castle. There is a lot to see and do in Ioannina — it is an enjoyable city.

Ioannina's roots lie in the early Byzantine era when the sixth-century Emperor Justinian ordered the city founded by the then homeless residents of Evroia, a nearby town that had been sacked by raiding Goths.First known as New Evroia, it took 100 years for the new settlement to become Ioannina, a name change most likely brought about by the prominence of the monastery of Agios Ioannis Prodromos, positioned in Ioannina and respected across the region.

The city's first 600 years passed rather uneventfully, save for a brief eleventh-century incursion by the Normans,but then in 1204 Epirus became a despotate and although Ioannina was not its capital, it soon became a wealthy and prominent town within the region. It even gained certain privileges, such as freedom from taxation. These and other privileges, including freedom of religion, continued even under Turkish rule, thanks to a deal struck between the city's nobility and their Ottoman occupiers; Ioannina surrendered without a fight and accepted a certain degree of autonomy in return.

Economic privileges were also granted, privileges that benefited the nobility to the extent that their position was threatened as much as the Turks' in 1611 when the religious leader Dionysios Skylosophus led a revolt that resulted in the capture of the city castle. The nobility betrayed Dionysios to the Turks; he was skinned alive. Following the revolt the Turks rescinded Ioannina's privileges yet the town continued to prosper, consolidating its commercial power and enhancing its cultural reputation.

1788 was the year that ushered in Ali Pasha, the most infamous of Ioannina's overlords and a man linked with most of the sights of the city today. His sad, bearded, almost benevolent face gazes out from many an Ioanninan picture postcard, but appearances can be deceptive. The Albanian-born Ali Pasha was dreaded by all throughout his 44 years of office. Duplicitous and ferociously ambitious, he would side with anyone — British, French or Turkish — in order to advance his own interests, all the time paying lip-service to the Turkish Sultan. His brutality was said to know no limits; Greek rebels could expect nothing but torture and death if captured. A popular (and believable) tale relates how he ordered the drowning in Lake Pamvotis of eighteen members of his harem including the mistress of his eldest son; the lady had refused his advances. Yet he was a great builder; most of what remains of the castle and old city today was constructed during his reign.

In 1820 Ali Pasha double-crossed the Sultan once too often; an army was sent west to dislodge him and in the subsequent battle the tyrant was killed in action. Ioannina gradually recovered and, on 21 February 1913, the city was liberated, an anniversary still celebrated today with parades and martial music along the streets of one of the most important cities of Greece.

The castle and the old city that is built beneath it stand on a promontory on Lake Pamvotis and make for a good first stop in the city. This is the place to taste a little of Ioannina's past. To reach the old city, walk down from the main square towards the water to arrive at a huge stone gate with thick iron doors — pass through it to see the charming tangle of Turkish style houses and cramped, cobbled streets. The old city has a lively bustle about it and seems worlds away from the noise and traffic. Many of the silversmiths — this is still one of the leading industries of Ioannina — have their work-shops here.

The streets lead up to the castle, built by Justinian and improved by later rulers, particularly Ali Pasha who gave the fortress its double walls. Set in a large, lush and flower-strewn area, are the unmarked and crumbling remains of outhouses, prison cells and cellars. Rusted and toppled cannons, left by the Turks, still point out over Lake Pamvotis from the ramparts, a popular spot for the young lovers of Ioannina.

The most impressive building stands opposite the entrance to the castle, just behind an Ottoman family grave claimed by some to be Ali Pasha's. This is the mosque, built by Aslan Pasha in 1618 as a symbol of Turkish domination after the failed revolt 7 years before; prior to this the Turks had agreed not to live or worship within the castle walls. The mosque has now been converted into a popular art museum; an appealing display of photographs, traditional cos-tumes, weapons and portraits of the battles and great leaders of the day.

More museums are to be found around what serves as the city centre, the bright and gaudy Platia Demokratius, home to the post office and the friendly and helpful tourist office. Walking down to the lake from there, on Averof Street, leads to the archaeological museum, just past a green and shady park. The museum's reputation is growing and rightly so; splendidly laid out, it displays the intrigu-ing finds from Dodoni and, on a more modern theme, some beautiful sculptures that include a perfect nude of Artemis. Heading back up towards the main *platia*, turn right on Mihail Angelou Street for the folklore museum, a pleasing collection of Epirot bric-a-brac. Thir-teen kilometres (8 miles) south of town is the Vrellis museum, a waxwork collection of figures representing significant events in Ioannina from 1611 to 1821. It provides another good guide to Ioannina's history.

If the bustle and general hubbub of the city gets too much, visit Nissi; the small island in the centre of Lake Pamvotis. Carless and

*Stalagmites in
the Perama
Caves*

quiet, it is the ideal retreat. Half-hourly boats make the 10 minute crossing from the old city over a lake which is 3,500 years old.

Pamvotis is Greek for 'feeding everything', an apt name as a whole variety of tasty fish fill the lake including carp, trout, and eel, although the numbers of the latter are rapidly decreasing. Overfarming is the problem; the eels are said to be the tastiest in all of Greece. However, with all this fish around, it is hardly surprising that every other establishment in Nissi is a restaurant and that every one of these specialise in fresh fish. The fish are kept in large glass tanks and the idea is that you pick your own. The restauranteer will happily make the choice for those unwilling to pronounce sentence on any one creature. Below the tanks, frogs hop about in nets — their legs are a speciality on Nissi. Note that on the island, restaurant prices get cheaper as one goes back from the harbour.

The island itself is lovely; green with willows overhanging the water on the shoreline and festooned with plane trees inland. Its small village was originally founded by Maniot refugees 300 years ago and is quiet and pleasant with no main street to speak of, just a meandering network of alleys.

There are four monasteries on the island, all visitable by ringing the bell. The monastery of Agios Nikolaos features well-preserved but stomach-churning frescoes depicting the sufferings of early Christians. The monastery of Agios Panteleimon houses a small museum in its grounds, built in the room where the desperate Ali Pasha made his last stand. He was shot from the room below, the bullets passing through the floor and into his heart; the bullet holes can still be seen. The rest of the museum is not particularly impressive although a dress on display there once belonged to his mistress, Vasiliki. The other two monasteries are the thirteenth-century Philanthropinon and the eleventh-century Diliou.

In 1940 the Italian Air Force subjected Ioannina to some terrible bombing raids, and residents from the city and its surrounds took cover among the nearby rocks and mountains. So it was that an old man discovered the Perama Caves, 4km ($2^1/_2$ miles) north-east of Ioannina and claimed to be the largest caves in all of Greece. Open daily, they are a must on any itinerary of Ioannina's sights, and are linked by frequent buses to the city. Tours of the caves (with a guide) last roughly 45 minutes and take visitors through clusters of stalactites and stalagmites and hidden caves. The guides have given some rather intriguing names to the rock formations; look out for 'Jaws', the 'Statue of Liberty' and even 'Ayatollah Khomeini'! At the exit stands a bust of John Petrochilis, speleologist and explorer of the cave.

Dodoni

This is one of the most beautiful and isolated ancient cities to be seen in Greece and is certainly one of the oldest. Dodoni was first settled over four millennia ago and its oracle to Zeus, in the form of an old oak tree, became famous across the land. Its ruins, dominated by a massive amphitheatre, stand only 22km (14 miles) from Ioannina.

Built in a deep valley in a wild and hilly region, Dodoni's choice as the site for this all-knowing oracle arose when a holy pigeon flew in from Thebes and reputedly declared from the branches of an old oak tree that this was to be a holy place. The choice of Zeus as a medium was easy. This most powerful god is said to have visited the town with one of his wives, Dione, from which the name Dodoni is said to be derived. Up until 500BC, no temples were built on the site. The oak tree alone was the focus of worship, speaking through the rustling of

Dodoni's amphitheatre, where performances are still held

its leaves and protected from evil spirits by copper tripods at its base and cauldrons hanging from the branches.

Pilgrims journeyed here from afar to ask questions which were not merely concerned with the outcome of war and strategic alliances; personal problems were also aired — whether a man's blanket was lost or stolen or whether his wife's child-to-be was actually his! Such questions, engraved in stone, were found during the excavations of Dodoni and can be seen in Ioannina's archaeological museum. In the meantime the city grew; a Temple to Zeus was constructed near the oak tree and, in 282BC, a huge theatre was built to host the Naia Games. However, in 167BC, the Romans sacked Dodoni and as Christianity spread in later centuries, the holy city died. In the fourth century, the oak tree was hacked down. The Dodonians fled to Ioannina.

The centrepiece of Dodoni remains the amphitheatre; marvellously intact, its dramatic presence is heightened by the site's isolation. Occasional performances are still held here during Ioannina's Epirus festival; ask at the tourist office in the city for details. The ruins above the amphitheatre are what remains of Dodoni's acropolis. Part of the Temple to Zeus still stands. It dates from 500BC and is enclosed within a courtyard next to an oak tree, planted by its archaeologists and adding to the site's aura. Near to this are the ruins of an early Christian basilica, possibly dating from the fourth century.

Getting to Dodoni by public transport can be a problem; only two buses leave daily for new Dodoni, opposite the site, and both turn around to head back to Ioannina on arrival. So you can either hitch, take a taxi or stay overnight in the small pension in Dodoni, taking the morning bus back to Ioannina.

The Zagorahoria

With a beauty that is sheer and spectacular, the valleys and mountains of the Zagorahoria region have no real equal in Greece when it comes to glorious panoramas. This really is a new world, bereft of the honking cars and *souvlaki* stalls of Ioannina yet only 1 hour's driving to the north. There are only snow-capped peaks, rocky canyons, gushing mountain streams and elusively hidden lakes; a part of Greece where one can still walk all day and not see another living soul apart from the odd wild goat and the large numbers of brilliantly coloured butterflies. Although a good deal of the Zagorahoria can be explored by car, the price of getting into its grand and peaceful interior is some occasionally strenuous hiking.

In recent years the area has been declared a national park and the forty-six villages within its boundaries classified as 'traditional settlements' — that is, being forbidden commercial development that goes beyond the needs of the inhabitants and the few visitors each village gets. Many of these villages date from the seventeenth century and before — those in consequent disrepair have been renovated by the Greek government into spotless little settlements, inhabited mainly by the aged. Many will find enchantment in these tidy, quiet and uniform villages, built from the grey slate that is indigenous to the area. However, it is the landscape and not the villages that draws visitors to the Zagorahoria.

Those intending to hike around parts of the region would be wise to do a little groundwork before setting off. Drop in at the tourist office in Ioannina for up-to-date information on routes, conditions and accommodation availability — trekking holiday firms have already begun to put Zagorahoria into the brochures. A visit to Robinson Tours, an Ioannian travel agency specialising in tours of the national park, may also prove worthwhile (ask at the tourist office for directions).

Pack a small rucksack with light provisions, a warm sweater (it can get bitterly cold above the treeline) and plenty of water. Be sure to wear strong boots — sports shoes will not be up to the task — and inform your hotel or pension where you are going and when you intend to come back. Those without cars should check in Ioannina on the bus schedules to either Papingo or Monodendri, the two most popular jumping-off points for hikes into the region; at times services can be down to only three or five per week.

For those hard-pressed for time, the quickest and most immediately rewarding hikes begin at the village of **Megallo Papingo**, 61km (38 miles) north of Ioannina, off the Konitsa road. Among the cobbled streets of this busy village one can find a smart guest house — an old mansion converted by the Greek Tourist Office for this purpose — that doubles as a useful information centre; some rooms to let and a couple of tavernas.

A twisting half-hour walk up to the sister village of **Mikro Papingo** leads into the courtyard of a small church where the asphalt ends and the trekking begins. Take a left at the church and walk up the village to a small signpost where the distances to all destinations are marked in walking hours; the first that needs to be reached is the refuge hut, nearly 2,000m (6,560ft) high in the mountains along a route clearly marked with splashes of red paint on the rocks. It is a 3 hour walk, continually climbing alongside buttes that look as if they have come straight from the set of *How the West was Won*!

Lush and green forests filled with flora are negotiated first, then the vegetation becomes scrubby and the treeline is passed leaving nothing ahead but bare mountain and the snowline, which is soon reached. The refuge hut is not far away from the snowline — it will be easily visible from there and the views upon reaching it are stupendous. Those who intend to stay overnight at the refuge can obtain the keys from the information centre in Megallo Papingo.

The splashes of red paint end at the refuge hut so, to continue, go past the hut and descend 50m (60yd) down a very steep and rocky path to a signpost whose destinations are again marked in number of walking hours. The nearest is to the north-east, an hour's squelching over the wet valley below and then a steep climb up to Dragonlimni, an icy lake secreted away amongst the snow-covered rocks of Mount Timfi. A stiff 3 hours' walk away is the hike to the 2,500m (8,200ft) high summit of Mount Gamila.

Another enjoyable trek that the region offers is the 7 hour hike through the Vikos Gorge, starting at Monodendri (connected by bus to Ioannina) and ending at Megallo Papingo, or vice-versa. Sleepy **Monodendri** is a grey village in every sense of the word but it does

Dragon Lake (Dragonlimni) in the Zagoria National Park

have two pensions, a small taverna and the monastery of Agia Paraskevi, nearly 1km ($^1/_2$ mile) away and open to visitors.

The gorge can be descended into from the beginning of the village or down the treacherous path that begins behind the church. The route is badly marked — it is a case of picking out your own path, partly along the rocks on the gorge's bed, partly along footpaths at the sides — but is made worthwhile by the flora and the sense of utter solitude.

At the point where the gorge widens keep going straight, past a small eighteenth-century chapel; Megallo Papingo is only 2 hours away. Do not be tempted by the stone steps that lead up and out of the gorge to the left at this point; they lead to the village of Vikos and to get to Papingo from here one has to either climb back down into the canyon or make the unwelcome 16km (10 miles) detour through the village of Astista to Papingo along an asphalt road. Those touring the region by car should note that the viewing platform just below the village of Vikos offers a striking panorama of the gorge.

At the very north of the Zagorahoria region and 63km (39 miles) from Ioannina, **Konitsa** is a 4,000 strong town and another good base for hiking, this time in the northern Pindos range. It is also worth a look around in itself. Built on the green slopes of Mount Trapezitsa, its lattice-windowed Turkish style houses stand alongside the post 1948 constructions, built to replace those destroyed in the Civil War.

Konitsa is only 12km (7 miles) from the Albanian border and was the scene of some fierce fighting in 1948 as the communists tried to take the town and establish a provincial government here. Take a look at its fine single-arched stone bridge, built in 1870 and the largest of its kind in the entire Balkans. To the south runs the Aoos river. There are several excursions to be made from Konitsa, the two most rewarding go east into the Mount Smolikas region and north to Mount Grammos.

Scene of some of the most terrible battles of the Greek Civil War, Mount Grammos towers at over 2,500 (8,200ft), gazing out east into Macedonia and west over the valleys of Albania. It is ascendable; take one of the daily buses from Konitsa to Plikati, where accommodation is available, and start the hike from here. The ascent should take no more than 4 hours but the route is poorly marked at points; try and get good directions before setting off.

An easier trip can be made east of Konitsa around the foothills of the second highest mountain in Greece, the 2,637m (8,650ft) high Mount Smolikas. A bus from Konitsa leaves daily for Pades, where a path leads upwards for 4 hours to the icy lake of Dragonlimni (not the same lake as that near Mount Timfi). The summit of Smolikas is a 1 hour walk from here, or you can take the path down the slopes to visit the monastery of Agia Paraskevi, a 3 hour walk.

From Pades a path is marked out to **Samarina**, a Vlach village in a beautiful setting. The highest village in Greece, it is enjoying a small renaissance with a flourishing artists' school. Visit Samarina in summer; its population numbers only one in winter; a shepherd left there to tend the sheep. Its main church, the eighteenth-century Panagia, draws hundreds of pilgrims annually for the celebrations of the Assumption of the Virgin Mary every 15 August. If you are in Samarina, consider making an excursion into Macedonia; it is connected to Grevena by a five times a week bus service between June and September.

Igoumenitsa and the Coast

The most appealing aspect of **Igoumenitsa** is that it is easy to catch a ferry out of. Regular services run from here to Corfu, Paxos, Italy and Yugoslavia with less frequent runs to the islands of Ithaca and Cephalonia further south. For the town is simply a busy passenger and cargo port, nothing more and nothing less, and although accommodation and eateries are available for those staying overnight and waiting to catch a connection elsewhere, there is not a great deal to entice the visitor to stay. There are a few attractions out of town, though; beaches at Kalami, 12km (7 miles) south, and Drepanos, 6km (4 miles) north. **Filiates**, 18km (11 miles) north of Igoumenitsa, is worth a look for the typical Epirot mansions scattered around the town; 4 km ($2^1/_2$ miles) outside Filiates is the thirteenth-century monastery of Giromerious.

Readers of the Greek-American author Nicholas Gage can make a literary pilgrimage of sorts 48km (30 miles) north of Igoumenitsa to the village of Lia, featured heavily in Gage's book — and the subsequent film — *Eleni*. A true story, the book is set during the Greek Civil War and centres on the struggles of Eleni, Gage's mother, to save her children from the *pedomazema* — the evacuation — by the communists of children to the 'sympathetic' states of Albania, Yugoslavia and Bulgaria. Eleni and her family lived in Lia; a small plaque marks her house.

Parga, 39km (24 miles) south of Igoumenitsa, is a lovely town with a pretty harbour hemmed in by the islet of Panagia and sited on a small peninsula behind a lush and fertile hill. The splendid remains of a Venetian castle look down from above the town. Its beaches and coves offer superb swimming and although Parga may be a little too developed for some peoples' liking, it is still a fine place for a few days' relaxation.

Like so many Greek towns and cities, Parga has its roots in ancient days. In the third century BC Ptolemy, a one-time general of Alexander the Great, recorded it as *Torini*, a town later sunk and lost forever, probably due to the effects of an earthquake. Yet, despite its fine harbour, Parga was not rebuilt until nearly 15 centuries later, when its founders sited it in today's location, behind a steep hill, to protect it from raids by Albanian gangs. The Venetians, then rulers of the Ionian Islands, claimed it as their own and held it until 1797 — except for a relatively brief period of Turkish rule in the sixteenth century.

The French, under Napoleon, then took Parga but, following their defeat at Trafalgar, lost it to the British in 1815. The British did not care much for Parga; in 1819 they sold it to Ali Pasha for 150,000 sovereigns and the Pargians, well aware of the tyrant's reputation, did not hang around to endure his rule. Virtually the entire population fled to the Ionian Islands. The Turks moved into the town in force and remained beyond the 1913 liberation until 1924 when they became part of the population exchange between Greece and Turkey.

Parga still retains remnants of its medieval past in the small houses in narrow streets stepped up a hill but this appeal is rather offset by the concrete breezeblocks of holiday homes and the glitzy clubs and restaurants that line the waterfronts. Yet it would be a surprise if the modern tourist-trappings were not there; Parga has some superb beaches, the best being Lihnos, a stretch of sand 3km (2 miles) to the south, and Valtos, beneath the castle and stretching for 1km ($^1/_2$ mile) around the bay.

An unusual sight can be seen at Agios Nikolaos Bay; an underwater spring just offshore spurts out fresh, if brackish water that forms a clearly discernable circle in the sea. If you swim the 150m (180yd) out to the islet of Panagia, the remains of a Napoleonic castle can be viewed. However, Parga's own Venetian castle is easier to reach, a short walk up from the bright harbour. Fronted by the Venetian symbol, a Lion of St Mark, only an empty shell remains yet it is still an impressive sight and once was the largest fortress in the region. Find time to take a look at the church of Agii Apostoli in the town, it is beautifully decorated and its icon of the Virgin Mary dates back 800 years.

In season, a daily caique leaves Parga for the tiny island of **Paxos** (or Paxi), Corfu's little sister to the south. Being so small — one can walk across it in a few hours — what tourist development there is is immediately noticeable, thus giving a rather misleading impression. To wander the quiet, olive tree festooned interior is to discover an island that has still managed to retain much of its own identity. It will probably remain that way because strings of hotels, luxury or otherwise, are simply not permissable on Paxos; the island has a severe lack of fresh water. Most of the tourists are day-trippers from either Parga or Corfu.

The Parga boat docks at Gaios, the capital of Paxos and a cramped but charming little town, packed by day with trippers but peaceful and serene by night. It has a picture-postcard type appeal best-appreciated from the guardian islet of Gaios, called Agios Nikolaos, which is easily reached by caique from the harbour. Most caiques, however, do not ferry visitors there for the view; they come to wander the empty shell of its ruined fifteenth-century Venetian castle.

Gaios also boasts a small sandy beach, usually packed with one-day visitors. The rest of Paxos can easily be explored from the capital, either by foot through the olive groves (Paxos is famed throughout Greece for its fine olive oil) or by the bus that trundles between Gaios and the island's other two settlements, Lakka and Longos.

Gaios is on the east coast of Paxos, Lakka is on the west, but there are only 7km (4 miles) separating them. An asphalt road links the two towns, forking right to Longos at the half-way point. Both Lakka and

Longos are small and pretty, busy only in season and with a pebbly beach or two to swim off. For a sandy beach one must head south to the islet of Mogonissi. Caiques for the trip can be hired at Gaios, as can caiques for the tour of Paxos' sea-caves at the south of the island. Set inside huge and sheer rocky cliffs, the gaping holes of their mouths make a dramatic sight. Ipapando Cave is another candidate for the home of Poseidon, the god of the sea.

A 30 minute boat journey from Gaios is the even tinier island of **Andipaxos**, inhabited by only 100 people yet still renowned for its marvellous wines; accordingly, the island is teeming with grape-vines. Its two beaches, Voutoumia and Vrika, are sandy and beauti-ful and consequently draw day-trippers keeping the tavernas that service each of them busy. Very few stay longer than one day on Andipaxos — no accommodation is available and the tavernas close after the trippers go, so a tent and provisions are essential items for those staying overnight. Camping on the beach has a real desert-island aura to it.

Avid readers of Greek mythology will know all about an ar-chaeological site 22km (14 miles) south of Parga — the Necromanteion of **Efyra**, where the dead made their entrance into Hades, the Underworld. Although deep Mani has a contender for this site at Cape Tenaro, Homer's account in *The Odyssey* gives this location the edge on authenticity, writing of a site where the river Styx and the river Acheron meet; they do so here. Unfortunately, the ruins are nothing special, consisting mainly of the remains of an oracle to the dead, through which the living could speak with the departed.

The rooms at which pilgrims spent the night can be seen, as can the ante-room where steps lead far down to the sanctuary underground where the actual communication took place. A long-receded lake once surrounded the sanctuary, which is known to be the only one of its kind in Greece, thus adding to its credibility. The nearest village is small **Mesopotamos**, just inland from the pleasant beach at Amoudia which has tavernas and several rooms to let.

Two routes now head south to Preveza, the coastal road and the inland road, the latter being the bus route and the one that passes within 4km (2¹/₂ miles) of Zalongo. Here, in December 1803, a momentuous event in the spirit of Masada took place that became a symbol of Greek defiance to Turkish rule. It featured the Souli women who were part of an independent-minded community, so independent that Ali Pasha determined to crush them once and for all after their sporadic uprisings against him.

A large Turkish army wiped out the male Souli defenders on the hill of Zalongo whereupon the sixty remaining women of the community fled to its summit with their children in their arms. They performed a ritual dance; then flung their children and themselves into the chasm below. A modern-art style monument commemorates their self-sacrifice. Beneath the hill is the monastery of Agios Dimitrios.

On the way to Zalongo, off the main road, one passes the ruins of Kassopi, a minor town built in the fourth century BC. Its remains mostly date from this era and consist of two theatres, a hostel for passing travellers, the old market-place and a tomb. The site is still being excavated. Preveza is only 17km (10 miles) south of here along a road that passes the wonderful beach at **Kanali**, lying below green slopes. It is now a mini-coastal resort with plenty of accommodation and restaurants.

Unfortunately, **Preveza** is a disappointing town for one whose history can be traced back to the third century BC; little remains of a past that featured the Romans, the Venetians, the Turks and the French, and most visitors arrive simply to take the half-hourly ferry across the Ambracian Gulf to Aktion. For those coming from Aktion there are regular buses to Igoumenitsa, Parga and Ioannina. Nevertheless, it is by no means insubstantial and has a population of 15,000, making it one of the largest towns in Epirus.

Anyone with an hour or so to spare while awaiting a connection elsewhere, can see the old Venetian clock tower in the city centre and its cathedral, Agios Ioannis, has a fine altar screen but, apart from these, its bright and well-stocked shops are the main attraction. There are some lovely beaches nearby, with plane trees meeting the sand, that draw many Greek holidaymakers. It is an active town culturally, particularly during the period between July and September when festivals and exhibitions run almost continually, ranging from modern art, to choral recitals, to childrens' festivals. It is also a very good base from which to explore the ruins of ancient Nikopolis, the 'Victory City'; only 7km (4 miles) around the bay from Preveza.

As its name suggests, **Nikopolis** (*nike* means victory and *polis* means city) was built in memory of a famous victory; a sea-battle where the Roman general Octavian — later the Emperor Augustus — routed his rivals Antony and Cleopatra in 31BC. Octavian had pledged to the gods Poseidon of the sea and Ares (Mars) of war that he would build a city to them should he be triumphant. Thus was Nikopolis founded, becoming a great Roman city with a population immense for the age — 300,000 — and a cosmopolitan make-up of Greeks, Romans and Jews. Culturally, it flourished too; the stoic Epictitus set up a school of philosophy here.

All went well until AD375 when an earthquake shattered much of the city and although it was rebuilt, it suffered a steady decline from then on. Sporadic raids from Goths began and although the Byzantine Emperor Justinian did much to strengthen the city in the sixth century, nothing could prevent its demise. By the eleventh century, Nikopolis was deserted and Preveza, established in a far more logical strategic point at the southern tip of the peninsula, became the region's major city.

The remains of Nikopolis are spread out over an extensive site just off the road; 3km (2 miles) of Justinian's walls still stand, as do the city's theatre and the Roman Odeon, still used occasionally for performances. There are several Byzantine churches, built from the stone of the old Roman temples and the Roman baths. Two tombs revealed a cluster of finds, most on display at the museum on site together with an array of busts and sculptures. A set of beautiful mosaics were unearthed during the excavations, some Roman and some Byzantine, the latter including a well-known mosaic depicting the earth's creation, crammed with plants and animals. The mosaics are currently being renovated and you have to ask at the museum to see them.

One of the most appealing towns in Epirus stands only 33km (20 miles) from Nikopolis; **Arta**, the region's second largest town after Ioannina and one that most tourists seem to skirt around. It has a lovely setting, sliced in two by the Arahthos river and surrounded on all sides by green and often snow-capped peaks. Parts of the town are an odd mixture of the old and the new; Turkish mansions and some wonderfully striking Byzantine churches standing beside modern stores and offices, particularly around the town square and the old quarter nearby.

The bridge for which Arta is famed has to be passed when entering the town. Spanning the Arahthos, this early seventeenth-century four-arched packhorse bridge is the largest of its kind in Greece. It has also become the subject of more than a few legends. The builder is said to have sealed up his wife in one of the bridge supports; the unfortunate woman allegedly still haunts the area today.

Arta began life 27 centuries ago as *Amvrakia*, founded by settlers from Corinth. Like that great city-state, it became a model of Hellenic democracy and gradually grew until, by the second century BC, it was made the capital of Epirus by King Pyrhus and became the centrepoint of resistance to the ever-encroaching Romans. The Romans did exact their revenge on *Amvrakia* though; in 168BC they sacked it and in 30BC levelled it completely so that the city was lost for over 1,000 years. Then it began to be rebuilt as Arta.

Like its predecessor, the new town quickly established itself. In 1204 it became the capital of the despotate of Epirus and despite being almost continually ravaged by calamities such as fire, flooding and disease, not to mention being eclipsed by Ioannina in importance, it remained an auspicious Epirot town up to its liberation in 1881 and beyond.

Apart from its bridge, Arta's main attraction is its collection of fine Byzantine churches, the best-known and most impressive of which is the Parigoritissa, a thirteenth-century six-domed structure that originally served as a monastery. It stands just off the main square of Arta (Skoufa) and is in use as a museum displaying various finds from the region.

A short walk away in the town's market area is Agios Vasilios, small but with some colourful ceramic decorations livening up its exterior. On the main Pirrou Street stands a church dedicated to the patron saint of Arta, Agia Theodora; built in the thirteenth century with grey stone, it is located in a shady, flag-stoned courtyard. The tomb of Theodora, the wife of the Byzantine Emperor Michael the Second, can be seen inside.

The monastery (now a convent) of Kato Panagia is a 20 minute walk away, east, on the Arahthos river. Another thirteenth-century construction, it is set among pines and planes on the banks of the river. It is beautifully ornate and open to appropriately dressed visitors (arms and legs must be covered). However, little remains of *Amvrakia*, only the ruins of a sixth-century temple and a small part of the old theatre. Both sites are located in the town centre. To the north-east of the city is a well-preserved Byzantine castle built on the site out of some of the stones of *Amvrakia's* old fortress.

From Arta it is a 66km (41 miles) journey north back to Ioannina, a route served by ten daily buses, although those with their own transport may wish to take the longer road back — travelling through a beautiful and very rarely visited part of Epirus. It is a hilly and lush region that passes small and tidy little villages, looking out over the valley through which the Arahthos flows and beyond that, to the east, the edge of the southern Pindos mountain range. After 46km (28 miles) Plaka is reached. Just beyond the village is a large and gracefully arched stone bridge that spans the Arahthos.

One can leave the Ioannina road here to travel east 17km (11 miles) past the busy little village of Pramanda, to the Anemotripa Pramandon Cave at the foot of 2,500m (8,200ft) high Mount Tzoumerka. Full of small individual caves crammed with stalactites and stalagmites and with an underground river coursing through, it is an eye-opening sight. One has to travel back to Plaka to continue on to Ioannina, 34km (21 miles) away along a twisting and mountainous road that eventually descends gradually past Lake Pamvotis into the capital of Epirus.

Instead of heading back to Ioannina, it is easy to reach southern Epirus from Arta, entering the area either across the Ambracian Gulf by ferry from Preveza or by the main road south. On this route **Amfilohia** is the first major town reached. It is built on two hills with a nice view of the gulf, a rather uninviting beach and little else. Better swimming is to be had a little north at Spartos. East of Amfilohia, along the southern edge of the gulf, are the towns of Vonitsa and Aktion.

Vonitsa is a pretty and quiet town, its streets coming together in shady squares as they lead down to the beach. A twelfth-century medieval castle stands above the town and is pleasingly intact. A road leads directly onto the island of Lefkada.

Aktion is another 16km (10 miles) east, on the tip of a peninsula facing Preveza. It is known mainly for its half-hourly ferry which shuttles across to Preveza and back across what is known as the 'Cleopatra Channel'. This was where the ships of Octavian clashed with those of Antony and Cleopatra in a famous battle that paved the way for Octavian's emperorship and led to the building of Nikopolis. From here you can travel onto Lefkada or head back the 54km (33 miles) east to Amfilohia to tour the rest of southern Epirus.

It is a straight road that leads south out of Amfilohia, passing the boggy shores of Lake Amvrakia and Lake Ozeros before bearing east to Stratos, where a few of the ruins of the ancient (fourth-century BC) Greek town that lies beneath the new village, can still be seen. Further on, at the small and inappropriately titled village of **Megallo Hora** ('Big Town'), a clue to its deceptive name can be seen; the ruins of a twelfth-century Byzantine castle stand just above it.

Only 6km (4 miles) on is **Agrinio**, busy and bustling, populated by 30,000 and the region's transportation hub and major commercial centre. Its primary industry is tobacco. There are several hotels, all catering for visiting businessmen rather than tourists passing through, and an airport with several flights a week to Athens.

Those with their own transport can use the town as a base for the pleasing day-trip around Lake Trihonida, a 76km (47 mile) journey through a lush and well-forested region with small and uncommercialised villages. The best place to break the journey is at **Thermo** where the extensive ruins of the once great Hellenic city of the same name can be seen. Plenty of imagination is needed to visualise the ruins as they once were but a small museum on site helps to fit the mental picture together. Back at Agrinio and continuing south, the pleasant town of **Etoliko** is reached, unusually built on a small island in the middle of a lagoon. Linked to the mainland by a stone bridge, it is a modern town in a lovely setting. Ten kilometres (6 miles) south is Messolongi.

Capital of Etoloakarnania, grid-planned **Messolongi** is a busy and noisy town with little of interest to the visitor beyond its association with the dashing English Hellenophile, the poet Lord Byron. It was in January 1824 that Byron arrived at Messolongi's small port with the task ahead of him to unite the various Greek rebel factions — a perpetually squabbling bunch — into a cohesive fighting force to expel the occupying Turks. It was a task that was to last only 3 months and end in tragedy — Byron died of a fever in April of that year.

Byron's death served to romanticise in Northern Europe the struggle for Greek liberation and the Great Powers were swayed into support of the rebels by fierce public opinion at home. Byron thus became one of the great heroes of modern Greece. His heart was buried in Messolongi, a spot marked by a small garden. The town hall houses a museum of the Revolution, featuring original paintings of the struggle and a small collection of Byron memorabilia.

The town is entered and exited through Exodus Gate, so-called as it was through here that the entire population of Messolongi fled in 1826 in the face of a large combined Turkish and Egyptian force. Tragically, most were massacred during their flight by Albanian gangs waiting in ambush. The dead were buried just inside Exodus Gate, their mass grave now being the Garden of Heroes. The survivors, nearly 2,000 in number, took refuge in the seventeenth-century monastery of Agios Simeon, 6km (4 miles) north-east of the town. The monastery hosts a boisterous festival every Whit Monday with dancing and fireworks, to give thanks for those who were saved.

The coastal road that leads north-west up to the entrance to Lefkada first skirts the Messolongi Wetlands, a huge morass of boggy and salty marshes centred by small islets surrounded by long reeds. Small and stilted fishermens' huts are everywhere. Indeed, the highly intensive fish-farming, the land reclamation along its northern edge and pollution have led environmentalists to voice concerns over the survival of these wetlands. Their demise would bring disastrous ecological consequences, particularly among the wildlife for which the region is famed. Already the waterbirds are decreasing in number, deprived of much of their fish diet. Yet for the time-being, the wetlands are a lovely sight. Little Katohi is the first village passed, then Lessini and Fraxos before arriving at Astakos 50km (31 miles) from Messolongi.

Astakos (which means lobster in Greek) is a relatively large fishing village, attractively located on the headland of a small bay and hemmed in by trees and vegetation. Its daily fish market is a noisy and jostling affair but there are quiet and sandy beaches near the town where one can escape to. Daily ferries leave from the harbour to the Ionian islands of Ithaca and Cephalonia.

Mitikas, the next village 34km (21 miles) up the coast, is more like a resort but is still wonderfully undeveloped. There are a few rooms to let for those wishing to enjoy its long pebbly beach for more than a day. Two small islets, Kastos and Kalamos, are easily visible from the shore; accessible by caique, they possess some lovely beaches which are visited by very few people.

Paleros, another small fishing village, 19km (12 miles) north of Mitikas, also has a good sandy beach. From here the road continues north up to Vonitsa; a 19km (12 miles) road south-east leads directly onto the island of Lefkada.

Lefkada

It is pleasing to know that there is at least one Greek island that does not have to be reached by bumping across the ocean waves in a ferry. Only 25m (30yd) separate Lefkada (or Lefkas) from the mainland and although it most certainly is an island, at one point in its history it was attached to the mainland. The narrow channel in between is man-made, most likely dug by Lefkada's original Corinthian settlers in the fifth century BC and now spanned by a military-style pontoon bridge. Previously, boats were dragged across by a clanking chain and pulley system. Yet, despite the easy access to Lefkada, its many charms remain unknown to most visitors to Greece. It is mainly Greeks that holiday here, thus allowing the island to retain much of its traditional atmosphere.

The island's past is not especially dramatic, particularly by the tumultuous standards of Greek history. Being founded by Corinthians, the allies of Sparta, it took up arms against Athens in the Peloponnesian wars and was ravaged by raiding Athenians. Several hundred years later, the great naval battle between the forces of

Octavian and those of Antony and Cleopatra was easily visible from its shores. It enjoyed a quiet existence under Byzantine rule but was lost to the Franks of Ioannis Orsini in 1300. It then went through the Epirot and Ioanninan cycle of rule by Venetians, Turks, Venetians again, French, Russian and finally British before being eventually ceded to the new Greek State in 1864, along with the rest of the Ionian Island chain.

There was one man, though, who tried to add a little spice to Lefkada's past — Wilhelm Dorpfield, a German archaeologist of the early twentieth century. Dorpfield was convinced that Lefkada was in fact the Ithaca of Homer's *The Odyssey* and that, therefore, the great undiscovered palace of Odysseus would lie buried somewhere on this island. Although all he unearthed were some Bronze Age tombs, interesting enough in themselves, he is remembered fondly by Lefkadians. After his death in 1940, a statue was built of him near the harbour at Nidri and the street that begins at Lefkada town's harbour was renamed Dorpfield Street.

After crossing the pontoon bridge the first town reached is **Lefkada town**, capital of the island and home to most Lefkadians. It gives few signs of the island's rather relaxed aura, being a busy commercial centre that owes its modern and rather flat appearance to the earthquakes of 1948 and 1953. Although it was not as hard hit as the Ionian islands further south, the earthquakes were strong enough to crumple the town's old Venetian and Turkish structures. It is now an earthquake-proof town, no building being higher than two stories, and has hardly any architectural appeal. The upper stories of buildings are an odd sight, gingerly constructed out of the lightest materials possible in order to put the minimum weight on the foundations.

Just prior to reaching Lefkada town, one passes the hulking remains of the castle of Santa Mavra which dips part of its formidable stone walls in the sea. Built in 1300 by Ioannis Orsini, its remains today are primarily the modifications made by later Venetians and Turks. The island was later renamed Santa Mavra, a name that stuck for nearly two centuries.

In the town itself, the only buildings worth more than a glance are the Venetian churches of the seventeenth and eighteenth centuries, usually with bell-towers built alongside them. However, there are a few museums to wander around; the town library features a collection of centuries-old icons and the archaeological museum displays a few local finds, including the artefacts unearthed by Dorpfield from the Bronze Age tombs. The phonograph museum is a little more unusual, a hotch-potch of old gramophones and colourfully-sleeved discs that were first cut up to 60 years ago.

A pleasant 60 minutes' walk west out of town leads steadily up to the Faneromeni monastery, now deserted but with grounds that offer wonderful views of Lefkada town and the northern coastline. The town itself has a range of hotels of varying quality and restaurants line the waterfront either side of the harbour. The island's main bus station can also be found near the harbour; there is a regular hourly service to the resort of Nidri on the east coast and twice-daily trips out to Vassiliki in the south and Agios Nikitas in the north-west. Alternatively, one should have no difficulty in hiring a car or moped in Lefkada town.

Travelling south along the island's east coast means passing a series of tiny fishing hamlets, picturesque but only coming to life when the day's (or night's) catch is being dragged ashore. Some of the houses seem rather too close to the sea for comfort and are perched rather gingerly on stilts. The landscape here is green and flat, in direct contrast to the stark and mountainous terrain of the interior.

It is a tranquil, somewhat sleepy route to **Nidri**, the number one resort of Lefkada and full of tourist villas and boutiques, night-clubs and restaurants. Surprisingly enough, the beach is nothing special but better swimming is to be had only a caique trip away on the islet of Meganissi, visible from the shore. Behind Nidri is the large plain where Dorpfield discovered his Bronze Age tombs. The archaeologist lived in Nidri during his stay on Lefkada and his statue stands by the harbour near to his old house. There are ferry connections from Nidri to Frikes on Ithaca and Fiskardo on Cephalonia.

Only a few kilometres south of Nidri is **Vliho** which marks a return to rurality. A quiet and cool village, it has the sandy and peaceful beach of Dessimi over the hill to the south. There are camping facilities there. Across the water from Vliho the peninsula of Agia Kiriaki juts out into the water and makes for a charming half-day excursion; it is an area brimming with wild flowers and lemon and olive trees, all set against the blue of the sea.

Poros, still further south and reached by a junction off the main road, has a few rooms and tavernas to cater for those enjoying its fine stretch of white pebble beach. Another good beach can be found at **Sivota**, a tiny hamlet in a lovely setting tucked into the bay of the same name. Ten kilometres (6 miles) west of here is the half-way point of any circuit of the island, the town of Vassiliki.

Maybe one day **Vassiliki** will become another Nidri but, for the time being, it is a resort with a pleasantly homely appeal. A cramped little town with plenty of places to stay and to eat, it has a pebble beach that boasts both waterskiing facilities and a windsurfing school. From here caiques bob over the water to the sheer white cliffs (after which Lefkada is named) of Cape Dukato, the southernmost point of Lefkada and the site of the island's sole mythological connection.

It was here that the poet Sappho, tormented by her unrequited desire for Phaon, became the Lover who made the original Leap, plunging down to her death in the ocean below. She was not the last to do so. Ancient Lefkadians performed an annual ritual on the cliffs of the cape which involved casting one person from the top into the sea as part of the worship of the god Apollo. The victim was usually a criminal or lunatic, who were believed, in those days, to be possessed. In order to give him a fair chance of survival, feathers and live birds were attached to his arms and legs supposedly to lighten the fall. During the Roman occupation, leaping from the cliffs became the ultimate game of 'dare' for the island's youths. A lighthouse that stands on the edge of the peninsula occupies the site of the old temple for Apollo.

The west coast of Lefkada lacks the lushness of the east. It is a dry and rocky landscape, sparsely populated and continually buffeted by sea winds. One has to travel north quite a way before arriving at the charming little village of **Agios Petras** and, further north, Kalamitsi from where a road leads down to the sands of Kathisma beach.

Agios Nikitas is just up the coast from here, a small resort town with sufficient tourist facilities and a large sandy beach that occasionally suffers, like all the beaches in the north-west of Lefkada, from powerful sea-breezes. There is another beach at **Tsoukalades**, where holiday villas are rapidly being built, and at **Giropetra** at the northern tip of the island and only 1 hour's walk from Lefkada town.

There are no real surprises in Lefkada's interior — just a few mountain villages — but **Karia**, connected by road to Lefkada town, hosts a boisterous festival dedicated to Agios Spiridon on the 11 and 12 August every year. It is a riot of feasting, folk singing and dancing for which the villagers wear their traditional Lefkadian costumes. Also in August is the International Festival of Arts and Letters, held in Lefkada town and featuring street exhibitions, music and live theatre, among other attractions, for its 2 week duration.

A small cluster of islets lie off the south-east coast of the island, a couple of which are accessible by boat from Nidri. Two, however, are strictly off-limits being privately owned; Madouri by a Greek poet and Skorpios by the Onassis family. Sparti is the northernmost islet, tiny and uninhabited. **Meganissi** is the largest of the group, only 20 minutes from Nidri and an islet which tourism, for the time being at least, seems to have passed by. There are three villages, the port Vathi, Spartohora and Katomeri and some lovely beaches, the best being at Ambelakia. The islanders make a living from the olive trees and from fishing although many supplement their income by renting out rooms to visitors struck by the peacefulness of the place.

Further Information
— Epirus and Lefkada —

Dodoni
The site
Open: 8am-5pm Monday to Friday, 8.30am-3pm weekends.

Ioannina
Ali Pasha Museum
Island of Nissi
Open: 9am-10pm daily.

Archaeological Museum
Off Platia Demokratius, heading for Nissi
Open: 8.30am-3pm daily.
Closed Mondays.

Folklore Museum
Open: 5-8pm Monday, 10am-1pm Wednesday.

Perama Caves
Village of Perama
Open: 8am-7pm daily.

Popular Art Museum
Open: 8am-3.15pm daily.

Tourist Office
Platia Demokratius
☎ 0651 25086
Open: 8am-1.30pm Monday to Friday.

Vrellis Museum
Open: 8.30am-7pm daily.

Igoumenitsa
Information Office
☎ 0665 22227

Messolongi
Museum of the Revolution
Town Hall
☎ 0631 22400
Open: 8am-2pm Monday to Friday.

Migallo Papingo
Tourist Office, traditional settlement/ information centre
☎ 0653 41088

Necromanteion of Efyra
Open: 9am-3.30pm daily, 10am-4pm Sunday.

Nikopolis
Open: 8.45am-3pm Monday to Saturday, 9.30am-2.30pm Sunday.
Closed Tuesdays.

Parga
Venetian Castle
Open: 7am-10pm daily.

6 • Northern Thessaly and Southern Macedonia

Introduction

There is no geographical or historical reason for placing northern Thessaly, southern Macedonia and Metsovo together as one area. For the visitor, however, it is very practical to do so. The road and public bus network makes it relatively simple to complete a circuitous tour of the region, a tour that incorporates some of the most spectacular sights in Greece as well as some of the least-visited towns. With big cities and small villages, mountains and beaches, Byzantine monasteries and nightlife, this is yet another part of Greece that caters for all tastes.

If arriving in the region from Athens, the city of Larissa, easily reached by either rail, air or road, is the ideal place to begin and/or end any tour. As one of the largest industrial and commercial centres in Greece, Larissa may not be everyone's cup of tea but it does have a very Greek nightlife and a road leading north to the historical village of Ambelakia.

From Ambelakia one can pass through the lovely vale of Tembi, sandwiched between the southern slopes of Mount Olympus to the east and Mount Ossa to the west, to the beaches of Platamonas which marks the border between Thessaly and Macedonia. The coast holds more beaches in store before reaching the charming town of Litohoro, set beneath Mount Olympus and the base from which to explore the highest mountain in Greece and the legendary home of Zeus and the immortal gods. On the slopes of Olympus are the remains of the great Macedonian city of Dion.

Katerini is the next stop north and from here the road cuts south to Elassona and then north, across the Aliakimonas river to the rarely visited town of Kozani (also accessible by road via Veria). A modern town with a prosperous past, it holds several sights of interest and some fine villages in its surrounds as does Grevena to the south-

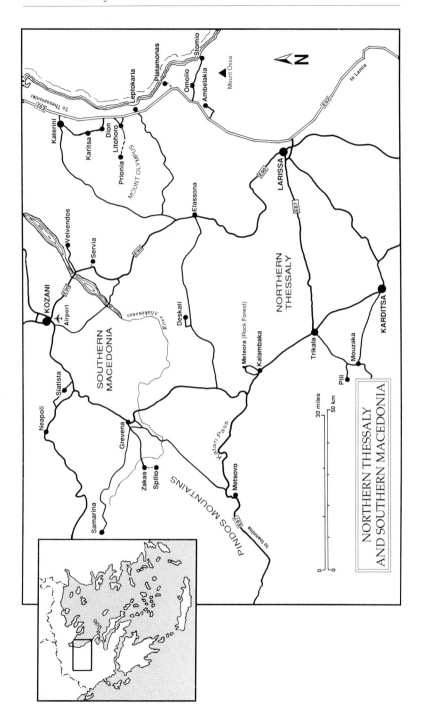

west, another town very much off the beaten track.

East of Grevena the Pindos mountains begin and some of the short walks between their villages are truly beautiful. From Grevena it is 65km (40 miles) by road south-west to Metsovo, a large mountain village inhabited mainly by the Vlach people and one which proudly preserves its traditions. The village is located at the mid-way point of the Katari Pass, the 1,700m (5,580ft) high road that provides the link over the Pindos between eastern and western Greece.

Travelling east through the pass, you descend to the plains just before reaching the stunning sight of Meteora; huge rocks climbing out of the plain reaching up to 300m (980ft) in height and with monasteries built painstakingly on top. These Byzantine monasteries, set inside this 'rock forest', form one of the most remarkable sights in Greece. The new town of Trikala, 20km (12 miles) to the east, is rather an anticlimax after this, as is Karditsa, the last major stop before heading back to Larissa.

Winters in the region can be cold and snowy and parts of the area impassable so any time between spring and autumn is a good time to visit. If you are intending to climb Mount Olympus be aware that the climbing season lasts from the beginning of May to the end of September. Also be aware that the months of July and August see the most tourists at Mount Olympus and Meteora, and that spring is the best time to view the region's startling array of wild flowers.

This is one of the easiest regions in Greece to reach; not only do Larissa and Kozani have airports with regular flights to Athens, but Katerini, Litohoro and Larissa all lie on the main E92 road that links Athens with Thessaloniki. The Athens-Thessaloniki rail-line also passes through these three towns but note that the express trains do not stop at Litohoro.

If travelling from Epirus in the east, cross the Katari Pass to either Grevena or Kalambaka (near Meteora). Getting around the region by public bus — at least between the major towns — is simple and there are train lines between Florina and Edessa (in north-west Macedonia) and Kozani and Kalambaka to Volos via Trikala and Karditsa.

Anyone travelling in this region may well be surprised at the vastly differing terrain. The territory is sealed in to left and right by mountains; Olympus in the east, Ossa to the south-east and the Pindos range running down its western flank. Yet the coastal area between Olympus and the shores of the Thermaic Gulf is one flat plain, as is a vast swathe of land around Larissa. The Larissa plain forms part of the agricultural backbone of Greece; almost every type of crop is grown, from cereals to tobacco, from rice to almonds.

However, the farming would not be possible were the plains not watered by several rivers — the Pinios, the Enippeas and the Aliakimonas.

It is in the mountains where the wildlife flourishes and the wildflowers bloom. Bears and wolves live high in the Pindos mountains west of Grevena and the rather less threatening figure of the tortoise is common around the rocks of Meteora. Meteora is also a good place to pick the herb that makes Greek mountain tea.

Yet it is on Mount Olympus where one can really appreciate the free-growing flora. Unusual in that it rises out of the Thessalian plain alone, with no surrounding range, the mountain is so near the sea that its lower slopes — very little grows near its icy peaks — are dense in vegetation with over 1,700 species of plant alone. Trees cover the slopes; black pines and Macedonian firs and herbs such as deadly nightshade and fireweed are common.

For flowers in the spring, look out for the orchids, irises and crocuses. For more information on the flora on this mountain, buy *The Flowers of Mount Olympus* by Arne Strid, a glossy book packed with photographs. Alternatively, ask to see the copy held at Refuge Hut 'A', halfway up the mountain.

Larissa and the Eastern Coastline

Eclipsing even the major port of Volos, **Larissa** is the capital of Thessaly and has all that one would expect from such an industrial and commercial powerhouse of a city. Positioned centrally on the Thessalian plain, its office blocks and wide, busy streets hold no particular allure for visitors except for the opportunity to observe a modern Greek city at first-hand. This is a pity, as this modernity tends to conceal its lengthy history. Archaeological evidence has shown that its site has been inhabited since 10,000BC — finds from the locality can be seen in the archaeological museum, and it is claimed that the founder of modern medicine, Hippocrates, died here.

During Byzantine times, the town was deemed important enough to warrant a castle which still stands and is open to visitors; and the Ottomans were to use Larissa as one of their local administrative centres. In the early 1980s the city was the subject of fierce controversy as the then Greek Prime Minister, Andreas Papandreou, fiercely and successfully resisted NATO plans to establish a base outside the town.

A popular place at the weekend for many Larissians is the Alcazar park; green, lined with colourful orange trees and with the Pinios river flowing alongside. It is a nice picnic spot if one has a couple of hours to spare in the city. Yet, the rest of this region is waiting to be explored. The route outlined here follows the E92 Athens-Thessaloniki road, running partway down the coastline and up to Mount Olympus.

Leaving Larissa and travelling north, the agricultural plain of Thessaly is left behind and replaced by the view of Mount Ossa, nearly 2,000m (6,560ft) high. After 28km (17 miles) turn left for another 5km (3 miles) to **Ambelakia**, a mountain resort town with cobbled streets, fine stone mansions and a lovely setting. This is a centre for a government scheme to promote greater equality between the sexes by sponsoring a womens' agricultural-tourist co-operative in the belief that a woman's financial independence is a pre-requisite for liberation. The women are involved in farming, re-introducing local crafts and encouraging tourism by renting out rooms in their own homes.

Those wishing to spend part of their holiday in Ambelakia, finding out more about the co-operative, can obtain a booking form by calling the number given in the Further Information section at the end of this chapter.

Ambelakia is in fact the ideal town for such a venture as it was here, in 1778, that the world's first industrial co-operative was founded, operating in the textile market. For a brief period of time it was world-renowned, with 6,000 members and branch offices all over the continent promoting the co-operative's skill in red-dyeing techniques, a skill that won them the contract to dye the fezes of the Turkish Army. The Turks themselves held the co-operative in high regard and it gradually became self-governing socially as well as commercially.

All profits began to be ploughed back into their increasingly prosperous community. Its wealth can still be seen today in the remaining thirty-six mansions, built in stone and sometimes featuring stained-glass windows and intricate wood carvings. The village once boasted hundreds of such houses.

Twenty-four of the old dye-houses still remain, many reconverted for the use of today's co-operative. However, Ali Pasha, tyrant of Epirus, all but levelled Ambelakia in 1811 and this, together with the advent of new technology in the dyeing industry, sounded the death-knell for the old co-operative.

The Schwartz mansion, named after the last president of the co-operative, is open to visitors and provides a good insight into the way of life that was once led here. Several of the churches are also worth a visit — Agios Georgios, Agios Athanassios and Agia Paraskevi — and while there, sample some of the local dry, red wine from which the town draws its name (*ambelia* is Greek for 'grape vines').

To return to the E92 and to head north again is to travel through the beautifully dramatic vale of Tembi, a narrow natural passageway between the mountains of Ossa and Olympus. Sheer cliffs tower on each side, offset by the vegetation along the banks of the Pinios that also runs through the vale. After 5km (3 miles) look up to the right to see the castle of Oria, built by the Franks to guard this vital strategic pass that provides the region's link between north and south.

A turn-off beyond Mount Ossa, but still in the vale, leads in 3km (2 miles) to **Omolio**, a typical small Thessalian town but one where ancient tombs have been excavated, and on to **Stomio**, a lovely coastal resort with hot therapeutic springs and a wonderful sandy beach. Near the beach is a free campsite, somewhat compensating for the limited accommodation that is available here. The town itself is splendidly positioned, built steeply onto the green slopes of Mount Ossa, and descending to the shore, thus giving it a semi-mountainous, semi-coastal resort appeal.

Back on the E92, the road cuts east and begins its run along the coastline of the Thermaic Gulf, a route followed until the road ends in Thessaloniki. Scrubby and sparse fields conceal both sandy and pebbly beaches for much of the way and developers have been unable to resist the temptation to turn much of the area into a tourist attraction. Half-completed constructions are everywhere, yet with so much shoreline it is not too difficult to find a secluded spot. Some of the towns are already firmly established as seaside resorts such as **Platamonas** which marks the border between Thessaly and Macedonia.

Apart from beaches, watersports, restaurants and hotels, Platamonas boasts a wonderfully intact Crusader castle, built between 1204 and 1222, which still dominates the countryside and the entrance to the Thermaic Gulf. Its location was of such strategic value to the Turks that the castle was spared the devastation of the other fortresses in the area that followed the Ottoman conquest of Macedonia in the fifteenth century.

Just keep heading up the coastline for more resorts, of which Skotina and Leptokaria are perhaps the most enticing. Only 10km (6 miles) inland from Leptokaria is Litohoro, the base for the ascent of the majestic Mount Olympus.

Mitikas, the highest peak of Mount Olympus

Mount Olympus

Towering hugely out of the flat coastal plain of Thessaly stands Mount Olympus, the mythical abode of Zeus and the eleven other immortal gods. Nearly 3,000m (9,840ft) high, it is the largest mountain in Greece and second only to Bulgaria's Mount Musala as the highest in the entire Balkan region. Its dominance of the area is emphasised by the fact that it is not part of any mountainous chain, such as the Pindos, but stands alone.

Tremendous in its beauty, lush and well-forested on its lower slopes; stark, rocky and alpine in its upper regions, Olympus lies along the route of European Long Distance Trail Number Four (E4), the great path linking the Pyrenees in Spain with Mount Taigetos near Sparta in the Peloponnese. As such, it can be climbed without any special training or equipment, although you will need to have a strong pair of legs and a good set of lungs — it is a long hard slog all the way. For those unwilling or unable to make the ascent there is still the opportunity to appreciate the charms of Olympus — there are plenty of paths where you can wander through its forested and flora-filled foothills.

For the vast majority of hikers the trek will begin at **Litohoro**, a relaxing little town that basks in the shadow of Olympus and is well-endowed with hotels, restaurants and a youth hostel. Getting there

The village square in Litohoro

is a simple matter; 61km (38 miles) from Larissa, 405km (250 miles) from Athens and 90km (56 miles) from Thessaloniki, it lies on both the Athens-Thessaloniki road and rail-line.

Those arriving by rail should note that the station is several miles out of Lithoro so one has to walk to the main road and wait at the bus stop for the Katerini-Litohoro bus. Once at Litohoro, you can prepare for the trek, whether you intend to walk up and down the mountain in a day (this is quite possible) or to savour the experience a little more and stay one or two nights on the mountain.

The climbing season on Olympus runs between May and October, actual dates being dependent on when the snow falls and melts in any one particular year. Unless you know Mount Olympus very well it is not advisable to climb outside of these months; snow covers the tracks and the chances of getting lost or being caught up in an avalanche are very high. Those who 'have' to climb out of season should enlist the services of a professional guide.

Climbers should carry no more than a light day-pack with essentials that include a hat, strong boots and as much water as possible. Also bring a sweater; although the heat can be searing on the lower slopes, up past the alpine line the howling wind is chilling. For those who intend to stay overnight on the mountain in one of the refuge huts, make a reservation the day before. Telephone numbers and names of these huts are given in the Further Information section.

Although Mount Olympus can be climbed from several points, the route that is safest and has the best facilities is from Prionia, 18km (11 miles) outside Litohoro and reached via an asphalt road from the town that soon becomes a dusty dirt track. The route up Mount Olympus that is outlined here provides an opportunity to spend the night on the mountain at refuge hut 'A'. This is owned by the Greek Mountaineering Club and is run by one of the foremost experts on Mount Olympus, Kostas Zolotas, and his family.

The route splits the ascent into two halves. The first over the lower slopes up to the refuge at 2,100m (6,900ft); the second to one of the main peaks of the mountain: Mitikas 2,917m (9,567ft), Stefani 2,907m (9,535ft), Agios Antonios 2,815m (9,233ft), Kalogeros 2,701m (8,860ft) and Skala 2,866m (9,466ft). Of these, Mitikas and Skala can be easily reached from the refuge hut and, together with Skolio, they are the peaks discussed here.

Unfortunately, there is still no public bus service between Litohoro and Prionia. Climbers must make their way there either by hitch-hiking (if so, start early in the morning), a crushingly tedious walk, or by taxi. If none of these options appeal, there is an alternative in a beautiful and exhilarating hike through the steep, green and butterfly-festooned Enippeas Gorge. In its own way, this trek can be as rewarding as the ascent of Olympus itself. From the central *platia* in Litohoro, follow the signs up a gentle slope to the youth hostel. Bear right as the path bears left for the hostel, continue out of Litohoro through deeply green fields for 15 minutes and just past the taverna at the end of the track is the first of many 'E4' signs, which guide hikers through the gorge and up Olympus.

It is not an easy hike, taking about 5 hours and full of steep ascents and descents but the scenery and sheer peace make it all worthwhile. The sparkling Enippeas river has to be crossed at several points. After about 4 hours, an unusual chapel is reached, Agios Spilio (the Holy Cave), built around a deep cave in the side of the gorge. Climbing out of the gorge, you will come across a huge, fire-blackened, gutted shell of a building, once the proud monastery of Agios Dionysos but destroyed by the German occupiers of Greece during the last war.

Thirty minutes walk from the ruined monastery is **Prionia**, with nothing of interest except for a small taverna with a limited menu, a large car park and a bridge over the river that leads to the path up Mount Olympus. This green and well-watered place is enchanting — the ideal spot to wander the mountain's foothills.

The path is steep but, initially at least, quite shaded and winds and

The Enippeas Gorge, Litohoro

twists its way through huge forests of black pines. Mount Olympus boasts a staggering variety of wild flowers and you can let your gaze wander as the landscape becomes more and more revealing during your ascent. Allowing for plenty of rest breaks, the climb to the refuge should take roughly 3 hours.

Having stopped to either stay overnight at the refuge or simply for a refreshing cup of mountain tea (made from herbs picked on Olympus), the ascent to the peaks and the throne of Zeus is only $2^1/_2$ hours away. This is also the part of the mountain where you have to be a little careful. The path that leads up from the refuge is only briefly wooded. After that it is real alpine territory, terribly barren but with breathtaking views. Much of the ascent is over loose rock — be careful not to twist an ankle — and try to stay away from ledges if you get nervous about heights; some of the drops are sheer.

To reach the three sister peaks of Mitikas, Skala and Skolio, simply follow the 'E4' signs. When you reach a right turn after about 1 hour, ignore it and continue straight unless heading for the Vrissopoules refuge which lies on this path. Maps will show that Mitikas can be scaled by taking this route and climbing after having walked for 45 minutes, but this is a dangerous option due to rock falls. In recent years there have been injuries and even deaths. So, following the 'E4' signs, you will eventually bear right around the side of a large valley and, mounting a hill, come to a long and spectacular ridge overlooking a deep chasm. Looking up from here, the peaks are easily visible and a straight, steep climb up until another ridge is reached means that you have ascended Skala peak. To the left is Skolio, a 30 minute walk away, and to the right, Mitikas, the highest peak. The only way to Mitikas from here is via the Kaka Skala (Bad Steps), a steep and narrow ridge that should not really be attempted by those who suffer from even mild acrophobia. If you make it up to Mitikas, do not forget to sign the visitors' book there, for this is the top of Greece.

Dion

Standing on the lower slopes of Mount Olympus and reached by returning to the E92 from Litohoro and taking the turn-off left after 2km (1 mile), is ancient **Dion**. Positioned just beyond the modern village of the same name, this was the sacred city of the Macedonians, the all-conquering people of the fourth century BC who, under Phillip the Second and then Alexander the Great, ruled the known world from Egypt to India. Excavations here have revealed some marvellous finds, showing the city to be a centre for sanctuaries to the gods, including Zeus, Dionysus, Aphrodite and Asclepius.

Several of the sanctuaries have been preserved, thanks to a series of earth tremors in the fifth century that caused mud to slide down off Olympus. The city had to be abandoned but the mud kept the structures free from decay. Also visible are several splendid mosaics, the city walls, the public baths and several buildings that showed Dion to be a living city as well as a centre for worship — houses, a sewerage system, workshops etc. A museum on the site contains some of the smaller items excavated — including jars, pottery, tools and gravestones. Also on the same site is a Christian church, evidence that the Romans also built here following their conquest of Greece in 168BC.

From new Dion, a minor road leads north past the villages of Karitsa and Nea Effessos to arrive after 15km (9 miles) in Katerini, a drab and modern town 70,000 strong and with road and rail connections to all points north and south. However, the Piera mountain range blocks all transit due west. To travel in this direction one must take the southern road past the western face of Mount Olympus for 70km (43 miles) to the town of Elassona before returning north to cross the Aliakimonas river en-route to Kozani, capital of the prefecture of the same name. The road south is a charming route, passing forests of bushy decidous trees.

Elassona, whose roots go back to the Bronze Age, is a pretty town, hemmed in by pale limestone. Those with a limited amount of time should be aware that Larissa is only 61km (38 miles) to the south and that the town of Grevena, due west, is also linked to Elassona by a 104km (64 miles) main road that runs via Deskati.

It is the E90 that links Elassona with Kozani, a road with a couple of interesting pit-stops en-route at the towns of Servia and Velvendos. This area sees hardly any visitors and an English-Greek phrasebook may well come in useful. **Servia**, was founded by the Byzantine Emperor Heraklius during the seventh century. The presence of several churches and a triple-walled fortress that remain from this age testify to the one-time importance of this town, which is 55km (34 miles) out of Elassona.

Velvendos, 6km (4 miles) on from Servia and 10km (6 miles) off the main E90, has some fine examples of Macedonian architecture. A market town, its close proximity to the Aliakimonas river makes it a well-watered and wooded place, full of peach and poplar trees. Returning to the main road, Kozani is only 30km (18 miles) away.

Kozani

In Hellenic times **Kozani** (population 23,000) was the northern frontier post of Greece, one of the first lines of defence against the Macedonians. Shifting borders mean that it now stands at the southern end of Macedonia. It is 720m (2,360ft) above sea level and flanked by the rolling Vourino, Askio and Vermio mountains. Excavations have revealed little about its ancient past but it is known that in 1650 the town began to flourish as a prosperous, commercial centre. This was chiefly due to a mysterious deal struck between the town's traders and their Turkish rulers, the result of which was the granting of virtual autonomy to the Kozanis — they paid no taxes and were not subject to conscription in the Turkish army. There was even a ban on Turks settling in the town.

The town's autonomy attracted scholars and Kozani became a haven for intellectuals — even today Kozani's sixteenth-century library, crammed with rare manuscripts, is second only to the national library of Athens in terms of importance. Maybe this virtuous history goes some way to accounting for the intense pride the town's citizens have in their heritage — and helps to explain the relaxed atmosphere that pervades in Kozani.

Today Kozani is a modern town but several examples of traditional Macedonian architecture can still be seen here and there; grandly built, with overhanging first floors and framed in timber. There are several squares, all attractive and leafy, the main one easily identifiable by the 1855 clock tower that dominates it. Behind the tower is the fifteenth-century church of Agios Nikolaos, richly decorated with icons and frescoes, and near to this stands the small archaeological museum, housing local finds.

The real attraction of Kozani, though, and one that should put it on any travel itinerary of the region, is the museum of natural history and folklore. Only recently opened, beautifully maintained and wonderfully presented, it provides a refreshing change for those weary of gazing at decapitated statues of former Roman emperors. There is a great deal more than its rather bland title suggests.

The spectacle begins two floors below the entrance, exhibiting a cabinet full of prehistoric animal bones; a selection of rocks and minerals found in Greece and an extensive array of dried flowers before moving onto an utterly staggering display of taxidermy. Wild boar, stags, wolves, bears, snakes and many more can be seen. The museum stresses that the animals were not killed for this purpose but were found dead in the region by locals.

Moving up the marble stairs, one reaches the world of *homo sapiens* with artefacts from the history of the Kozani region — weapons, jewellery, farm tools, musical instruments, house interiors and a whole row of reconstructed eighteenth-century shops. It ends with an exhibition depicting the liberation of Kozani from German rule in World War II. This is a beautiful museum and, judging by the signatures in the visitors' book, one rarely visited by non-Greeks.

The region of Kozani was once well-known for its production of saffron and the art is still practised today in the nearby villages of Krocus and Karaditia. In these villages, as in Kozani itself, Shrove Tuesday is festival day. Near Kozani one can visit the Zavorda monastery, constructed in the sixteenth century and with a pleasing display of frescoes. It was here in 1959 that a priceless thirteenth-century manuscript was discovered, containing pieces from Classical literature that had previously been considered lost.

Beyond Kozani

Kozani serves as the transportation hub of southern Macedonia. It has an airport to the east of town with daily flights to Athens and a rail link with Ptolemaida and Florina in the heart of Macedonia and on to Yugoslavia. As a major crossroads, it has direct routes to Florina, Thessaloniki, Larissa and Ioannina in Epirus.

Taking the Ioannina road to the south-west in the direction of Grevena, a stop can be made at **Siatista**, 5km (3 miles) off the main road, 25km (15 miles) from Kozani. Like Kozani, this is a town that

The barren, inhospitable uplands of the Pindos Mountains, Epirus (ch5)

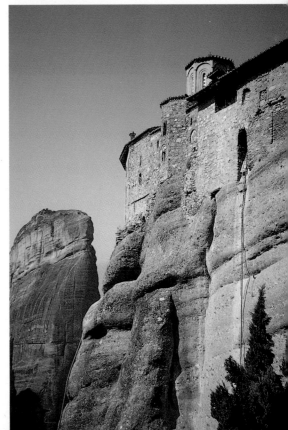

The convent of Rossenau, perched on top of the 'rock forest' at Meteora, Thessaly (ch6)

Cannons, left by the Turks, point out over Lake Pamvotis from Ioannina castle, Epirus (ch5)

The green and beautiful Enippeas Gorge, near Litohoro (ch6)

prospered greatly under Turkish rule and the many wooden-framed and overhanging eighteenth-century Macedonian mansions bear witness to its former wealth. Unfortunately, many are in a rather dilapidated state, but others have been well-maintained with stained-glass windows and interiors covered with wall and ceiling murals, most concentrating colourfully on the theme of nature.

Siatista has a famous son in John Trabandzis, an entrepreneur who left the village to emigrate to Romania where he accumulated a large fortune, part of which he donated to Siatista to found and maintain its school, the Trabandzian Gymnasium. Trabandzis was just one of several Macedonian emigrés who amassed wealth abroad and used a good deal of what they made for the benefit of their home villages. Similar parallels can be drawn today with the hundreds of thousands of Greeks who live and work abroad, often in Australia or America, and who send home remittances to their villages. These provide a lifeline for the local economy but burden the Greek economy as a whole because it is impossible to tax remittances.

Up until the 1930s Siatista was a thriving centre of the grape-growing industry but disease wiped out the vineyards and its residents were compelled to turn to another source of income; in this case, fur trimming. Sights to see in the town include the carved, exquisitely worked wooden altar in the eighteenth-century church of Agia Paraskevi; and those staying overnight can do so at a renovated and converted Macedonian mansion, the Arhontikon Hotel.

Anyone who is in the town on the afternoon of 23 December can witness a happy and charming Christmas festival, performed in memory of the shepherds who watched their flocks on Christmas night. The children of the village gather in their neighbourhood square, bringing sticks and tinder with which they light a large fire. Then, tinkling bells and singing loudly, they dance around the fire, often joined by the adults and with musicians providing accompaniment to the singing. This exuberant festival is enacted in a number of other villages across Macedonia.

From Siatista those partial to local Greek cheeses may care to make a 30km (18 miles) round-trip detour to the village of **Neapoli** before returning to the Grevena road. The town is one of the dairying centres of the region and its soft cheese can be bought almost anywhere. Back on the main road, it is another 28km (17 miles) to Grevena, another important but relatively unknown town of the region.

Grevena

Capital of its own prefecture, the town of **Grevena** is rarely featured in tourist guides to Greece and receives scarcely any attention from travel agents; as such, it welcomes only a tiny handful of tourists every year. This is quite a surprise as, although Grevena is in itself very much a modern Greek town, if a little more relaxed than most, it is also the eastern gateway to the Pindos mountains, that great range that stretches down northern Greece through Macedonia and Epirus. The surrounding mountains and villages are beautiful and untouched by tourism, the people are welcoming and it is very firmly off the beaten track.

It is believed that settlements have existed on the site of Grevena since Hellenic times. However, as no actual archaeological discoveries have been made in the vicinity, its early history is unclear. Not so its more recent history, for this was a major stronghold of the Greek nationalists during the 1821-27 War of Liberation and although Grevena, as with the rest of Macedonia, was not incorporated into the modern Greek state until 1912, the Turkish occupying forces received some terrible blows from the Andartes. Leader of the Greeks was the formidable Georgios Zakas (1798-1882), a local hero, whose bust gazes severely across the main square of the town.

As usual, it is in the main square that most of the essentials can be found. The banks are located here and, just off the square, is the town hall which doubles as an unofficial tourist office. The town has a few hotels, one of which, the 'D' class Hotel Aegli, can be recommended. It is a basic place but clean and is run by a helpful and friendly family.

As for sightseeing, ask a local if there are any tourist attractions in Grevena and you may well be directed to a brand new 'ancient theatre'. This is built in the style of the theatre of Dionysus in Athens and, unfortunately, is a sorry-looking set of concrete blocks already being covered in red graffiti. It is a nice walk there, though; leave Grevena by crossing a bridge over a small river and continue for 20 minutes past a large and thick pine forest, ideal for a short ramble or for picnics.

Back in Grevena, Friday is market day, the best day to be in town as villagers from across the region stock up on their goods for a week. In the past there was a weekly animal bazaar on this day but fruit and vegetables are now the main wares sold. Grevena's mobile hamburger salesmen, gliding around on bulky tricycles, do a brisk trade.

It is the surrounding mountains and the villages that lend the Grevena prefecture its appeal. Sparse and rocky in some places but usually covered in fir, pine and beech trees thanks to the abundance of water, the undulating landscape is encountered immediately upon leaving the town. Many of the villages are located high in the mountains, up to and over 1,000m (3,300ft) above sea-level, positioned high as protection from pirates and gangs of brigands. They also sheltered the Greek Andartes during the War of Liberation and served as sanctuaries for Greek members of the resistance during World War II. Because of their latter role, the Germans razed many villages to the ground.

Residents of the villages make their living from farming — goats, sheep and cereal crops — and increasingly from traditional crafts that are gradually being reintroduced. The cottage wool-weaving industry is a good example. Craftsmen and women specialise in the production of *kilimia*, a patterned woolly rug. A particularly beautiful village is **Samarina**, which has a population of 600 and is 1,500m (4,900ft) above sea level, but at 55km (34 miles) from Grevena, it is a long and winding day trip. Equally lovely, though, are the villages of Zakas and Spilio, easily reached from Grevena, marvellously unspoilt and constantly providing glimpses of Greek rural life.

Zakas is 14km (8 miles) out of Grevena, built at an altitude of 900m (2,950ft) and angled onto the slopes of Mount Orlakia. The mountain is green and pastoral at this point but as you follow the asphalt road out of town, it becomes a sheer sheet of rock. Although Zakas is a pretty village, Spilio, 3km (2 miles) on, is even more charming and the walk there is pure delight. The road snakes around Mount Orlakia, at one point running through a tunnel carved out of the rock, and the only life likely to be seen is the shepherd leading his sheep and goats out to pasture for the day. The wolves and bears that live on this mountain keep well away.

After 2km (1 mile) you reach the spot where Georgios Zakas won a cunning victory over the Turkish occupiers during the War of Liberation. Perched on the top of Orlakia, Zakas and his men filled barrels with rocks and rolled them down onto an unsuspecting Turkish force as they passed by underneath. Many Ottoman soldiers lost their lives. The road curves to the right as it enters Spilio, passing a sixteenth-century church that is said to have miraculous powers because it can cure the insane. Ask in the village for the key and, as English speakers are rather thin on the ground here, it may be helpful to know that *kleethee* is Greek for key and *igleezia* means church.

Spilio is a real throwback to the eighteenth century. Five hundred strong and built 60m (200ft) higher than Zakas, its wide, cobbled streets, flanked with low houses that lead down the slopes to the pastures below, give the impression of a village trapped in time.

Zakas village, built high on the slopes of Mount Orlakia

From one angle it faces the dramatic cliffs of Mount Orliaka, seen from the other side and filled with caves. However, it is the view east that takes the breath away, particularly if one takes the trouble to ascend a short but steep hill, immediately to the left as one enters the village, to reach a ramshackle viewing platform. There, the Greveniot Pindos range stretches out as far as the eye can see and there is nothing to do but just sit and stare at what is certainly one of the finest panormas in northern Greece.

Those with their own transport will have no difficulty getting to and from Zakas and Spilio; those without will need to make an early start. At present (and there is no reason for this to change), there are just two buses a day from Grevena to Zakas, at 6am and 2.30pm. Both continue to Spilio before immediately turning around to return to Grevena. The morning bus is by far the better option; the mountains look even finer at dawn and you can always catch the afternoon bus back. Alternatively, hitch-hiking is always an option; locals are well aware of the limited bus service and do what they can to help.

A view over the Meteora rock forest towards Kastraki

Meteora

Seventy kilometres (43 miles) south of Grevena is one of the great wonders of Greece, if not of Europe. The 'rock forest' of Meteora is a sight that no traveller to Greece should miss. With over 1,000 granite teeth soaring out of the lush countryside and each rock seemingly in competition with the other for sheer dramatic presence, the neighbouring town of Kalambaka is utterly dwarfed. Yet this spectacle is not only a miracle of nature — man has also left his mark on Meteora, as, perched on top of what appears to be the most inaccessible rocks, are monasteries. These were tortuously constructed by monks as the perfect sanctuary during the dark days of the thirteenth century when the Byzantine empire was crumbling under the onslaught of the Moslem Ottomans. At one stage there were twenty-four monasteries in operation — six are still inhabited today and are all open to visitors, regardless of age or sex.

Up until 80 years ago the monasteries could only be visited by the terrifying usage of primitive scaffolding, winch-hauled baskets and swaying rope ladders. Today, thankfully, an asphalt road links all six, snaking its way through the rocks in a 21km (13 miles) circuit from Kalambaka and allowing for perfect exploration, either by car or by foot. The latter means is probably the best way to experience Meteora — it offers numerous opportunities to get off the asphalt and wander the old mule paths that criss-cross the area. Look closely in the spring and summer as wild tortoises can be seen, the dense vegetation of the lower regions making a perfect habitat for them.

Before setting off, remember that each monastery (except Varlaam) charges an admission fee and that the appropriate dress standards are maintained, i.e. trousers for men, skirts of at least knee-length for women, who must also have their arms covered. Also consider packing a picnic lunch as the monasteries close for a lengthy siesta between 1pm and 3.30pm before closing their gates at around 6pm.

Tourist buses do not normally begin to arrive in Meteora until midday, so to view the monasteries in peace, get an early start. Take the well-marked road out of Kalambaka, go through the small village of Kastraki (there are three campsites and several restaurants here), and reach a sign pointing at the uphill path to the first 'living monastery', Agios Nikolaos. Constructed in the fifteenth century, its narrow chapel features the colourful frescoes (wall paintings) of the Cretan monk, Theophanes. Particularly charming is the one depicting Adam naming the animals. The ruined monastery nearby is Agia Moni, deserted since the 1850s.

One kilometre ($^1/_2$ mile) further on is the convent of Rossenau, built in the fourteenth century on a great toothpick of a rock which is so steep that its only access is via a bridge from an adjacent rock. The chapel contains stark and bloody frescoes; painted in the sixteenth century, they portray the gruesome deaths of the early Christian martyrs, a feature that is shared by the great monasteries of Varlaam and Transfiguration (Grand Meteoron). These are reached by taking the left fork as one descends from Rossenau, on the side opposite to the one ascended.

It is a tough slog up to the wonderfully photogenic Varlaam — there are nearly 200 steps — but it is well worth the effort. Very little sunlight enters the chapels, with the result that the frescoes are still preserved in all their dazzling colours. Although gory death is the dominant topic, other subjects are featured, including the Last Supper and the Transfiguration. A saintly looking man in white is depicted on a pillar to the left as one enters the narthex; this is Varlaam the Hermit who lived on this rock over 100 years before the actual construction of the monastery in 1517.

Grand Meteoron is the best-known of all the monasteries and not only because it is the largest, and at 613m (2,010ft) above sea-level, the highest. It is also because that for centuries, this monastery has dominated the others in terms of riches, status and prestige.

Founded in the thirteenth century by the great monk, Athanassios, its wealth was derived from a Serbian prince who abandoned his name and his heritage to live the monastic life here as Jasaph. With these two leading figures directing the monastery's development, Grand Meteoron soon began to eclipse the others and assume a prominence that it has maintained. Its cool and shady interior comes as a welcome relief after the steep climb up to the entrance.

The enchanting sixteenth-century chapel has a striking, twelve-sided dome. The monastery also houses its own museum containing ancient books and manuscripts, as well as some astonishingly intricate wood-carved crosses, one of which took 14 years to complete. The carvings are the work of the monks themselves. Unfortunately, most of the treasures of the Grand Meteoron have now disappeared, either by theft or by misguided monks of the past offering them for sale to raise funds for the monastery but at prices way below their actual market value.

Continuing the tour, return to Rossenau, keep left and the road will lead to Agios Triada (Holy Trinity), a monastery that is over 500 years old and one that has recently been re-opened. A series of stone steps lead up under an over-hanging rock to the fortress-style entrance. The frescoes inside were painted by the monk Nikodemos towards the end of the seventeenth century.

From this monastery it is only a short stroll to the convent of Agios Stephanos; cool and airy and a relative 'youngster' at only 200 years old. That is only the buildings though; monasteries and hermitages have existed on this site, peering down at Kalambaka, since the twelfth century. The central church is dedicated to St Charalambos, an early Christian who was martyred in the second century. There is a small gift shop and museum displaying some of the tiny icons that were not destroyed by communists during the Greek Civil War.

To return to Kalambaka one can either keep on the asphalt road for 5km (3 miles) or retrace one's steps to Agios Triada and make the steep but rewarding descent down a dirt path through the rocks. It is a very pleasant 40 minute walk and red splashes of paint on the rocks clearly mark the path. It ends at the top of Kalambaka town.

Kalambaka itself is a town that thrives solely on its proximity to Meteora and is a lively, pleasant place with plenty of shops, hotels and restaurants. Its modern appearance derives from the fact that it was destroyed by the Germans during World War II and had to be rebuilt. Most of the hotels are located near the main square but some visitors may prefer to put up with a small drop in quality and facilities and stay in one of several small tavernas at the top of the

The bell-tower of Kalambaka's eleventh-century Byzantine church

town. In these you can eat in front of a roaring open fire, drink *chipola*, the local hootch, and listen to the bouzoukis playing before retiring upstairs.

Also at the top of the town is an ancient Byzantine church, modelled on the Sancta Sophia in Istanbul and with a huge central pulpit, an unusual feature in Greek churches. Known as the church of the Dormition of the Virgin, its site has been a place of worship since 200BC, originally as a temple to Apollo. It was converted into a church in the fifth century and the present buildings date back a millennium. The church is most definitely worth a visit, particularly during services when the blackened frescoes, dim lighting and chanting of priests all combine to recreate an air of Byzantine mysticism.

The church of the Dormition of the Virgin, Kalambaka

Metsovo

From Kalambaka one can either continue the circuit to Trikala, only 19km (12 miles) away, or make the 116km (72 miles) round-trip to the little town of Metsovo on the E87 to Ioannina. Ignore the distance and enjoy the journey as there is little doubt that the E87 west of Kalambaka is one of the most spectacular routes in Greece. It runs up to 1,700m (5,580ft) through the Katari Pass, the great chasm that cuts across the snow-capped Pindos mountains to link Thessaly with Epirus. To drive through is a breathtaking, ear-popping experience as the road twists around the sheer drops into the pass. It is easy to see why this road was of such strategic importance during both World War II and the Greek Civil War. During the winter months, snow ploughs are kept continually busy keeping the road to Ioannina open. Halfway along its route is Metsovo, an unusual village in many ways and a great place to break the journey.

Metsovo straddles the Katari Pass at over 1,000m (3,300ft) above sea-level. It has a distinctly alpine appeal that is enhanced by the low stone and wooden houses with their over-hanging roofs, steep and tiny alleyways and a striking view over the white-tipped Pindos range. Initially at least, it would seem to be equally at home on a Swiss or Italian mountain top. Yet this village is Greek with a difference, a difference immediately noticeable in the traditional costumes

worn by young and old alike; women in red and black checked shirts
and shawls and men in black from head to toe — caps, jackets,
leggings, skirts and rather dainty clogs topped with furry pom-poms
on the toes. For these costumes are not Greek, they are Vlahi.

The actual origins of the Vlahi people are unclear. One school of
thought suggests that they were brought from Vlahia in Romania by
the Romans to be trained as guards for the Via Egnatia, that great
road that linked Constantinople (Istanbul) with Rome. This would
explain the many Latin words used in the native Vlahi language,
which is still spoken here. Another theory argues that Epirus, including southern Albania, has always been the Vlahi homeland.

Whatever their origins, the Vlahis have clung fiercely together,
despite sporadic attacks on their culture by more nationalistic Greek
governments. They live in several villages around the Katari Pass, of
which Metsovo is the largest, and derive their income mainly from
agriculture and sheep farming.

Many Metsovians make their living from tourism, which is hardly
surprising as the deeply traditional nature of the town has an inevitable appeal for visitors. Organised tourist buses stop in Metsovo
daily during the summer and the souvenir shops around the main
platia are kept busy, leading some to claim that Metsovo practises
'tradition for tourism's sake'. This is hardly a fair accusation as
anyone who arrives outside the summer months will see, but there
are many facilities for tourists.

The only street in the town has several hotels, some rather enticing
restaurants and shops that sell souvenirs, antiques and wooden
handicrafts. Several shops sell Metsovo cheese, an absolute must for
anyone who likes their cheese hard and tasty and a real feast when
accompanied by the local *retsina*. Metsovo honey is also a popular
buy. Note the carpentry workshops where the old Vlahi art of wood-
carving is still practised. Some of the work is superb — just go in and
ask to look around.

The reason that many of the traditional and local industries of
Metsovo have been maintained is that a certain Baron Tositsas, an
extremely prosperous Swiss banker with roots in the village, willed
his wealth to Metsovo. A museum has been established in his name,
located in the old family mansion just up from the main street. The
museum is a real throwback to the eighteenth century, preserved as
it was and filled with the furniture, utensils and other handicrafts of
the age.

Other places of interest in Metsovo include an art gallery featuring
the works of contemporary Greek artists and, beside the clock tower,

The Vlahi village of Metsovo

Metsovo: the old mansion of the Tositsas family, now a museum

the fifteenth century church of Agia Paraskevi. Both are located in the main *platia* but if neither appeal, just wander the steep, cobbled alleyways.

A 15 minute walk down the hillside leads to the small and serene monastery of Agios Nikolaos. Ring the bell for the caretaker who is happy to open the chapel to allow visitors to see the beautiful post-

Byzantine frescoes painted there. You can also visit the monks' cloisters to get an idea of how materially stark and rigorous the monastic life is. However, be warned, the climb back up to Metsovo is an exhausting experience, particularly during the hot summer season.

Trikala

Built along the banks of Litheos river, **Trikala** is one of those bright and lively new Greek towns that, while offering little of immediate appeal to tourists, makes for a very pleasant half-day visit just shopping and strolling around the busy central *platia* and seeing its few sights. With a population of 35,000, it is one of the larger, more important towns of the region and evidence suggests that it has always been so, built as it is on the site of ancient *Trikki*. The Hellenes deemed *Trikki* important enough to warrant a castle, built on the town's highest point and a fortress still occupies the spot today. However, its well-preserved remains are Turkish, built over the earlier Byzantine and Hellenic structures.

It is this fortress that serves as Trikala's main tourist attraction and tour buses en-route to Meteora regularly pull in here for a brief stop. What the tour groups never get to see, though, is the intricate network of closely packed, Turkish-style houses at the foot of the hill on which the fortress stands and the large and mystical Greek Orthodox churches in the vicinity. On most days a fruit and vegetable open-air market spills out onto the streets.

The area immediately below the castle is an attraction in itself, offering public gardens with a childrens' playground at the bottom and a shady walk through woods to the summit. On the slopes one can find the ruins of a sanctuary to Asclepius, god of healing. This find has prompted experts to suggest that Trikala, along with the island of Kos and Epidavros in the Peloponnese, may well have been one of the founding centres for the worship of this god.

While in Trikala, a pleasant excursion can be made to the large village of Pili, 21km (13 miles) away and renowned for its local yoghurt. Easily reached by car or by regular bus from Trikala, the road follows the Portaikos river south-west, passing the turn-off for the village of Gomfi. There is nothing remarkable about Gomfi now but the ancient town of the same name, north-west at Paleokastro, was once a hill-top town of vital strategic importance, heavily fortified and guarding the eastern entrance to Thessaly. It was destroyed in 48BC by the troops of Julius Caesar.

Pili itself is a pretty village but its main attraction is 1km ($^1/_2$ mile) further on and beautifully located at the mouth of a gorge. This is the Byzantine church of Porta Panagia; built in 1283, surrounded by an empty moat and with gorgeous mosaics and frescoes that have been untouched since their completion 700 years ago. The church will almost certainly be locked but the key can be obtained by knocking on the door of the low house on the hill nearby. Pili has a hotel, the Babanara.

The town of Karditsa can be easily reached from either Pili or Trikala. From Trikala take the signposted main road south-east for 30km (18 miles). From Pili head due south for 5km (3 miles) to Mouzaka, then take the eastern road through a string of rural villages for 31km (19 miles).

Karditsa

Karditsa is an important commercial centre for the region, employing its residents in agriculture (cereal crops and cotton) and in the tobacco industry which employs up to 6 per cent of the entire Greek workforce.

Built alongside a tributary of the Pinios river, the town has few attractions except for the green and pleasant Pafsilipo park, ideal for an afternoon stroll. Yet Karditsa is a good base to explore the large man-made lake of Nea Plastira, the water source of the entire region and set at an altitude of 800m (2,624ft), high in the Agrafa mountains. Making a circuit is the best way to see the lake, which is fast attracting the attention of travel agents, but it can only really be made by those who have their own transport or who are extremely determined and very fortunate hitch-hikers.

Nea Plastira is 20km (12 miles) outside Karditsa on the western road and it is a rolling, peaceful experience travelling around its 48km (30 mile) circuit through the villages of Neraida, Kastania and Filakti. Rooms to let are available in most of the villages for those who wish for a few days of unhurried calm before returning to Karditsa.

From Karditsa, a direct road leads north-west for 60km (37 miles) back to Larissa where one can rejoin the E92 Athens-Thessaloniki highway. If returning to Athens, though, a pleasant route is to make the 88km (54 miles) journey south-east to the town of **Lamia** which also touches the E92. A little more relaxed than its modern, grid-plan lay-out would suggest, the town is dominated by the ruins of a fourteenth-century Catalan castle and, with plenty of hotels, makes a good place for an overnight stop. Those who do so will be following the example of storks and other migrating birds who use Lamia as a stopping-off point on their routes north and south.

Further Information
— Northern Thessaly/Southern Macedonia —

Ambelakia
Schwartz Mansion
Open: 9.30am-3.30pm.
Closed Tuesdays.

Womens' Agrotourist Co-operative
☎ (0495) 31495

Dion
Site and museum
☎ 0351 53206
Open: 9am-3pm daily.
Closed Mondays.

Grevena
Tourist Information
Town hall, just off main square
Open: 8am-2pm Monday to Friday.

Katerini
Tourist Information
Platia Eleflarios
☎ 0351 33000

Kozani
*Museum of Natural History
and Folklore*
Open: 8am-2pm daily.

Archaeological collection
☎ 0461 26210

Tourist Information
Platia 28 Oktovriou
☎ 0461 39979

Litohoro
Tourist Information
Agios Nikolaos 15
☎ 0352 82288

Metsovo
Tositsas Museum
Main street
Open: 8.30am-1pm and 3-5pm
daily.
Wait at the door until the guide
appears on the half hour, every
half hour.

Art Gallery
Main square
Open: 9.30am-1.30pm, 4-6pm.
Closed Tuesdays.

Mount Olympus
Refuge Hut 'A'
☎ (0352) 81800
Owner: Kostas Zolotas
☎ (0352) 81329

Refuge Hut 'B'
(Vrissopoules)
☎ 01 323 4555

7 • Western Macedonia

Introduction

T he homeland of Alexander the Great and the base for his vast empire that stretched from Ethiopia to India, western Macedonia today still retains an air of independence from the rest of Greece. Indeed, it was only 90 years ago that Greek and Bulgarian rebels were fighting in its hills to expel the Turkish occupiers and establish a separate state of Macedonia that would incorporate its Greek, Bulgarian and Yugoslavian sections. Yet, today, western Macedonia is proudly Greek and is the area where one can discover a part of the country that has been virtually untouched by the influx of foreign tourists; from its bright and wealthy capital of Thessaloniki in the east, to the west, where bare hills mark the Albanian frontier.

This is not the area where one can embark on an endless round of beaches and sightseeing; its beaches are confined to a few strips of sand south of Thessaloniki and its archaeological sites, with the exception of Pella, are good without being outstanding. The nightlife is often limited to sitting in the smoke-filled town or village café (*kafenion*), sipping *ouzo* or *retsina* with the locals. You sometimes have to work hard to travel here; English-speakers are often very thin on the ground. Yet it is a part of Greece that few get the chance to experience.

The main gateway into western Macedonia is Thessaloniki, positioned at the top of the Thermaic Gulf and the second largest city in Greece. Most of its overseas visitors only pause here long enough to get a connection to Athens or Istanbul. However, it is a fine city in its own right, kept cool by the sea breeze and with plenty of attractions. These include a superb archaeological museum and an old city that holds the atmosphere and architecture of nineteenth century Macedonia.

Thessaloniki is a prosperous place, its wealth accumulated independently of tourism. From the city a trip lasting a day or more can be made to the town of Kilkis and its surrounds — lush and very

Colourful woven rugs are a distinctive feature of Greece

A whitewashed house in a quiet corner of Kastoria (ch7)

Statue of Aristotle in Stagira, his birthplace (ch8)

Ruins of ancient Pella, with the new city in the background (ch7)

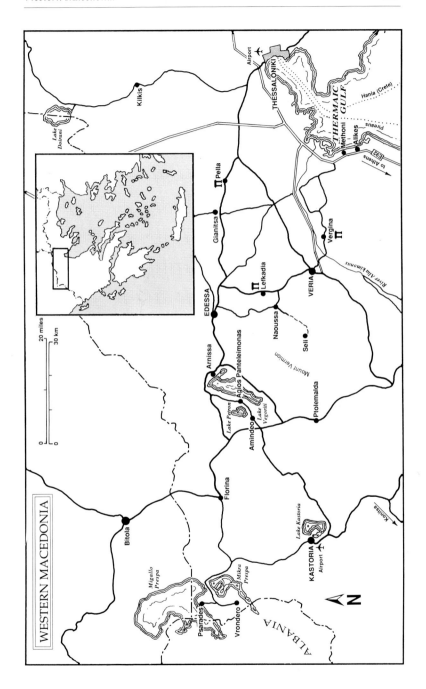

popular among nature-lovers. West of Thessaloniki are the extensive remains of ancient Pella, birthplace of Alexander the Great and capital of his kingdom. Beyond Pella, there is Edessa, located high in the hills and a popular spot among Greeks for its gushing waterfalls, the *katarrakton*.

Travelling west out of Edessa, one heads into territory that is largely untouched by tourism, skirting around Lake Vegoriti towards the high and attractively located town of Florina, in the top left-hand corner of Greece. Continuing west over the hills, one arrives at one of the finest natural attractions of Greece, Migallo Prespa (Big Lake) and Mikra Prespa (Little Lake) both set in the base of a bowl of beautiful mountains that straddle the borders of Greece, Yugoslavia and Albania. A wonderful area for boating, fishing, walking and swimming, these 'Great Lakes of Greece' remain unknown to all but a handful of visitors.

South of Florina is Kastoria, a town full of history, built on the shores of its own lake and the long-time centre of the Greek fur industry. Heading east from Kastoria, one crosses a mountainous landscape on the way back to Thessaloniki, dropping in on the towns of Naoussa, which is said to produce the best wine in Greece, and Veria, an old and atmospheric Macedonian-Turkish town. Near Veria are the excavated tombs of Vergina, where the skeleton of the Macedonian King Phillip the Second was unearthed, together with a fantastic collection of priceless artefacts now on display at Thessaloniki's archaeological museum. If a relaxing swim sounds appealing after all this touring, there are several beaches on the coast near Veria, reached via either Eginio or Katerini. The beach at Methoni has the most facilities.

For most people, Thessaloniki will be their point of entry into western Macedonia. The city has excellent road and rail links, whether from Athens in the south or from almost any point in northern Europe. Flights from the major European centres regularly touch down at its airport, as do frequent services from Athens and a whole host of Greek islands. Kastoria also has an airport with several connections a day to Athens.

If entering the region from Epirus, there is a direct road link between Konitsa and Kastoria. Note that if arriving from western Yugoslavia, one can cross the border by road or rail at Bitola, 17km (10 miles) north of Florina. Travel to and from Albania is totally forbidden and even boating too close to its shores on Migallo or Mikra Prespa is to invite being shot at by the Albanian border guards.

The region is easy to travel around by public transport. Buses seem to run to most places, although not particularly frequently to the more minor towns, and there is a useful rail line as a slower and cheaper alternative. The tracks run from Thessaloniki to Florina, via Veria, Edessa and Amindeo and from Florina to Kozani via Amindeo and Ptolemaida. One can hire cars in either Thessaloniki or Kastoria. Climatically, the region can be distinctly chilly during winter-time and more than a little gloomy. The best time to visit is between spring and autumn, with summer being preferable if one intends to do any swimming in Migallo Prespa.

Macedonian influence in ancient Greece first became apparent in the seventh century BC when Perdikkas gained control of the region and established his capital at *Aiges* (Vergina). Although *Aiges* had given way to Pella as the Macedonian capital by the end of the fifth century BC, it still remained the traditional burial place of the Macedonian kings, most of whom met a violent death at the hands of their opponents for the leadership. Yet, despite these brutal power struggles at the top, the region grew culturally, commercially and in military might. By 336BC, King Phillip the Second had conquered all of Ancient Greece and united it as a powerful force with which to attack the invading Persians. Like so many of his predecessors, though, Phillip was assassinated and it was his son, Alexander the Great, who in a 13 year reign covered in glory, led the Macedonians in conquering what was then the entire known world.

Alexander died of a fever in Babylon, Persia in 323BC and the Macedonian Kingdom splintered immediately into factional in-fighting. In time, some of its old stature was regained; the Macedonians fiercely resisted the Roman legions in 168BC but were eventually subdued by the Latin victory at Alikes that year. Western Macedonia was very important to the Romans; the Via Egnatia, the Rome-Constantinople road, passed through here on its way to the sea-route which would link it to Brindisi in Italy.

The Goths, Slavs and Bulgars created a lot of problems for the Byzantines during their rule of Macedonia. From the fourth to the tenth centuries, the region was constantly defending itself against attack from these raiders, particularly the Bulgars who claimed the territory as their own, a claim that persisted up until the end of World War II. A furious war in the tenth century against the Bulgars was conducted by the Byzantine Emperor, the appropriately named 'Basil the Bulgar-Slayer'. He achieved lasting notoriety by blinding an entire Bulgar army of 10,000 men; the Bulgar king was said to have died of shock after seeing his men arrive home in such a condition.

The Turks over-ran Macedonia in 1430 and began a rule that was to last 483 years. Although often brutal and repressive, some cities did prosper, including Kastoria and Thessaloniki; the latter grew into a thriving cosmopolitan city. Yet the Macedonians rose against the Turks during the 1821-27 War of Liberation and although they were defeated, took to the mountains again from 1870 onward to conduct a guerilla war against the Turks. These guerilla units (the Andartes) proved vital to the Greek victory over the Turks in 1913 that united Macedonia with Greece. However, the region was soon to be occupied again; by the Bulgarians during the two World Wars. Yet, with their defeat in 1945, the Bulgarians renounced all claims to Macedonia and the region became unalterably Greek.

The mountains and hills of western Macedonia proved to be wonderful havens for the Greek rebels fighting the Turks, particularly where they are at their highest along the Yugoslavian and Albanian frontiers. Here the mountains effectively provide a natural border. Lesser hills roll across the region's interior, occasionally dipping down to the shores of calm lakes such as Kastoria, Vegoriti and Petron. Some of the region's wildlife can be seen at the two major lakes of Macedonia — Migallo and Mikra Prespa. The wild bears, boars and wolves keep themselves hidden away in the surrounding mountains but pelicans and cormorants can often be seen around the lake itself. In spring, numerous wild flowers are in bloom here.

Thessaloniki

It may raise a few eyebrows that **Thessaloniki** be deemed as off the beaten track. It is, after all, home to over 1 million people; is the largest city in Greece after Athens and the transportation hub for the entire Balkan region. In addition, there is a whole wealth of attractions including an attractive old Turkish quarter, splendid churches, a lively nightlife, plenty of Roman remains and an archaeological museum that ranks as one of the finest in southern Europe. Yet most of the hotels are filled with Greeks doing business in this wealthy, commercial centre and the vast majority of tourists seem to take one look at the dilapidated buildings; the crowds and the frantic roads and head off; usually east into Turkey or south to Athens and the islands. They are missing a great deal.

Ever since its establishment 23 centuries ago, Thessaloniki has been a city of great stature and importance; it has its location to thank for this, standing at the junction of Europe and Asia and served by both the sea and two sizeable rivers, the Gallicos and the Axios. It was undoubtedly these strategic reasons that prompted Kassandros, a Macedonian general, to found the city in 315BC. He named it after the

Psarades, a village on the beautiful lake of Migallo Prespa

woman he married; Thessalonia, sister of the conqueror of the then known world, Alexander the Great. During this era, Pella was capital of Macedonia, and Thessaloniki, 40km (25 miles) away, wasted no time in establishing itself as the kingdom's second city and the base for its navy.

Thessaloniki positively boomed under Roman rule. It became a vital staging post on the Via Egnatia, the Rome-Constantinople road, and so Paul had no difficulty travelling here from Phillipi to preach the Christian faith. He was well-received and the city became an early stronghold of the new faith. Indeed, Paul's two epistles to the Thessalonians praise them for their steadfastness. However, later Christian leaders did not enjoy the same level of tolerance from their Roman rulers. Dimitrios, a Roman officer and lay-preacher, was arrested, imprisoned and martyred in the third century to the outrage of a Christian community who successfully pressed for his canonisation. He is the city's patron saint and defender of Thessaloniki from war, plague, famine etc.

Thessaloniki passed through the Byzantine era in the same manner as most of the rest of Greece — long periods of calm followed by short periods of violent strife. In AD904 the city was raided by Saracen mercenaries from the east who conducted a 10 day orgy of slaughter and pillage. For 20 years in the twelfth century Thessaloniki became the capital of the Crusader Frankish kingdom.

The year 1430 brought stability, although hardly in the way that the city wanted. This was the year the dark curtain of Ottoman conquest was drawn over the city and 500 years of crushing civil oppression began; bringing with it enforced conscription into the Turkish army, the conversion of churches into mosques and high taxes. However, following the Balkan Wars of 1912-13, the city was incorporated into Greece. Four years later, almost all vestiges of its past were destroyed in a huge fire, causing the city to be rebuilt in the fashion that it is today.

One of Thessaloniki's greatest tragedies was to come during World War II. The occupying Germans rounded up the city's 44,000 Jews, most of whom had fled here from Spain following Ferdinand and Isabella's expulsion of all Jews from that country in 1492, and transported them to the extermination camps. Only one synagogue remains in Thessaloniki today.

There are four ways to get to Thessaloniki—by road, rail, air or sea. Of the four, by boat is the worst option. Only two passenger ferries serve Thessaloniki, one departing every Saturday for Pireaus via Lesvos and Chios, the other every Monday for the long haul to Hania, on Crete. However, the road and rail networks link Thessaloniki directly with most major cities north, south, east and west and the airport is Euro-international, with flights to many European capitals. It also maintains a busy internal schedule with services to Athens, Patras and Iraklion (Crete) among others. Note that although no public bus services make the 16km (10 mile) journey to the airport, Olympic Airways buses depart from outside their main office on Nikis Street 90 minutes before each flight.

Just as getting there is relatively easy, getting around Thessaloniki should rarely pose a problem. Its grid-plan layout makes for easy orientation and, with the help of the detailed map handed out by the tourist office, it is pretty easy to get from A to B. The city is centred around the three main streets that straddle it and, conveniently, each one services visitors in a different manner. Nikis Street, which runs along the waterfront, is where Olympic Airways and most travel agents are located; Tsimiski Street (two blocks up) is home to the banks, the Greek telephone organisation and the post office; and Egnatia Street, another two blocks away from Tsimiski, is where most of the hotels can be found, catering for all tastes and budgets.

It is difficult to wander around Thessaloniki without coming across remnants of its history, as the new city has been built virtually right on top of the old. The rather incongruous result of this is that most of its important archaeological sites are located next to the chaos of daily street life. There are few opportunities to explore the past in peace. The old Roman market and theatre, splendidly preserved in what is now Law Courts Square, is only a stone's throw away from five-lane Egnatia Street which is the old Via Egnatia of two millennia ago.

The finely engraved arch of Galerios, built in AD300 by the Roman emperor Galerios in celebration of a successful military campaign in Asia, stands at the corner of Gounari and Egnatia Streets, and the second century Roman baths are on Aristotelus Street, north of the law courts. What remains there are of the palace of Galerios lie in the north of the city, near Navarino Square. From a later era, the downtown area around Egnatia and Tsimiski Streets contains a number of large and impressive Byzantine and post-Byzantine churches.

For most visitors, sightseeing in Thessaloniki begins at the city's archaeological museum and quite rightly so. Arranged in a simple, chronological and educational fashion and clearly marked in both Greek and English, it exhibits a startling array of mosaics, sculptures and busts dating from the prehistoric to the Roman eras. The museum's central attractions, however, are the artefacts excavated in 1977 from the Royal Tombs of Vergina, burial place of Phillip the Second, under whose leadership Macedonia conquered Greece. The finds include some beautiful examples of figurines and crowns handcrafted in gold. At the entrance to the display, in a glass cabinet, lies the grotesquely charred skeleton of Phillip himself.

Another museum is only a 5 minute walk away from here, housed in what has become the symbol of Thessaloniki, the White Tower. Stand at almost any point on the waterfront and this sixteenth-century Turkish construction is clearly visible, a giant chesspiece of a monument standing in a cool and shady park. Originally built to aid the city's defences, it soon earned the title of the Bloody Tower, due to the Turkish practice of putting convicts to a gory death on its ramparts as a warning to others. Yet in 1890 it changed both its name and its colour, thanks to a rather unusual deal struck between the prison authorities and a prisoner in which the latter was told that if he whitewashed the building he could go free. Not surprisingly, the prisoner set to with bucket and brush and eventually gained his release. The museum inside houses a collection of Byzantine relics but, with all the artefacts being labelled in Greek, a visit can be a confusing experience for non-Greek speakers.

Currently undergoing the completion of a major renovation programme is the museum of the struggle for Macedonia. Covering

A typical Macedonian street, made up of closely packed houses with overhanging eaves

the modern historic period, it is more of an exhibition than a museum and provides a useful means of understanding this much quarrelled over territory. Also worth a visit is the ethnological and popular art museum; 250 years of history seen from a folk-orientated, cultural viewpoint. The museum has a fine display of the traditional clothes of northern Greece.

For a glimpse of what could be termed a 'living museum', visit the *kastro*, the old Turkish quarter of Thessaloniki and an area untouched by the 1917 fire. Reached either by public bus 22, a 45 minute walk from the law courts or, most conveniently, by taxi, this quarter is composed of traditional Macedonian style buildings, clumped closely together and crowned by the remains of a castle built by the Byzantines in the fourteenth century. The panorama over new Thessaloniki is vast, if not exactly beautiful, and there is a feeling of being away from the city's bustle. The nearby Vlatadon monastery is open to visitors. To get a further flavour of the Turkish occupation of Thessaloniki, you can visit a museum maintained by the Turkish consulate. It is a 20 minute walk from the *kastro* and the house in which it is displayed is the birthplace of the great statesman, Kemal Ataturk, founder of modern Turkey.

The Byzantine churches of Thessaloniki are mainly positioned in the downtown, commercial areas and most merit a quick visit at the very least, particularly the two best-known; Agios Georgios and Agios Dimitrios. The latter is the largest church in the whole of Greece and is dedicated to the city's patron saint who was confined in what is now the crypt in AD303. The crypt is open to visitors until 3pm daily, except Tuesday. The most impressive feature of Agios Dimitrios is perhaps its sheer size but it also has a brilliantly decorated dome that was restored in 1948. The church was constructed in the fifth century but was destroyed by raiders and rebuilt in the seventh century and the delicate and faded frescoes in the small northern chapel date back to that second construction.

The church of Agios Georgios is better known as the Rotunda and it too has a very lengthy history. Standing next to the Arch of Galerios on Egnatia Street, it was built in AD305 as a part of the arch and to serve as a mausoleum for the emperor himself. However, the Byzantine Emperor Constantine ordered its conversion to a church and centuries later the Turks converted it again, this time into a mosque, giving this circular building its minaret. On the liberation of Thessaloniki it was reconverted into a church. Unfortunately, the building cannot be entered — restoration work, necessary since the 1978 earthquake, is still underway at the time of writing. For the latest information on this, phone 031 213627.

One church that can be visited despite the fact that it is undergoing restoration, is Agia Sophia, modelled on the great Agia Sophia of Istanbul. It is a large and lovely building although the scaffolding severely hampers the views of the frescoes; it is located on the corner of Ermou and Agia Sophia Streets. Other Thessalian churches of interest are Panagia Halkeon (eleventh-century), Agii Apostoli (fifteenth-century) and Agios Nikolaos Orfanos (fourteenth-century), all decorated finely and still in operation today.

Thessaloniki is packed in September when its international trade fair comes to town, held at the exhibition grounds at the end of Egnatia Street. Several festivals immediately follow this, making it a frantic time of year; a film festival, a Greek song festival and the Agios Dimitrios festival which features a series of cultural events.

The swimming around the city is not particularly clean although there are beaches at Agia Triada and Nea Mihaniona east of the city. For better bathing, travel either south on the E5 to the beaches around Litohorio or to the prongs of Kassandra or Sithonia in Halkidiki.

Some of the tourist literature available waxes lyrical about the delights of Panorama, a small village 12km (7 miles) east of

Thessaloniki with a fine view over the city and the Thermaic Gulf. It is hardly possible to enjoy the view in peace, though, the road that cuts through the village is a frantic one and the over-priced restaurants and bars are packed with locals.

An interesting and peaceful excursion can be made to the prefecture of Kilkis and its capital town of the same name, lying only 50km (31 miles) north of Thessaloniki. Very few non-Greeks set out for this unspoilt and uncommercialised region, a fine spot for nature-lovers.

The town of **Kilkis** is pleasingly located among the green hills and valleys, kept lush by the Axios river that divides into two and sandwiches the town. This is an excellent river for fishermen. There is no need to travel all the way south back to the coast to swim; 35km (21 miles) north of Kilkis is Mouries, from whose beach one can swim in the blue waters of Lake Doirani which marks the border with Yugoslavia. While in the town of Kilkis, take a look at the long, large cave at the north of the town with its rocky patterns over the ceiling and walls. It lies about 300m (360yd) from the little church of Agios Georgios.

West of Thessaloniki

It takes quite a while to leave the sprawl of Thessaloniki behind as you exit the city on the north-western road to Edessa but eventually the breezeblocks give way to the flat and green Macedonian plain. After 40km (25 miles) travelling along this road, great columns can be seen to the right, and it is a good idea to stop the car or get off the bus to explore the ruins of the most important city of Macedonian times — **Pella**. This city took over from *Aiges* (Vergina) as the capital of Macedonia at the end of the fifth century and, following the conquest of the rest of Hellas by the great military strategist Phillip the Second, became the capital of the entire Hellenic Federation. It was here that Phillip the Second was assassinated and Alexander the Great was born.

Strategically it seems an odd site for a capital — there are no defensive hills surrounding it and no outlet to the sea — but during these times Pella was connected to the sea by a long silted-up river. The city's importance was such that it seems odd that it was only rediscovered by accident in 1957.

The site itself is extensive, stretching from the roadside back towards the nearby and unexciting village of Nea Pella, and shows the city to be a large one, particularly by the standards of the age. Excavations are still in progress so some parts are firmly off-limits

but the wide streets, houses and large palace/government administration building are all clearly discernable.

It was in the palace, fronted by the tall columns, that the cream of
the finds were made — a whole series of mosaics of which three have
been left untouched. One depicts a stag hunt, another a battle between a Greek and an Amazon, and the third the rape of Helen. All
three are quite remarkable, exquisitely worked in softly coloured
stones and with real drama.

More mosaics of equal beauty can be seen in the small Pella museum on the other side of the main road — Dionysus astride a
panther, and a lion hunt. Other smaller artefacts from the excavations are also housed here. Note that Pella is simple to visit by public
transport — buses run half-hourly from Thessaloniki's bus station
on Anagenniseos Street and stop at the small café just before the
museum. All buses to Edessa make a stop here.

Towards the end of the 38km (23 mile) journey from Pella to Edessa
the flat plain gives way and the road begins to climb steadily,
twisting its way around the cherry-tree covered foothills of Mount
Vermion before entering the 15,000 strong town of **Edessa**. You do
not have to spend too much time here before realising it is one of the
prettiest 'new towns' in Macedonia; full of small but very well-kept
parks, leafy and with tiny streams bubbling almost everywhere (its
name means 'the waters' in Slav).

It is not difficult to see why Edessa is a popular spot for day-
tripping Macedonians who mainly come to see the town's foremost
attraction, the *katarrakton* (waterfalls). These are actually quite dramatic and well-worth a look. To reach them is a simple enough task
— just follow one of the streams down to their meeting place at the
end of the town where they all unite in a charming little park before
disappearing over the end of a cliff to splash down 24m (79ft) below
in a cloud of spray.

A path that leads down the side of the falls provides the best views.
Follow it down far enough and you will arrive at the town's hydro-
electric plant which is serviced by the main waterfall and two other
smaller ones. The area around the top of the falls is full of tourist stalls
selling postcards and local handicrafts and also serving as a good
introduction to the Macedonian fondness for furs and taxidermy.
Stuffed foxes and birds peer glassily at passing visitors.

Unlike Kastoria or Siatista in Macedonia, the fur industry is not a
major employer in Edessa. Carpet-making is, though, and several of
the shops along the main street are devoted to this local industry. The
main street, home to the banks, the post office and several of Edessa's

Weaving on a traditional loom

more reasonably priced hotels, is called Egnatia Street. Edessa, like Kavala and Thessaloniki, lies on the route of the old Rome-Constantinople road, in this case being a staging post on its journey to the Adriatic Sea. Few remnants of ancient Edessa remain although excavations at its original site 5km (3 miles) north of the town have uncovered a few relics such as a Byzantine church and a colonnade.

In the town itself, there are several examples of its more recent past — some crumbling but still grand eighteenth-century mansions, an old Byzantine bridge at the north of the town and, positioned behind the clock tower, a fifteenth-century mosque dating from the Turkish occupation of Edessa.

Due west out of Edessa, the Florina road heads directly into the heart of Greece's lake district, a lush and surprisingly uncommercialised region where English-speakers are rare and tourists few and far between. It has attractions in abundance, the first of which lies on the northern shores of Lake Vegoriti, 18km (11 miles) out of Edessa, at **Arnissa**. There are no actual 'sights' here; it is simply a pretty village in a lovely location, sprinkled with white apple blossom in spring. There is a beach from which you can swim in the lake's blue waters. The great peak of Mount Kaimaktsalan towers to the north, it straddles the Greece-Yugoslavia border and was the scene of some vicious battles during World War I.

For a similar village in a similar setting, make the 16km (10 mile) round-trip detour to **Agios Panteleimonas**, on the lake's eastern shore. It was here that a Russian archaeological team unearthed 376 prehistoric graves, the finds from which are displayed in a museum in Istanbul, Turkey. However, as with Arnissa, the appeal of this town is aesthetic and nothing more. Five kilometres (3 miles) before Florina itself is **Armenohorio**, an unremarkable town but one where important archaeological excavations have taken place; finds unearthed here date back four millennia to the early Bronze Age. The artefacts can be seen in the Florina archaeological museum.

Florina and the Lakes

Capital of its own prefecture, **Florina** is tucked away in a deep valley in the north-west corner of Greece and although it is not the most charming town in Greece, it certainly has a lovely setting and a friendly atmosphere. There has been human habitation here since the early Bronze Age although little evidence of the original Florina, on the nearby chestnut-covered hill of Agios Panteleimonas, remains — the Hotel Xenia now occupies the site. The artefacts discovered there, as well as others from digs across the district, can be seen in the archaeological museum, a 2 minute walk from the train station. Small but well-presented, the museum also features a large display of grave steles (engraved headstones) dating from the third century AD when the Romans occupied the region.

Apart from this museum, a small zoo and an evening fish, fruit and vegetable market, there is little reason to linger too long in Florina. Its smattering of hotels, though, makes it the ideal base from which to explore the Prespa Lakes, one of the most beautiful and isolated regions of mainland Greece and the perfect retreat for the tourist-shy traveller. The journey there is a delight in itself. The road twists its way alongside the valley past isolated farmhouses and, at certain points, touches the snowline.

After 22km (13 miles) Mount Pissoderi's ski slopes are reached, the ski centre there has a ski school and rental service. The road continues towards the Albanian and Yugoslavian frontiers before bearing right at Karies where the flat and calm waters of the Prespa Lakes become visible, a full 850m (2,790ft) above sea-level and forming the base for the bowl of mountains that surround them.

At over 5 million years old, these two lakes were around long before humans began to bicker about who actually owned them. However, bicker they did and today Mikra (Little) Prespa is mostly within Greek territory, with a small sliver belonging to Albania while Migallo (Big) Prespa is mainly Yugoslavian but with sizeable chunks being Greek and Albanian.

To their credit, the Greeks have resisted the strong temptation to develop this area and turn it into a major tourist attraction; instead, they have declared huge tracts of land here nature sanctuaries. The consequence of this is that the region, always wild and sparsely populated, is destined to remain so. The bears and wolves can still roam unmolested in the surrounding mountains; and the pelicans and cormorants — the latter being the largest known of the species in Europe — can live around the lakes. The lakes themselves are the freshwater fisherman's dream; full of eels, bass, trout and carp.

The best and least tiring way to explore the Prespa Lakes is by car but those without wheels have no reason to despair. Two buses daily (currently 6am and 2.15pm) leave Florina for the sleepy hamlet of Agios Germanos. This is only a couple of kilometres from the Yugoslavian frontier, and is known for its Byzantine church dedicated to the saint after whom the settlement is named.

Get off the bus at Lemos, a small village just before Agios Germanos, and strap on the hiking boots. A sizeable part of the area can be explored in this way, especially when considering that although few vehicles pass by, those that do tend to stop to give walkers a ride. Be sure not to miss the last bus back — around 3.30pm — as accommodation is very hard to find and, at 50km (30 miles) from Florina, its a long hitch back.

At the turn-off to Lemos, there is a road leading west, ominously signposted 'Albania'. Flat, straight and 5km (3 miles) long, this road bisects the two lakes. At its end are a small taverna, a larger restaurant and a wonderfully long and clean sandy beach, with a small campsite just behind, on the shores of Migallo Prespa. Western Macedonia does lack good bathing spots but this one helps to compensate. Incongruously, this is a small part of Greece that is forever England — just before the taverna is a monument dedicated to Flight Lieutenant L.B. Buchanan D.F.C. of the Royal Air Force, killed in action here during World War II.

Here the road separates again, into the high and the low. The high road runs over 6km (4 miles) of tremendous mountains to the wonderfully photogenic village of **Psarades**, located in a valley, on Migallo Prespa's shores. A fishing and farming community, its older inhabitants still speak Macedonian and, like that language, it has an almost forgotten aura. Local fishermen offer boat trips around the lake and there are two tavernas, both noted for their fish dishes.

The low road runs for 14km (9 miles) alongside Mikra Prespa via the villages of Pili and Vrondero. After 2km on this road, a dirt track leads to a small jetty where there is a possibility of hiring a boat to Agios Ahilis, a tiny islet in the middle of the lake where the remains of a thirteenth-century Byzantine church stand between its many caves and inlets. It is on Mikra Prespa that the majority of the area's waterbirds can be seen.

Kastoria

Another fine base from which to explore the Prespa Lakes is **Kastoria**, 68km (42 miles) south of Florina through a dramatic landscape of hills and mountains. Try not to be put off by the rather brash and modern appearance of this 15,000 strong town; it has a long and distinguished history that is easily noticeable, most obviously in the Byzantine churches around the town.

Built on a small delta of a peninsula protruding into the sadly polluted waters of Lake Kastoria (or Orestias), and overshadowed by the often snow-capped peak of Mount Vitsi to the north, Kastoria began life in ancient times as the town of *Keletron* and grew to prosperity during the Byzantine era as *Justinianopólis* after the sixth-century Emperor Justinian the Great. It endured 527 years of Ottoman occupation before being liberated in 1912 as Kastoria, a name derived from the Greek for beavers, who were once plentiful along the lake's shores.

The beavers' demise stems mostly from the contamination of Lake Kastoria but also from the fact that Kastoria has been the major centre of the Greek fur industry for centuries. Rather than trapping, the furriers concentrate on fur-trimming — piecing together furs to make garments that are both for the domestic market and export. It is a vital industry for Kastoria and is the town's major employer. Many of the shops sell local furs.

The remains of Kastoria's eighteenth-century prosperity can still be seen in the fine old Macedonian mansions of some of the leading fur traders — Nantzia, Tsiatsapas, Sapoundzis, Immanuel and Nerandzis — mostly in and around the town's old lakeside quarter, Kariadi. Nerandzis is now the home of Kastoria's folk museum

The historic town of Kastoria

which displays the mansion as it once was. By enquiring here you may be able to gain access to the others to see their high carved wooden ceilings and colourful wall-paintings.

Those who appreciate experiencing the solemn and mysterious aura of a Byzantine Greek Orthodox church will want to take a look at some of the many Kastoria has. There are over sixty in all and most are open to visitors but, as is usual in Greece, you have to find a caretaker who will hold the keys to several.

Of the churches, the ones most worth visiting are Taxiarches, which is the oldest, built during the tenth century, and has four-teenth-century frescoes; Agia Anagyri which boasts thirteenth-century frescoes and the tiny domed Panagia Koumblelidiki, damaged during World War II but now restored and with excellent sixteenth-century frescoes. All three are located around the Kariadi quarter — ask at one of the nearby cafés for the keys, otherwise try the folk museum or the police.

Anyone who has gained a taste for post-Byzantine icons while visiting the churches can also visit the Byzantine museum which houses a large collection of these religious paintings. Alternatively, it is possible to get away from buildings altogether, by taking a long walk around Lake Kastoria itself along a quiet and shady footpath.

To leave Kastoria, take the road signposted to its airport and then bear east at the suburb of Dispili. Twenty-three kilometres (14 miles) later, take a right turn to Klissoura along a rather poor road to Ptolemaida. It is a wise decision to by-pass this very heavily industrialised town with its huge thermo-electricity plants and chemical fertilizer factories and head due south to Kozani (see Chapter 6) before making the 61 km (38 mile) journey north-east to Veria. This is a lovely little journey, full of interest en-route. The road climbs steeply initially, with startling views to the right of Mount Olympus, the highest mountain in Greece, and other peaks linked to the Piera range such as Katafigio.

At the well-watered and very attractive village of **Zoodochos Pigi** ('Fountain of Life'), built at nearly 1,400m (4,600ft) above sea-level, the road begins to descend steadily and to run alongside the river Aliakimonas, which keeps the region lush, fertile and well-forested.

Not far from Zoodochos Pigi is **Kastania**, a pretty village built on the slopes of Mount Vermion. Its main attraction is its monastery of Panagia Soumela, open to visitors and built by refugees from Asia Minor following the disastrous Greek-Turkish war of 1921-22. It hosts a great festival on 15 August, the Assumption of the Virgin Mary and one of the holiest days in the Greek calendar. While you are there, take a look at the miraculous icon the refugees brought with them, they claim it was painted by St Luke himself.

Capital of the prefecture of Imathia, **Veria** is a large, 30,000-strong town with a heady atmosphere and a history that goes back a full 25 centuries. It is this history that lends Veria its appeal, despite the glossy rows of shops and offices that make up most of the town centre. Founded in the fifth century BC, it survived the Roman occupation to grow into one of the capitals of Macedonia by the third century AD during the reign of the Roman Emperor Diocletian. The Apostle Paul came here in the intervening years to spread the word of Christianity, following his success in Thessaloniki.

Veria flourished under the Byzantines and, during the Ottoman occupation, became a centre of the cotton-weaving industry. The Turks certainly left their mark on the city. For a flavour of this, be sure to visit the old bazaar quarter. Do not expect to see any 'sights' as such, it is just fun to wander the shady, narrow streets gazing up at the balconies and wooden frames of the nineteenth-century Turkish-style houses. Post-Byzantine churches are everywhere here, usually tucked away down side-alleys and more often than not in a sorry state of disrepair. Others, however, are still very much in use, such as Veria's two cathedrals, one old and one new. Unfortunately, most of the churches are locked — try enquiring at the nearest café for a caretaker with a key.

Veria has two museums, one a folk museum displaying the usual nick-nacks from bygone days — embroidery, tools, clothing etc; the other an archaeological museum, exhibiting mainly Roman artefacts.

The archaeological site of **Vergina** is best visited for a sense of what it was rather than for what can be seen. The few remains that can be seen tend to confuse rather than impress. Nevertheless, Vergina was the first Macedonian capital, the burial place of Phillip the Second and the site from which marvellous treasures (on display at Thessaloniki archaeological museum) were excavated. Those who wish to see the site will want to make the quick 13km (8 miles) journey from Veria. Buses from this town run regularly out to the site, there is also a frequent service from Thessaloniki, 75km (46 miles) away.

According to legend, *Aiges*, as Vergina was then known, was founded by Perdikkas, a king from Argos in the Peleponnese in about the seventh century BC. It definitely served as the capital of Macedonia until the fourth century BC when Pella took over the role. The reason that its importance is beyond doubt is due to the sheer wealth of the finds unearthed during the excavations in 1977. The finds were made in three large, royal tombs. The first tomb was sadly looted long ago, yet has a wall-painting depicting the Rape of Persephone who was carried off by Hades into the Underworld to be his wife. In the second tomb, the bones of Phillip the Second were discovered. Their discovery, along with the fabulous golden treasure-trove within, ranks as one of the most important finds in Greece since the great digs of the nineteenth century that unearthed Mycenae, Knossos and Corinth. Both of these tombs lie just outside the new village of Vergina. The third is a little further away, along the same road, and contains a carved marble throne — it is known as the 'Tomb of Vergina'. Here, a signpost points directions to what remains of the Palace of Palatisa. Dating from 300BC, a lovely floor mosaic remains in situ.

Those who have had their appetite for Macedonian tombs whetted will be pleased to hear that another can be seen, at **Lefkadia**, 25km (15 miles) north of Veria on the Edessa road. Known as the Great Tomb, this is the largest temple tomb discovered to date in Macedonia and is believed to have been constructed 23 centuries ago. The marvellous fresco of a soldier being led to the Underworld by Hades, and other frescoes depicting battles, have led archaeologists to con-

Rowing on Lake Kastoria

clude that the tomb was the resting place of a great general. Three other tombs are nearby but these are unfortunately closed to the public.

By backtracking for 4km ($2^1/_2$ miles) on the Veria road, and then turning right, one can visit **Naoussa**, built on the slopes of Mount

Vermion and one of the lushest towns of the region thanks to the profusion of tiny streams. It is a town famed for its apples and peaches but most of all for its fine red wine, reputed to be the best in Greece. It also hosts a boisterous carnival during the week before Lent. Twenty-six kilometres (16 miles) of steady climbing south of the town leads to **Seli** where a ski centre and two mountain refuge huts are located.

Back on the main Veria-Edessa road, head north and bear right at a junction in the dry and unenticing town of Skidra, 15km (9 miles) from Edessa. From here the route leads directly back, via Pella, to Thessaloniki. From Thessaloniki, heading south along the E5, several beaches can be visited — Nea Agathoupoli, Methoni and Alikes — the latter near to the remains of ancient **Pydna**, where the final decisive battle was fought between the Romans and Macedonians for control of the region in 168BC. The remains of an ancient fortress, possibly dating from this battle, can be seen.

Further Information
— Western Macedonia —

Florina
Archaeological Museum
Near the railway station
☎ 0385 28206
Open: 8.45am-3pm.
Closed Mondays.

Kastoria
Folklore Museum
Open: 9am-12.30pm daily.

Byzantine Museum
Church of Agios Spirodon
☎ 0467 26649
Open: 8.30am-3pm Monday to Friday

Tourist Information
Town hall
☎ 0467 22312

Kilkis
Archaeological Museum
☎ 0341 22477

Pella
Site and Museum
☎ 0382 31160/31278
Open: 8.45am-3pm daily, 9.30am-2.30pm Sunday.
Closed Mondays.

Thessaloniki
Archaeological Museum
Opposite the YMCA on the extension of Desperai
☎ 830 538 or 831 037
Open: 8am-7pm daily, 8am-6pm Sunday.
Closed Tuesdays.

Ataturk Museum
Apostolou Pavlou St (next to Turkish Consulate)
Admission only on production of passport.
Open: 9am-1pm, 4-6pm Monday to Friday.

Church of Agios Dimitrios
Aghiou Dimitriou St, above
Dikastirion Square
☎ 031 27008
Open: 8am-12 noon daily, 4-7pm in
season.

*Ethonological
and Popular Art Museum*
68 Vas. Olgas St
☎ 830 591 or 844 848
Open: 9.30am-2pm Monday to
Friday. Closed Thursdays.

Museum of the Macedonian Struggle
23 Prox. Koromila
Agios Sofias
☎ 229 778

Tourist Office
8 Aristotelous Square
☎ 031 222935/271888
Open: 8am-8pm Monday to Friday,
8am-2pm Saturday.

Tourist Office
Thessaloniki Airport
☎ 031 425011 (extension 215)

White Tower Museum
White Tower
☎ 267 832
Open: 8.30am-7pm Monday to
Saturday, 10am-3pm Sunday.
Closed Tuesdays.

Vergina
Archaeological Site
☎ 031 830538
Open: 8.45am-3pm daily, 9.30am-
2.30pm Sunday.
Closed Mondays.

Veria
Folklore Museum
Open: 9am-2pm, 5-8pm daily.

Archaeological Museum
☎ 0331 24972
Open: 9am-3pm daily, 10am-4pm
Sunday.
Closed Mondays.

Tourist Information
Periptero Elias
☎ 0331 26383

8 • Eastern Macedonia and Thrace

Introduction

T ucked away high in the top right-hand corner of Greece and
bordered by Bulgaria to the north, Turkey to the east and the
North-East Aegean Sea to the south, lie eastern Macedonia and
Thrace. It is not only the Nestos river that divides these two regions;
they also differ considerably in the number of visitors they draw.
Eastern Macedonia has the more obvious attractions; the sandy
beaches of Kassandra and Sithonia (both prongs on the Halkidiki
peninsula and now pushed firmly onto the beaten track); the island
of Thassos, covered in pine trees and also with fine beaches; the
astonishing cave at Petralona and the ruins of ancient Phillipi. Thrace
is quite simply the least visited region in Greece. The vast majority of
its visitors are in transit, rushing through on the train or bus to
Istanbul or back again. Yet Thrace has a lot of appeal, particularly in
some wonderful towns made all the more intriguing by the curious
Greek-Turkish mixture of their populations.

Taken together, there is more than enough in these two regions to
keep the inquisitive traveller and the dedicated sun-seeker busy and
happy. For most visitors, the first port of call will be the Halkidiki
peninsula which is a rounded chunk of land with three prongs
pointing down into the Aegean. This area of contrast is the homeland
of Aristotle; one can enter the spectacular Petralona Cave where a
skull over 700,000 years old was discovered; explore the tiny villages
of its beautifully lush and hilly interior; or soak up the sun and revel
in the night-life at the beach resorts of Kassandra and Sithonia.

If you are male and over 18 it is possible to visit the third prong of
the peninsula, Mount Athos, a devout and austere monastic community made up of 1,600 monks living in and around twenty Byzantine
monasteries. It is an area from which women have been barred since
the eleventh century and for which non-Greek males need a permit

A horse with a primitive saddle, Mount Athos

to enter. Obtaining the permit is not difficult and to walk its dirt tracks, staying overnight in the monasteries and eating with the monks, is one of the most fascinating experiences to be had, not only in Greece, but in Europe as a whole.

East of Halkidiki is the bright and busy port of Kavala from where ferries leave for the 90 minute journey to the greenest island of Greece, Thassos. Near Kavala are the extensive ruins of the once-great city of Phillipi, famous for the letter written to its inhabitants by the Apostle Paul. Thirty-two kilometres (19 miles) east of Kavala, you cross the Nestos into Thrace. The first Thracian town reached is Xanthi, a bustling mixture of Greeks and Turks in a lovely setting and with a fine old quarter. Komotini, reached via Lake Vistonia, also seems as much Turkish as it is Greek.

From Komotini the road cuts south to the coast and several pleas-ant beaches before reaching Alexandropoulis. The last major Greek town before Turkey, this is a busy and noisy place but the only point of departure to Samothraki; a small, rocky and isolated island with a lot of charm and a fine archaeological site, the Sanctuary to the Great Gods. Just beyond Alexandropoulis is the river Evros, mark-ing the border between Europe and Asia.

This is an easy region to reach, particularly if one is coming from northern Europe. Thessaloniki airport is international and handles flights from all major European cities, as well as several connections a day to Athens and less regular links to a number of islands. Kavala and Alexandropoulis also have airports, with less frequent flights to Athens. Travelling by rail presents few problems and Thessaloniki lies on the main E92 road which runs through Yugoslavia to Athens.

If arriving by sea from Chios, Lesvos or Limnos, you will dock at either Thessaloniki or Kavala. Travelling to the region from Turkey is equally simple as Istanbul and Thessaloniki are connected by road and rail, the latter passing through Alexandropoulis, Komotini, Xanthi, Drama and Seres. Parts of the journey are lovely, especially between Xanthi and Drama as the line skirts the edge of the Rodopi mountains.

It is cheaper (but slower) to travel by train in eastern Macedonia and Thrace although the public bus services between the major cities are far more frequent. Bus services to the outlying areas, however, are often down to one or two a day. Cars can be hired in Thessaloniki, Kavala and Alexandropoulis, as well as in some of the Kassandrian and Sithonian resorts. The best time to visit this area is between late spring and early autumn; the winters are very long and wet.

Human habitation of this region can be traced back a staggering 700,000 years; the age of the skull discovered at Petralona. One has to jump 696,000 years for further evidence of settlement in the region, to the clay pots unearthed in the area around Drama. However, it was not until the seventh century BC that the cities of Macedonia and Thrace began to be formed — at Avdira, Maronia, etc. None achieved the military might and influence of the city-states of the south although Democritus, the father of democracy, was born at Avdira, south of Xanthi.

Operating from Pella in the west, the Macedonians of Phillip the Second swiftly gained control of the region around 355BC and the Thracians became loyal members of the Macedonian army. Macedonia and Thrace were vital territories to the Romans — the Via Egnatia, the road that connected Constantinople (Istanbul) to Rome, passed through — and Phillipi became a major centre and the first foothold for Christianity in Europe, due to Paul's preachings here.

Under the Byzantines both Macedonia and Thrace had to defend themselves continually against attacks from Bulgars, Serbs and Goths. A stability of sorts was only achieved when the Turks took control after the fall of Constantinople in 1453. Many Turks settled in the region and their descendants still live here today as Thrace was the only region (with Istanbul) not included in the heart-rending population exchange that followed the Turkish defeat of the Greeks in the 1920-22 war.

Although on the surface both communities appear to peacefully co-exist, there is an underlying tension; many Turks (or, more properly, Greek Moslems) complain of discrimination. The Greeks also feel they have a demographic problem in that the Turkish population is growing faster than the Greek and may one day form the majority in the region, thus opening up inevitable questions concerning sovereignty. Because of the ever-present tension between Greece and Turkey, the military presence, particularly in Thrace, is very tangible.

Eastern Macedonia and Thrace are primarily agricultural areas — tobacco and wheat being the main crops — and the area's fertile and flat plains are highly productive. Yet it is also a region of mountains – tall and imposing and covered with a huge variety of trees, the pine being the most common. The mountains stretch mainly along the northern border and in the past provided a huge strategic barrier against the Bulgarians who once coveted Macedonia and Thrace and who only gave up their claims on the area in the twentieth century. Fine walks can be had among the mountains, particularly around the towns of Drama and Xanthi.

Lakes are here in abundance — Koronia (Vassilios) and Volvis together forming the 'eyes of Halkidiki'; Kerkini north of Seres and Vistonia near the village of Porto Lagos in Thrace. During spring and autumn Vistonia is a resting-place for thousands of migratory birds such as storks and herons, as are the Evros Wetlands, at the southeast of the region on the border with Turkey. These are internationally famous wetlands, renowned for their fantastic variety of birds and small mammals but intensive fish-farming and over-hunting is rapidly driving away many of the species. Some, such as the otter, have already disappeared.

At the village of Monoklissia (Macedonia) and Petra (Thrace) an unusual role-reversal festival takes place on 8 January — Midwife's Day. On this day, the men take over the traditional role of Greek village women (staying inside and looking after the house) while the women take over the traditional role of Greek village men (sitting in the cafés chatting to their friends).

The women elect their own government for the day and two edicts are pronounced; one, that no woman may return home until dawn, two, that any man seen in the streets will be stripped and thrown in cold water. In the evening the women hold a feast with bawdy songs and dancing and the festivities end with the village midwife being dragged through the streets on a carriage. It is a lively and boisterous event and fun to watch — if you are a woman!

Eastern Macedonia

Halkidiki

Situated twenty-two kilometres (13 miles) north-east of Thessaloniki, the large village of **Langadas** is unremarkable and, for most of the year, certainly worth by-passing. However, those who happen to be in the area around 21 May should waste no time in making a bee-line directly there. For 21 May is the festival day of Constantine and Helen and, in celebration, villagers dance barefoot over a bed of burning, red-hot coals. Inexplicably, they emerge from the ritual unscathed.

Although the origins of the ritual are hazy, some have suggested that it is in memory of a fire in a church in the village of Kosti in Thrace around 1250. Desperate to salvage the church's icons, villagers entered the inferno and, clutching the holy works of art, came out unmarked. Although the leaders of the Greek Orthodox Church remain stolidly unimpressed, viewing it as some form of satanic ritual, the rest of Greece is fascinated. The villagers of Langadas repeat the festival over the two following nights and charge an admission fee. If attending, be sure to arrive by at least 6pm — seats fill up very rapidly.

For most people, a visit to the region will probably begin with a journey south to Halkidiki, that three-pronged clump of land shaped like a giant turtle escaping from the mainland. This is one of the many regions of Greece that has just about everything; gorgeous scenery; ancient remains; beautiful caves; long and sandy beaches; quaint villages and, on the eastern prong of the peninsula, Mount Athos, solely the preserve of monks and visitable only by male permit-holders.

Not surprisingly, travel agents and developers have transformed great chunks of the region into premier tourist resorts, most notably the coastal areas around the western and central prongs of Kassandra and Sithonia. Nevertheless, parts of the region remain happily off the beaten track and even some that are slightly better-known are well worth viewing. For a good example of the latter, visit the **Petralona Cave**.

It is 67km (41 miles) from Thessaloniki to Petralona, taking the Nea Moudania road and bearing left at Eleochoria. The site lies just beyond the modern village of the same name. Buses link Eleochoria with Petralona in season; during the winter months one must either hitch-hike or make the 7km (4 mile) walk. Its attraction is that this is the oldest inhabited place known to man — controlled fires were lit

here by prehistoric man a staggering
700,000 years ago. As a subterranean
beautyspot, it is one of the finest in
Greece. The stalactite and stalagmite
formations are awesome.

Discovered accidentally by villagers
from Petralona in only 1959, the cave can
only be viewed by guided tour. Entering its dank and clammy
interior through a narrow passageway, it seems unimpressive at first
until it opens out into Aristotle's Hall, a great mass of rock formations that set the imagination whirring as one tries to pick out
distinctive shapes from the sheer curtains of rock. The rest of the tour
continues in this vein, moving into the Great Hall and on to a spot
where, in 1960, the best-preserved skull of primitive man ever found

was discovered. It is, in fact, the skull of a woman, and is believed to date back 700,000 years.

To view the skull, though, one must travel to the University of Thessaloniki where it is housed in the palaeontological collection. Bones of creatures long extinct to the region have also been found here — lions, bears, hyenas, rhinoceroses — and are exhibited in the small museum on the site, together with a display of Stone Age tools. The museum is only open in season (from May to September).

From Petralona, one must head south to Nea Moudania, the gateway to Kassandra, to make any further progress into Halkidiki. The road passes the small village of Zographou, named after the monastery on Mount Athos, and with a stone Byzantine tower that dates back to the fourteenth century.

Nea Moudania itself doubles as the major commercial port of Halkidiki and, as a glossy coastal resort, offers a taste of things to come in Kassandra. In season, Nea Moudania is connected by hydrofoil to Skiathos, Skopelos and Alonissos, three islands of the Sporades chain. As for Kassandra, this is the most popular spot in northern Greece in terms of tourism and, as such, is not covered here.

For those with an interest in history, a 6km (4 mile) excursion south to what remains of **Potadia** will prove rewarding. First colonised by the city-state of Corinth in the seventh century BC, Potadia fell to the Athenians in 429BC after a lengthy battle in which the great philosopher Socrates fought. Viewed as a vital strategic point, due to its position at the mouth of the Thermaic Gulf, successive conquerors — the Macedonians, Romans, Huns, Byzantines, and Venetians — continued the fortification of the town until it was finally laid to waste in 1430 by the Ottomans.

The few ruins seen are of the castle walls and date back to the year AD600. To reach Potadia, one has to cross a bridge that spans a manmade canal cut across the neck of the peninsula, believed to have been dug in the first century AD. The modern town nearby is called Nea (new) Potadia and is, inevitably, a coastal resort.

Back at Nea Moudania, a road heads east, passing the turn-off for the small town of Agia Mamas; host to a bustling open-air farming machinery market between 1 and 3 September every year. After 5km (3 miles) you reach the left fork for **Olynthos**, another new town with ancient remains nearby. Between its destruction by the Persians in 480BC and its final razing by the Macedonians of Phillip II in 348BC, this was the foremost city in Halkidiki.

The ruins excavated include the ancient *agora* (market place), the civic centre and several houses, neatly arranged into blocks of ten.

The site here has no museum and the finds are divided between the museums of Thessaloniki and Polygiros. Also excavated here was an eleventh-century Byzantine church, Agios Nikolaos, whose impressive remains stand at the eastern end of the site.

Back at the turn-off for Olynthos, the road continues east for another 9km (5 miles) before dividing; straight on leads south for the central prong of Sithonia; due north takes you 13km (8 miles) to Polygiros — capital of Halkidiki. Although Sithonia is firmly off the beaten track compared with Kassandra, it still attracts many sun-seekers, particularly at the large resort of Porto Carras, a popular haunt for the very rich and famous and priced accordingly. Nevertheless, some relatively secluded spots can be found — try **Metamorfossis**, 24km (15 miles) from the turn-off to Polygiros, or the small beaches that dot the southern tip of the peninsula between Sarti and Koufos.

Polygiros is built around the base of Mount Holomon in a lush and green, olive-growing region. A friendly and rarely-visited town, 4,000 strong, its hub lies along the main street where one can find the bus station, the banks and post office. Accommodation is notoriously difficult to find here and what is available is terribly over-priced — it is therefore better to view Polygiros as a stopping-off point en-route elsewhere.

Find time to visit the archaeological museum, near the bus station, which houses Halkidikian finds that include the beautifully decorated sarcophagus from *Acanthos* (now Ierissos) completed 25 centuries ago, and the male and female statues of Stratoni dating back to the first century AD.

A proud boast of Polygiros is that it was the first town in Halkidiki to rise against the Turks at the outbreak of the War of Liberation. The price paid for this was the destruction of the town. Following its rebuilding, it soon grew in status as an important commercial centre and became capital of the region in 1869.

From Polygiros take the northern road for 11km (7 miles), bear right at Paleokastro and begin a spectacular 30km (18 miles) journey through the green hills and valleys of Halkidiki. The road ends at **Arnea**, a small town and a regional centre for northern Halkidiki. Little is known of its early history but it is certainly one of the most attractive towns of the region. The traditional, balconied Macedonian houses; dominating clocktower; eighteenth-century manor house that still stands solidly; and the shops selling woollens hand-woven by the town's womenfolk all make for an hour or so's happy wandering. The town has good bus connections standing on the

*The clock tower in
Arnea, Halkidiki*

Thessaloniki-Ouranopolis route.

Fifteen kilometres (8 miles) east of Arnea is **Stagira**, built along both sides of the main road and famous as the birthplace of one of the greats of ancient Greece, Aristotle. The philosopher's statue is beautifully located on a grassy hill just before the town. There are compelling views out to sea and it makes an ideal site for a picnic.

The ruined wall near the statue is all that remains of the fortress of Madem Aga, a representative of the Ottoman Sultan who oversaw the silver mining for which the area was once famous. Madem Aga was killed in 1821 and his fortress destroyed as the people of Stagira rose in rebellion with the rest of Greece.

From Stagira the road continues on to Stratoni where one can bear south and hug the eastern coastline of Halkidiki until **Ierissos** is reached. This is an important regional fishing and boat-building centre and is blessed with great stretches of sand to swim off. It is another small town with a long history, although its current site lies to the south-east of the original, following an earthquake of 1932 that shattered the old town.

Little remains of the old Hellenic city, known then as *Akanthos* (meaning thorn), but excavations in and around the cemetery there have proved successful — the finds are housed in the archaeological museum in Polygiros. Most of the ruins still standing at old *Akanthos* today date from the Byzantine era.

Still going south in the direction of Mount Athos, the growing beach resort of **Nea Roda** is passed, standing at the narrowest neck of the peninsula and on the site where the Persian king Xerxes attempted to cut a canal in 480BC to assist his invasion of Hellas.

Further on is **Tripiti**, a small anchorage with a few houses from where boats leave regularly to Amouliani, a tiny islet just offshore whose inhabitants support themselves through the fishing industry. Most visitors to **Amouliani** are day-trippers, there to enjoy its beautiful crescent-moon of a beach. However, there is a campsite, a taverna and several rooms to let for those planning to enjoy its peace a little longer.

A seemingly never-ending stretch of sand leads down to **Ouranopolis**, a relaxed and unimposing coastal resort with two sandy and inviting beaches. What immediately catches the eye, though, is the fourteenth-century Tower of Prosphorion that stands on the shore just beside the jetty and was originally built as a look-out post for the Mount Athos monastery of Vatopediou. It was inhabited in 1928 by the Lochs, a Scottish-Australian husband and wife missionary team who did sterling work in assisting the inhabitants of Ouranopolis, which was only established in 1922 by bewildered and poverty-stricken refugees from Asia Minor.

A 30 minute walk south of town through the farms of local residents eventually leads you to an imposing, barbed-wire topped, concrete wall. This is the wall by which the monastic communities of Mount Athos cut themselves off from the rest of Greece, and to get behind that wall is a fascinating experience.

Mount Athos

It is ironic that while two of Halkidiki's prongs harbour some of the most hedonistic spots in Greece, the third should be a devout, serene and restricted strip of land dedicated solely to the worship of God. This is the Holy Mountain of Athos, the 'Agion Oros', home to over 1,600 monks living in and around twenty Byzantine monasteries and maintaining the austere, intensely spiritual way of life that has been led here for centuries.

Sealed off from the rest of Greece by a barbed-wire topped, concrete wall that stretches across the neck of the peninsula, Mount Athos has no commerce, no asphalt roads and hardly any electricity. There is one small town, Karies, the monasteries are only accessible

An unusually tiled dome, Mount Athos

by dirt track and the mule is the most common form of transport. Even ancient timing is used — when the sun sets, it is midnight.

Mount Athos belongs to ages past, stuck firmly in a medieval time warp of its own making yet in a way that suits the other-worldly life-style of its inhabitants. These monks jealously guard the autonomy and isolation granted to them in 1063 by an edict of the Byzantine Emperor Constantine. It is this ruling, bolstered by a decree of the Greek government in 1926, that is in force today, guaranteeing the status of Mount Athos as the great bastion of the Greek Orthodox Church.

There have been settlements on the peninsula since 300BC yet the history of Mount Athos up to around AD800 is very hazy; in the intervening years the region was constantly ravaged by pirates and raiders who destroyed all written records. What is known is that the first monks began to seek sanctuary here in the seventh century, usually alone in solitary hermitages. From these early pioneers the community grew, aided by the arrival of such great theologians and builders as Paul the Xeropotamite and Athanassios the Athenian. Their presence served to attract others and the ecclesiastical prestige of Mount Athos grew until, in AD885, Emperor Basil I declared it an area solely for monks.

Seventy-five years later, Megista Lavra, the first monastery, was completed and others rapidly followed until the number of monasteries reached 40 and the monastic population an estimated 20,000. In line with its new status, the region was declared autonomous by Constantine in 1063.

Little has changed on Mount Athos since this edict, despite the major political upheavals of the last millennium — the collapse of the Byzantine Empire, the Crusader conquests, the Turkish occupation and the Greek War of Liberation. However, in 1926 the Greek government felt it necessary to update Constantine's ruling. That year Mount Athos was declared a Theocratic republic, setting the parameters for where government authority ends and monastic independence begins.

The system of self-government on the Holy Mountain is quite straightforward. All the relevant decisions are made by the Holy Community, a committee made up of a representative from each of the monasteries on Mount Athos.

The Mount Athos terrain is unquestionably the wildest and most unspoilt in Greece. Fir, pine and chestnut trees grow unchecked, sprawling over the hills and mountains like a giant green blanket. However, a serious forest fire in August 1990 caused extensive damage. About 3,000 acres of forest were burned, including 625 acres of wild chestnuts. In the south looms the peak of Mount Athos itself, over 2,000m (6,500ft) high and snow-capped throughout the year.

A visit to Mount Athos could easily be one of the most enduring experiences of a visit to Greece. Unfortunately, it is an experience to be savoured by males alone. Women have been barred from entering the Holy Mountain since Constantine's edict and before. The reasons for this are obscure. Some simply say that the presence of women would serve to distract the monks from their spiritual pursuits; others cite a legend relating how the Virgin Mary, shipwrecked on the peninsula and struck by its beauty, declared it to be her own Holy Garden upon which no other woman could step. Even female domesticated animals are barred and the closest that women can get to Mount Athos is to view the monasteries at a distance, from the decks of the pleasure boats that leave from Thessaloniki and from Limenarias on the island of Thassos.

As for males, those who hold a Greek citizen's identity card can enter freely whenever they choose. Those who do not must go through the time-consuming but ultimately worthwhile process of obtaining a visitors' permit from the Ministry of Northern Greece in Thessaloniki (see the Further Information section for details).

Iviron monastery, which dates from AD980

Strictly speaking, only those with a proven scientific or religious interest can be granted permits — students of Byzantine history, art or architecture; clergymen; journalists or those who are ambiguously classified as 'men of letters'. However, in practice the rules are a good deal more relaxed, particularly if applicants use the 'men of letters' clause. Either way, all applicants will require a letter of recommendation from their embassy or consulate in Greece, which are obtainable on the spot for a fee. Both Great Britain and the USA have consulates in Thessaloniki (see Further Information section).

Only ten foreign visitors are allowed in Mount Athos on any one given day and places fill up quickly in summer. Those visiting Greece during this period should write well in advance to the Ministry of Northern Greece, reserving their date of entry to the Holy Mountain. Those with long hair may well consider having a haircut or tying their hair up, as the monks disapprove of 'long-hairs'.

Vatopediou monastery and a characteristically unspoilt stretch of coastline

Entry to Mount Athos can only be made from the sea, thus making Ouranopolis or Ierissos, both pleasant beach resorts just north of the neck of the peninsula, the starting points for any visit. Boats leave daily from these towns to Mount Athos; from Ouranopolis to the port of Dafni on the west coast; from Ierissos to Iviron monastery on the east. Of the two, it is better to catch the Ouranopolis boat which has a fixed departure time of 9.30am, the schedules from Ierissos tend to be erratic. From both points the journey is roughly 2 hours.

Visitors arriving at Dafni will find a bus (looking as if it also dates from the Byzantine era!) to transport them to **Karies**, the capital of Mount Athos and no larger than a village. Here, yet another permit must be obtained. At the time of writing, this costs £9 ($15) and grants the guest permission to eat and sleep at any of the monasteries for up to 4 nights, free of charge. Those wishing to stay a little longer should apply for a permit extension at this stage. They are usually granted.

The permit takes about 1 hour to issue so, while waiting, take a look at the Protato, the cathedral of Karies, an imposing structure with fourteenth-century frescoes and sixteenth-century icons. Just up from the cathedral is a tiny street with a café and two shops selling soft drinks, postcards, cigarettes and guide books. Guests will have their passports given back (these will have been taken from them on the boat) when they receive the accommodation permit.

The monasteries themselves can be reached only by foot or, if sited along the coastline, by a rather sporadic motor boat service. They are all signposted clearly but in Greek so a little knowledge of the Greek alphabet can come in more than useful. Numerous dirt paths offer tempting short cuts but to take them is to risk getting hopelessly lost, something which is not recommended.

When arriving at a monastery, ask first for the *archtonari*, a monk whose task it is to welcome visitors and to display the hospitality for which the monasteries are renowned. Guests are always offered a cup of coffee or a glass of brandy on arrival and a slice of *lougoumi*, a small, Turkish delight-type sweet. Warm and comfortable sleeping arrangements will be made.

As for eating, this will depend on which type of monastery you are staying at, *cenobitic* or *idiorhythmatic*. *Cenobitic* monasteries practise the concept of communal living; worshipping together and eating together at set times. *Idiorhythmatic* monasteries allow their monks to live more of an individual lifestyle, choosing their own times for prayer, study and eating. Therefore, guests at the *idiorhythmatic* monasteries will eat together, not with the monks, and normally enjoy a large and satisfying meal with wine.

At *cenobitic* monasteries guests and monks eat together; their table, however, can be rather spartan, particularly during fasting periods, so visitors may care to bring some of their own food to supplement their diet. No meat is ever served, as it is said to increase carnal desires. If possible, the *archtonari* will find an English speaking monk for guests to talk with. Be sure to arrive in good time at the monastery you intend to sleep at, allowing enough time to get to another if all the beds are taken. All monasteries lock their gates firmly at sunset.

The evening meal at the monasteries is normally taken around 6pm with 'lights-out' being an hour later; the lights will be hand-carried oil lamps. At 3am all will be awakened by the curiously compelling beat of wooden hammers on wooden blocks, calling the monks to the first service of the day in the same way that Noah gathered his animals to the Ark. The service will last until 7am. Attendance is not compulsory for guests but it is an enchanting experience with the incense swirling and the strange but melodic chanting of the monks.

Of the twenty Byzantine monasteries on Mount Athos, seventeen are Greek, the remainder being Russian (St Panteleimona), Bulgarian (Zographou) and Serbian (Helandrariou). Founded in 1169 and only one hour's walk from Karies, St Panteleimona is particularly worth a visit. Its huge belfry contains the world's second largest bell, 3m

The imposing Dohiariou monastery

(10ft) wide and weighing 13,000kg. Its Catholicon (main chapel) is a festival of gold.

As for the Greek monasteries, Iviron and Megisti Lavra are the best-known. An *idiorhythmatic* monastery, Iviron was founded in AD980 and takes its name from the monks from the Iberian peninsula who settled here. It has a glorious display of frescoes in a chapel that contains such holy treasures as a large, lemon tree-shaped, solid silver candlestick.

Megisti Lavra was the first monastery founded on the peninsula, and consequently it is the most influential. It is famed for its library which boasts over 2,000 volumes, some of which date back to the monastery's inception. Its frescoes were painted 500 years later and are the work of the Cretan Theophanes, the master-painter whose frescoes also adorn many of the chapels of the Meteora monasteries.

St Panteleimona, Megisti Lavra and Iviron attract more visitors than most, so, if possible, try to put some of the smaller, lesser known monasteries on the itinerary. The tenth-century Stavronikita is built fortress-like on a rock gazing out to sea; its frescoes, including a colourful portrayal of Christ's entry to Jerusalem, are also the work of Theophanes. It stands 1 hour's walk east from Karies. The Bulgarian Zographou, built and rebuilt over the years due to fire and the destruction wreaked by invaders, notably the Catalans, has services still conducted in the Slavic tongue. Agios Paulou is one of the strictest, most austere *cenobitic* monasteries on the Holy Mountain. It also boasts the largest monastic population and is still growing.

For more detailed information on the monasteries of Mount Athos, try *Mount Athos*; part of the 'Greek Places' series and available in Ouranopolis.

Good hikers may also want to ascend Mount Athos itself. The 5 hour climb begins at the small community of Agia Anna (the nearest monastery is Agios Paulou). Climbers can stay overnight, admittedly under spartan conditions, at the church of the Panagia, 1 hour below the summit, before rising early the following morning to make the final push to the peak and view the sunrise over the entire peninsula.

Those hiking around the peninsula will come across many small, battered and windswept stone houses and huts. These are *seats*, houses granted by a monastery to a single monk for the remainder of his life. The monk supports himself by selling his own handicrafts. A cluster of such houses will be a *skite*, a type of mini-monastery with its own chapel and representation within the wider monastic community. Hermits live in the wildest and most inaccessible areas; praying continually, often fasting for days on end and practising fully the monks' dictum that they 'die in life to live in death'.

How many and which monasteries the visitor to Mount Athos visits is of course dependent on the amount of time that he has available. To stay as long as possible will obviously provide the more complete experience. Yet even those staying one night only can, with good hiking and an early start, visit Koutloumousious (15 minutes from Karies), Iviron and Stavronikita. They can stay the night at either of the latter two before hiking back through Karies in the morning to St Panteleimona. From there it is a 2 hour walk back to Dafni in time for the day's only boat to Ouranopolis at 12noon.

Kavala

Kavala has always been one of the most important towns of eastern Macedonia, dating back to the Roman occupation when it was named *Neapolis* and served as a vital port on the Via Egnatia, the road that provided the link between Rome and Constantinople. Its most famous visitor, St Paul, landed here in AD49 en-route to spread Christianity in Phillipi nearby. In later years the various occupiers of Greece recognised Kavala's vital strategic location and the town remained unmolested; the Turks in particular held it in high regard.

Today it is a large, bustling town, a major centre of the tobacco industry and home to nearly 50,000. Although nothing remains of ancient Neapolis, there are plenty of remnants of Kavala's Turkish past in and around the steep and cobbled alleyways of the old town, built on a small peninsula just east of the port.

Built underneath the well-preserved ruins of a thirteenth-century Byzantine fortress, the old town is a rabbits' warren of shaded, narrow and atmospheric streets flanked either side by nineteenth-century Turkish houses. The latter are balconied and have front doors that open out onto the street. Some of the streets lead directly down to the sea. Be prepared to ask directions to the sights; these include the fortress with commanding views out to sea, the Kamares Aqueduct, built in the sixteenth century to bring water down from nearby Mount Simvolo to the town; and the house where, in 1769, Mehmet Ali was born.

Mehmet Ali was made King of Egypt by the Ottomans and his line lasted until Nasser's 1952 revolution. At one time it was possible to look around this fine example of a Turkish mansion; now it is closed and its dilapidated condition and overgrown gardens give the impression of a haunted house. Next to the house is a dramatic but graffiti-festooned bronze statue of Mehmet Ali astride his horse, curved sword in hand. To the right of this is the Imaret, once a mosque and school for Moslem theologians. Another impressive building, admission is again impossible; it is now a tobacco warehouse.

The busy streets and brightly-lit shops of the new town seem rather uninspiring after the old but there are a couple of places of interest. The archaeological museum contains some of the finds from the excavations at Phillipi, and the folk art museum nearby hosts a display of traditional Macedonian costumes and some of the works of the Thassos-born sculptor, Polygnotos Vigas. There is a tourist office in the main square.

The town beach is strewn with breezeblocks and patrolled by hungry-looking stray dogs. However, good swimming is to be had west of Kavala where a string of small resorts have been established, patronised mostly by Greeks. Kalamitsa, Batis, Nea Iraklitsa and Nea Paramos are served by hourly buses from Kavala station in season.

Seventeen kilometres (11 miles) out of Kavala, on the Drama road, are the ruins of ancient **Phillipi**. The city was founded by Phillip the Second of Macedonia, father of Alexander the Great, as a base from which to protect the region's gold mines from the attacks of fierce Thracians.

The city gained fame on two counts. The first of these is that it is on the site of a major battle of the Roman civil war in 42BC, between the followers of Brutus and Cassius (murderers of Julius Caesar), and Antony and Octavian, the eventual victors. Secondly, the city is where St Paul began to spread Christianity in Europe and where he was imprisoned accordingly.

The remains of Phillipi are substantial and it is easy to build a vivid picture of how the city once was. There is a sixth-century basilica; part of the Roman forum; what is reputed to be the prison of St Paul and his companion, Silas; the theatre (where performances are still given every July and August) and the public toilets. The road — the old Via Egnatia — splits the town in two. There is a small museum on site.

On the same road as Phillipi, only 2km (1 mile) out of Kavala, is the small and modern monastery of Agios Silas, named in honour of St Paul's companion and built on the site where both supposedly rested en-route to Phillipi. Just ring the bell outside and one of the monks will be happy to show off the bright chapel; the lovely view over Kavala; the spot where Silas and Paul slept; and a menagerie of pheasants, peacocks and pigeons, kept in the courtyard. The monastery is only open at certain times (see the Further Information section) and skirts and shawls are provided for those incorrectly dressed.

Another monastery that can be visited is Eikosifinissas, 44km (26 miles) west of Kavala via the town of Eleftheropoulis at the head of one of the gorges of Mount Pangeo, with a summit nearly 2,000m (6,500ft) above sea-level. A popular spot for climbers, it has two mountain refuge huts, one of which serves as a ski centre.

Thassos

For years Thassos was one of the untouched islands, a green and mountainous sanctuary in the Aegean Sea, yet still just 1 hour by ferry from Kavala. Then an enterprising travel agent arrived and, before long, gift shops and car-hire firms began to spring up in the two main towns, together with truckloads of cement which were soon converted into some surprisingly pretty hotels. However, visitors seeking to escape the throng should not be discouraged; Thassos has just the right amount of tourist-awareness to make a stay there a comfortable one but has lost none of its intrinsic identity. Indeed, most of the island is as Greek as the olive-oil that is its main produce.

Thassos is an island of trees. Pines and olives alone account for more than 60 per cent of its land mass and walnut, cherry and apple trees also thrive. Deeply green hills swoop down to the dark blue Aegean, providing a striking colour contrast that becomes even more pronounced in May when the wild flowers bloom. The forests are home to wild goats and rabbits and also to the *amoditus*, a highly venomous snake of the horned-viper variety and apparently unique to Thassos. Do not worry about it though — it is rarely seen and recorded attacks number precisely zero.

Finding a place to stay should never be a problem. The hotels in Limenas, Limenaria and Potos are amply supplemented by the 'rooms to let' signs that line the coastal road and official campsites abound, often located on hillsides with sparkling views. Freelance camping is technically forbidden although the local police seem to tolerate it. What is not tolerated, however, is lighting campfires — huge chunks of western Thassos were devastated in a 1985 forest fire and islanders have no wish for a repeat experience. Those starting a campfire can expect to spend time in jail.

One hundred kilometres (60 miles) of coastline mean that the watersports enthusiast is well-catered for, from the waterskier to the fisherman who can hire a boat for the day. Scuba-divers, however, may wish to holiday elsewhere as diving is prohibited to protect the many antiquities that lie submerged offshore. For those preferring their sport on terra firma, there are tennis clubs at Markryammos and Skala Prinos.

Most visitors to Thassos will take the Kavala ferry to the uninspiring port of Skala Prinos rather than make the 40 minute journey to Keramoti to catch a boat direct to the capital Limenas. Regular buses connect Skala Prinos with **Limenas** (known as Thassos to the locals). This is an attractive town with a good deal to offer beyond its tourist facilities and one which preserves its history in a pleasing, contemporary fashion.

The town's ancient theatre hosts Greek comedies and tragedies performed by the State Theatre of Northern Greece during the months of July and August, a full 26 centuries after its completion. It can be reached by climbing a moderately steep path that begins at the archaeological museum. This displays finds from the acropolis, and from the ancient town of Thassos, the remains of which lie conveniently next to the museum.

As for the rest of the island, it is best-explored by circumventing the coastal road, cutting inland when necessary. Buses shuffle slowly along the route and it is better to hire a car or moped in Limenas. This allows for leisurely exploration of not only the tiny villages and hamlets, but also of some splendidly isolated coves that are ideal for the uninhibited skinny-dipper. For those short of drachmas, hitch-hiking is usually good.

Leaving Limenas by the eastern road, the first settlement reached is the large village of **Panagia**, graced by its church at the top of the town. Within its walls is the banner of Richard the Lionheart, King of England from 1189 to 1199. This is a rather unusual artefact but one that seems to confirm the islanders' claim that Thassos was a resting place for weary Crusaders en route to the Holy Land.

Two kilometres (1 mile) on is **Potamia**. It is hard to imagine that this small village has its own claim to fame within the world of the arts but claim it has, and a proud one at that. This is the birthplace of Polygnotos Vigas, the twentieth-century sculptor who, despite living most of his life in New York, bequeathed his life's work to Greece, preferably to be housed in a museum on Thassos. In 1980 his wish was granted and the Vigas museum today stands next to the church at the south of his village.

Further down the coast is the rather anonymous hamlet of **Kinera**. Anonymous today, that is; in ancient times it was the centre of a thriving gold mining industry. The small island of Kinera lies 1km ($^1/_2$ mile) offshore and can be reached by boat or by some strenuous swimming.

At the south-eastern tip of Thassos is **Aliki**, built on a tiny peninsula, its houses below a small hill strewn with the ruins of two early Christian sanctuaries and a fifth-century church. The peninsula is flanked by two sandy, sheltered beaches. Three kilometres (2 miles) on is the monastery of Archangelou, staring across the sea to the Holy Mountain of Athos, under whose jurisdiction it is. The monastery is open to appropriately dressed visitors (arms and legs must be covered).

Potos is the next stop, a town rapidly becoming a resort due to its fine beaches, and is followed by **Limenaria**, the second town of Thassos. Boats leave here daily in the summer for cruises around the Mount Athos peninsula. The road continues up the west coast from here to Limenas, a route far less scenic than that on the east coast due to the ravages of the 1985 fire, but one that passes some delightfully quiet beaches.

The real tranquillity of Thassos is to be found inland in hamlets such as Kastro, home to only three families and snuggled up close to the pines. Theologos is beautifully set in the hills and bisected by a tiny stream, and Maries is the base for those wishing to drive up Mount Ipserion, at 1,000m (3,300ft) the island's highest point. Its

41km (26 miles) of dirt-track are best attempted in a four wheel drive vehicle. Those with good shoe leather and strong lungs can make the shorter ascent on foot from Potomia.

Thrace

Xanthi

If Kavala has a Turkish past then **Xanthi**, 56km (35 miles) east in Thrace, has a Turkish present. The muezzin calling the faithful to prayer in the mosques, women clad in all-enveloping Islamic garb and spicy aromas emanating from local kitchens, all lend the impression that one is being slowly pulled into Asia Minor. Even the town's local delicacy, roasted chick peas, is very much a Near-Asian dish. Yet Greek Orthodox and Moslem seem to happily co-exist in this bright and almost totally uncommercialised town. Set at the end of a green valley, bisected by the Kossinthos river and with the rolling Rodopi mountains covering the 40km (25 miles) north to the Bulgarian frontier, it has a lovely setting, an easy-going atmosphere and a charm that the heavy military presence does nothing to diminish.

As with Kavala, Xanthi is divided between the old and the new; and the mostly Turkish inhabited old town has more to offer. To get there, go east from the spacious, clock-tower dominated main square, push through a curtain of video arcades and *souvlaki* stalls and climb its first cobbled street. The nineteenth-century Thracian houses are a mass of different pastels and have distinctive iron-railings, overhanging balconies and bright window shutters; several have small, well-tended gardens.

The large, rectangular and well-secured buildings are the old tobacco warehouses, part of the industry that made Xanthi prosperous and is still the town's principle employer. Often built next to their owner's mansions, they have an air of faded elegance.

An old tobacco merchant's mansion has been converted into a folk art museum, and is about the only way to get inside one of these splendid buildings. The wooden floors and staircase and the high ceilings covered in fine paintings and portraits are certainly worth a look. Even the toilet is decorated. As a museum, it houses a large selection of traditional costumes from Thrace and as far away as the Black Sea. Also of interest is a 1 tonne painted marble fireplace and a lovely selection of turn-of-the-century postcards.

Of the three Byzantine monasteries that stand on the densely covered hills and forest just north of Xanthi, only two are still in operation; Panagia and Taxiarches. The third one, Kalamou, is now deserted. All three are linked by an asphalt road that turns right off the main highway to the town of Stavropoulis to the west, and both Panagia and Taxiarches are open to visitors until sunset.

Although Kalamou is locked and bolted, it does mark the starting point for a 5km (3 miles) refreshingly tranquil walk through the plane-tree forests, overlooking the green valley through which the Kossinthos flows, before arriving back in Xanthi.

To get to Kalamou, take the Stavropoulis bus and ask to be let off at the turn-off to the monasteries. Climb steadily uphill for 30 minutes until the sadly dilapidated Kalamou is reached (its grounds, however, shelter a pleasant and shady picnic area) and then take the narrow dirt path that falls steeply down just before the main gate. It is all downhill from here, brushing through the thick forest along a path well-marked with red splashes on rocks, before eventually arriving at a viewing spot overlooking the old town. A road leads downhill from here, crossing the bridge over the Kossinthos and heading back into new Xanthi.

Leaving Xanthi on the Komotini road east and bearing south after 8km (5 miles) at Vafika, takes you past the hot spas of Genissea and a series of small, mainly Moslem-populated villages before arriving at **Abdira**.

There are three very good reasons for making the trip here. Firstly, Abdira itself is an old and timeless Thracian village, its traditional houses lining the cobbled streets and leading up to a main square that is centred around a small fountain. Secondly, 7km (4 miles) south is a huge stretch of sandy beach, totally undeveloped save for a solitary taverna and with just a few small fishing vessels bobbing around in its tiny harbour. Thirdly, a 5 minute walk from the beach leads to the ruins of ancient Abdira, birthplace of Protagoras, the sophist and Democritus, father of democracy.

As archaeological sites go, this one is initially unimpressive — most of the ruins do not get past knee-height — but with the help of the map shown on site, one can distinguish the baths, the storerooms, the theatre and all other remains of the major third-century BC town. Most of the transportable finds are in Kavala's archaeological museum. As excavations are still in progress, it is still one of those sites where you can wander around, looking at the pieces of broken pottery. Be warned, though, that they cannot be taken home because of Greek customs regulations.

An interesting place to break the 56km (35 mile) journey east along the main E5 highway to Komotini is **Porto Lagos**, unusually located on a narrow strip of land that separates Lake Vistonia from the sea.

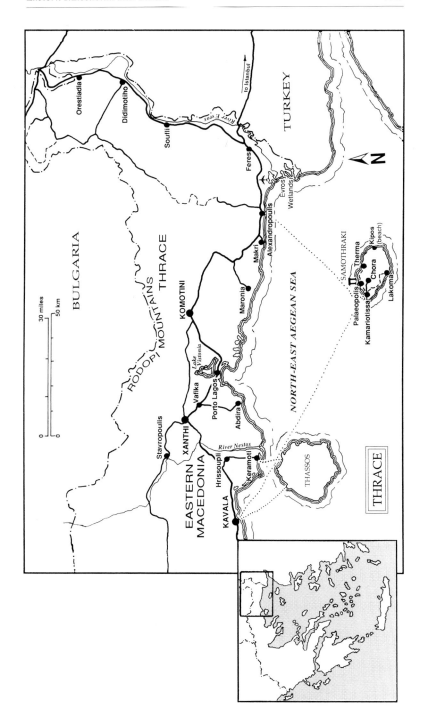

A large fishing village, its charm has been diminished in recent years due to increasing industrial development but the abundance of water and soft reeds still make it a popular rest-spot for migratory birds en-route to warmer climates. In winter the area is crammed with geese, ducks and herons.

A 20 minute walk east out of town leads to Agios Nikolaos, a small whitewashed monastery picturesquely positioned on the lake itself and reached via a small footbridge.

Komotini

Komotini lies on the south-eastern edge of the Rodopi mountain range and is another town that manages to happily combine both East and West, as well as old and new. There is not a great deal to see in terms of sights, although the archaeological museum at the town's entrance has an excellent collection of Thracian finds. However, it is a great town for just rambling around, particularly on Tuesday, the colourful market day.

The Moslem presence is a good deal more pronounced here, with over a dozen operating mosques, but there are also a number of fine traditional Thracian houses, often incongruously squeezed between the uniform, squared-off new constructions. In the middle of this is the neo-Classical, Victorian-style building of Nestor Tsanaklis, tall and grand with arched windows and finished in steely grey.

If it is open, the 1800 church of the Panagia is also worth seeing, particularly for its portrayals of Paradise and the Original Sin in frescoes. Komotini is a good place for an overnight stop, with several nice hotels.

Fans of Homer's epic, *The Odyssey*, have the chance to pay a literary pilgrimage of sorts to **Maronia**, a pleasant traditional-style village 32km (19 miles) south of Komotini near the coast. For, just beyond the town, stretching down to a sandy beach, are the ruins of the walls, temples and houses of ancient Maronia, the Homeric *Ismaros*.

This was the town where the local Priest of Apollo presented Odysseus with twelve jars of fine wine. The wine was dark, mellow and irresistible and used by Odysseus to lure the man-eater Cyclops into a drunken stupor so that the hero and his crew could put out the monster's eye and escape from his cave. This stalactite and stalagmite filled cave can also be visited, at the small fishing village of **Makri** which lies on the route of the E5, 12km (7 miles) before Alexandropoulis.

Linking Komotini with Alexandropoulis, the E5 which ends in Turkish Istanbul, runs partway along the Thracian coastline at this point and passes several coastal resorts patronised almost exclusively by Greeks. Makri, Nea Hili and Messimvria all have long, sandy beaches, hotels and rooms to let. It may be better to stay overnight at one of these three rather than at Alexandropoulis which, despite being capital of the Evros district, has little to attract visitors.

Alexandropoulis, the easternmost major Greek town, is a modern but already crumbling port only 44km (27 miles) from the Turkish frontier. As such, the military presence here is more pronounced than in any other Thracian town. Some may find its twin personality (Greek and Turkish), its grid-plan easy layout and its bright shops appealing. Others will simply use it as a convenient base from which to travel to the island of Samothraki, 2 hours away, or to visit the Evros Wetlands, 30km (18 miles) to the east.

Keen ornothologists will already know about the Evros Wetlands, a large and marshy delta and one of the most important spots in Europe for the viewing of migratory birds. At the last count, 263 different species had been recorded here; from ducks, swans, pelicans and herons to rarer species such as the majestic sea-eagle. The area has several shelters from which to view the birds in peace but, unfortunately, most of the Wetlands are closed off to visitors. This region lies directly on the Turkish border, making it a highly sensitive military point.

Samothraki

There are very few Greek islands further off the beaten track than Samothraki. Part of the North-East Aegean chain, this small and rocky island stands alone in the north-eastern corner of Greece and has no airport and no inter-island ferry connections. The only means of entry is by boat from Kavala (twice weekly — 4 hours) or from Alexandropoulis (daily — 2 hours).

Quiet and unspoilt, Samothraki's remoteness has kept it well off the main tourist routes, yet it still manages to draw a small amount of visitors annually. In ancient times Samothraki was the centre for the worship of the mysterious and all-powerful Great Gods, rulers of the world and Underworld. The remains of their sanctuaries can still be seen today, 26 centuries after their completion.

The island's name has easily-defined origins: 'Samo', as it was believed to have been originally settled by adventurers from Samos; and 'Thraki', indicating its proximity to Thrace. By 500BC it was a powerful island, this was mainly due to its Sanctuary of the Great Gods which attracted pilgrims in droves. The Great Gods themselves were deemed to be even more powerful than Zeus and the other

Castle ruins above a village on the island of Samothraki

immortals; they were centred around the Great Mother, the lesser god Kadmilos and the terrible twins, the Kaviri. There is no written record of the style of worship that took place at the Sanctuary, but the rites here concentrated on fertility and, judging by the clay lamps and food bowls found during the excavations, took place at night and were followed by a huge feast. Several of the ancient greats — such as Lysander the Spartan and Phillip the Second — are known to have worshipped here. Yet as the Great Gods declined in popularity, so did Samothraki. It never regained its former prominence. It just passed through the centuries uneventfully, before becoming part of Greece in 1912.

All visitors to Samothraki will first put in at **Kamariotissa**, a small port fronted by a string of cafés and restaurants and with a pebbly beach. Although Chora is the capital of the island, Kamariotissa is the transportation centre of Samothraki. The island's three bus routes all

A panorama across the rooftops of Xanthi (ch8)

Many Greek boats, like these at Ierrissos, are built to a traditional design (ch8)

A house in the old city, Xanthos (ch8)

Donkeys play a crucial role in the everyday life of rural Greece

go via here and caiques shuttle passengers to the more remote spots on the island's eastern coast. There is a hotel and there are several rooms to let, more so than in Chora, the island's most populous town, 6km (4 miles) away to the east and reached by an asphalt road that meanders its way steadily up the slopes of Mount Fingari.

Chora is a quiet and sleepy town, with only the sadly crumbled ruins of a Byzantine castle standing over its red-tiled roofs offering anything like a 'tourist attraction'. Yet it is the host to Samothraki's post office and OTE (the Greek telephone company). The Sanctuary of the Great Gods is within walking distance.

It is also possible to make the ascent of Mount Fingari from Chora. Also known as Mount Soas or the Mountain of the Moon, it is, at 1,670m (5,480ft) above sea-level, the highest peak in the entire Aegean. It provided the perfect vantage spot for Poseidon as he stood on top of Fingari and watched the great clashes of the 10 year Trojan War, over the sea to the east. The mountain can be climbed but it is a strenuous 6 hour pull. A guide is essential; some of the tracks are unmarked and it is all too easy to get lost.

The **Palaeopolis**, or Sanctuary of the Great Gods, can be reached from Chora or from Kamariotissa, on the main north-eastern road out of the port. Visit the on-site museum before wandering the ruins themselves in order to get the best mental picture of how the Sanctuary both looked and functioned and to see some of the finds excavated here. Afterwards, the well-labelled ruins make much more sense. There is the Anaktoron, where worshippers were believed to have been initiated into the ceremony and the Arsinoeion, at 20m (65ft) in diameter, the largest known circular building in Ancient Greece. In addition, there is the Temenos, the feasting spot and the five columns and stone benches of the Hieron, the holiest site and one restored by the Romans 17 centuries ago.

The Winged Victory of Samothraki once stood on the Nike Fountain in the Sanctuary. Discovered by a peasant in 1863, it was 'sold' to the French Consul Champoiseau and eventually ended up in the Louvre in Paris where it resides today. A copy of this beautiful nude female marble statue was donated by the French to the museum at Palaeopolis.

The eastern road out of Palaeopolis arrives in 9km (5 miles) at **Therma**, one of the lusher villages of this barren, granite island, and a popular summer spot amongst Greeks for its hot springs in which you can bathe. A better, easier ascent of Mount Fingari can be made from here. On the southern side, reached from Chora, are a series of villages; Alonia, Xiropotamos, Profitas Elias and **Lakoma**. All are quiet and unspoilt and from the latter a 2 hour walk south-east leads to Pahia Ammos, a great swathe of sandy beach nearly 1km ($^1/_2$ mile) long and a destination, in season, for the caiques from Kamariotissa. Another good beach, **Kipos**, accessible only by caique, lies out on the far eastern coast. Sandwiched midway between the two beaches are the Kremasto Nera (coastal waterfalls).

Eastern Thrace

Back on the mainland, one can either begin the long haul back to Thessaloniki or start a tour of what is certainly the least-visited region of mainland Greece; eastern Thrace. This hugs the Turkish frontier and moves upward in a great thumb-like shape between Bulgaria and Turkey. It is not only for its remoteness that this region is rarely explored; it is also because this pretty but thinly-populated, predominantly agricultural area does not have much to catch the visitor's eye. Nevertheless, **Feres**, 33km (20 miles) east of Alexandropoulis, has a Byzantine church dating from 1152 and modelled on the great Agia Sofia in Constantinople (Istanbul).

Soufli, another 65km (40 miles) north, is the silk-producing centre of Thrace, the silk being processed mainly through cottage industries. **Didimotiho**, 31km (19 miles) further up, boasts a history going back 10 centuries that is reflected in its traditional-style Thracian houses and ruined Byzantine walls. **Orestiada**, again just north, is a pleasantly lush and green town with a small folklore museum. However, aside from these, most other inhabitation is in small farming communities and hamlets; some Greek, some Turkish, and all very quiet.

Back to Thessaloniki

The route back to Thessaloniki is a long one — 337km (209 miles) on the southern route via Kavala and skirting the top of Halkidiki — and 358km (222 miles) over an alternative northern route, picked up where the road divides at Xanthi on the road signposted Drama. This is a pretty journey, running alongside the undulating green landscape before arriving at the dull and dusty town of **Drama**, which stands at the foot of lush Mount Falakro, over 2,100m (6,890ft) high.

From Drama, take the Nea Zihni road south-west and then bear right to **Seres**, a bright and modern town with a Byzantine castle and church to reflect its 800 year history.

A small diversion can be made to **Lai Lia**, 25km (15 miles) north. This small town is set in green forests on the slopes of Mount Vrondou and is a marvellous area for just strolling around. The springs here are fresh and pure and the water is used in the making of the local *lougoumi*, a sticky and soft sweet. Lai Lia also has a ski-run and refuge. Return to Seres, and from there it is a mostly straight 77km (48 miles) to Thessaloniki.

Further Information
— Eastern Macedonia and Thrace —
Eastern Macedonia

Kavala
Archaeological Museum
☎ 051 222 335
Open: 8.30am-3pm.
Closed Mondays.

Folk Art Museum
☎ 051 227820
Open: daily 9-11am, 6-9pm.

Monastery of Agios Silas
Open: daily 7am-2pm, 4-8pm.
Ring the bell.

Tourist Office
Eleftheria Square
☎ 051 228762/222425
Open: Monday to Friday 8am-1.30pm, 5.30-7.30pm;
Saturday 8am-1pm.
Closed Sundays.

Mount Athos
To obtain permission to visit, apply either to:
Ministry of Foreign Affairs or
Ministry of Northern Greece
(see below).

British Consulate
8 Venizelos Street
Thessaloniki
☎ (031) 269984
Open: Monday to Friday 9am-5pm.

Ministry of Foreign Affairs
2 Zalokosta Street
Athens
Open: Monday to Friday, 11am-1pm.

Ministry of Northern Greece
(Room 218)
Dikitiros Square
Thessaloniki
☎ 031 270092
Open: Monday to Friday, 8am-2pm.

U.S. Consulate
59 Nikis Street
Thessaloniki
☎ (031) 266121
Open: Monday to Friday, 9am-5pm.

Petralona Cave
Near Petralona
☎ 0396 31300
Open: daily 8.30am-3pm.

Polygiros
Archaeological Museum
☎ 0396 31300
Open: 8.30am-3pm.
Closed Mondays.

Phillipi
Site and museum
Open: daily, dawn to dusk.
☎ 051 516470

Thassos
Archaeological Museum
Thassos town
☎ 0539 22180
Open: 8.30am-3pm.
Closed Mondays.

Vigas Museum
Village of Potomia
Open: April to October, 8am-
12noon, 5.30-9pm; Sundays 8am-
3.30pm.
Closed Tuesdays.

Thrace

Alexandropoulis
Ecclesiastic Art Museum
Open: Monday to Friday 9am-
12noon.

Archaeological Collection
☎ 0551 26785

Tourist Information
Leofaros Dimokratius 296
☎ 0551 24998

Komotini
Archaeological Museum
☎ 0531 22411
Open: 9am-3pm.
Closed Mondays.

Olynthos (Halkidiki)
Archaeological site
☎ 0373 21862
Open: 8.30-3pm daily.
Closed Monday.

Samothraki
Palaeopolis
(Sanctuary of the Great Gods)
☎ 0551 41474
Open: 9am-3pm daily. Sunday
9am-2.30pm.

Xanthi
Folk Art Museum
The old town
Open: Monday to Friday 5-7pm.

9 • Chios

Introduction

'All Chiotes are foolish. Some more, some less'. This old eighteenth-century proverb is more likely to have arisen from envy rather than from maliciousness. For the island of Chios, with the exception of an awful massacre by the Turks in the nineteenth century, has always been happy, well-respected and prosperous — it remains so today.

The fifth largest of all the Greek Islands, Chios has a sizeable population (50,000) and a diverse and profitable economic base. The latter encompasses grapes and vines, citrus fruits, almonds, livestock and cattle-breeding, olives, mastic (the island is unique worldwide in its production of this gummy resin) and, most important of all, shipping. The island has produced some of the most successful shipowners of the day — John Karras and Kostas Lemos, for example — and shipping is now the number one employer for the men of Chios.

In recent years, another string has been added to the island's economic bow — tourism — albeit on a very minor scale. The few charter flights, mostly from the Netherlands and Scandinavia, all arrive between mid-July and the end of August and all are bound for Karfas, the only tourist resort of the island. Chios has plenty of summer visitors, though, the overwhelming majority — over 80 per cent — being Greeks in the know.

It is surprising that Chios has remained off the beaten track for so long as the island has all the ingredients for the perfect Greek island holiday. It has a good climate; averaging 29°C (87°F) in the summer; sandy and popular beaches and secluded little coves; a fair nightlife (in Karfas and Chios town); a medieval castle; some astonishingly beautiful villages in the south and a Byzantine monastery that ranks as one of the most important in the world.

The island's interior is green and rolling, despite being damaged by a series of forest fires in the 1980s, and its coastline is bursting with beaches. Yet there are two reasons why Chios has remained un-known to travel agents and almost untouched by developers. The first is that Chios has been wealthy enough not to want or need tourism; the second is purely strategic. Positioned in the North-East Aegean Sea, Chios is over 4 hours sailing away from Samos and Lesvos, the two islands it is loosely sandwiched between, yet only 8km (5 miles) from the Turkish coast. The Greek army therefore maintains a large presence on the island and was active in discour-aging the promotion of tourism to Chios.

Times have changed and in the last year the Greek Tourist Office has been heavily promoting the island; yet, even with three or four times the number of overseas visitors it gets today, the unfussed, easy-going atmosphere of the island is unlikely to change.

A rectangular island, Chios can easily be split into north and south with Chios town, the capital, marking the divide. The north is not as immediately attractive as the south, having been ravaged by recent forest fires, but is home to some of the island's best beaches and offers fine, solitary walks. The south is more populous and is drenched in wild tulips in the spring. It has some of the more popular beaches and a series of medieval villages, built in the thirteenth century and virtually unchanged over the years. Together, these villages of the southern interior form the Mastichoria, the heart of mastic produc-tion on the island.

Chios has been known since ancient times for the production of mastic, a sticky crystallised resin that is drawn from the trunks of the gnarled and bushy mastic tree and is used in a multitude of products such as paints, varnishes, face creams, toothpaste and chewing gum. Mastic products are everywhere on Chios and make good souvenirs. The chewing gum is particularly popular, despite the fact that some claim it is like chewing incense.

Curiously, southern Chios is the only area in the world where the mastic is formed in the tree. The trees were planted in northern Chios and although they grew well, they yielded no mastic. It was the mastic that made Chios a favourite island of its medieval occupiers — the Genoans and the Turks — and the industry still thrives today, most of the mastic being exported to Iraq to be converted into alcohol.

Confusion surrounds the origin of the name Chios. Some say it is Syrian for snakes (these were once common on the island); others that it is named after the mythical nymph Chioni. Still more claim it is from the Greek *chioni* which means snow. Similarly, nobody knows if this really was the birthplace of Homer; Chios is one of

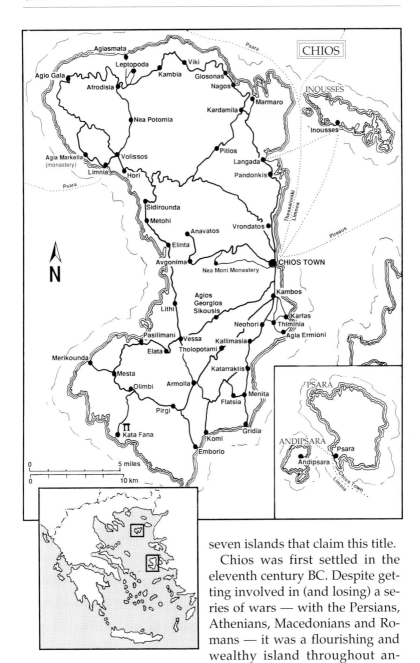

seven islands that claim this title.

Chios was first settled in the eleventh century BC. Despite getting involved in (and losing) a series of wars — with the Persians, Athenians, Macedonians and Romans — it was a flourishing and wealthy island throughout ancient times, an important trading and commercial centre that was known for its vineyards and fine ceramic pottery. However, under the stagnant rule of Byzantium, Chios slumped and was frequently raided by pirates and, in the eighth century, by the marauding Saracens, who sacked much of the island.

Despite these events, prosperity was just around the corner, and in 1346 the Genoans captured Chios and ruled the island for the next 220 years through a trading company called Maona, especially created for this purpose. During their rule the island boomed commercially. Vast quantities of mastic were produced, the ancient silk industry was revived and made profitable and the vineyards produced fine wines. The villages of southern Chios were established, and many were decorated with *xysta*, geometric black and white designs that arose from the Genoan influence.

Genoan rule was by no means benign; in fact, it was often harsh and many Greeks were put to work as slaves building mansions for the Genoese nobility, mansions that can still be seen in southern Chios today. The island was a fine prize for the Turks who over-ran the island in 1566.

Unlike many areas that fell to ruin under Turkish rule, Chios prospered further. Its commercial base was consolidated and expanded and the islanders gained a reputation as fine traders and navigators. The Turks had a particular fondness for mastic and produced huge quantities of it; it was even used to freshen the breath of ladies of the harem.

The favour the Chiotes enjoyed under the Turks made their punishment doubly worse when they rose against their occupiers in March 1822 and joined the Greek War of Liberation. Within 2 weeks a huge Turkish army, led by Kara Ali, landed on the island and, in one of the worst atrocities ever committed in this region, there began a systematic slaughtering of the population that lasted 15 days. Over 30,000 Chiotes lost their lives and 40,000 were taken away to be sold into slavery. Even today, it is argued that Chios has never recovered from this tragedy. Only the villages of the south, needed for their production of mastic, were spared.

Delacroix's masterpiece, *Massacre at Chios*, and Victor Hugo's poem, *The Child of Chios*, added fuel to the flames of European outrage at this genocide and the alarmed Turks relaxed their rule, inviting those who had fled during the slaughter to return. Yet, in 1881, another disaster rocked the island in the form of an earthquake that killed over 3,500 people. Again Chios picked up the pieces. In 1912 it was won for the new Greek state and its population replenished by the Greek refugees from Asia Minor.

Chios is an easy island to reach but by sea it normally involves a long journey. There are daily connections to Pireaus (10 hours) and Lesvos (4 hours) and at least weekly links to Samos (4 hours) and Thessaloniki (17 hours) via Limnos. All boats dock at Chios town. There is an airport to handle the summer charters and the daily flights to Athens and less regular services to Samos, Lesvos and Mykonos. Book well in advance for all flights and this also applies to accommodation, at least in season. Although rooms to let are becoming more and more available, there are simply not enough hotels.

Those who do not want to bring a tent should check in the Further Information section at the end of this chapter for the names and telephone numbers of some hotels. Please do not view them as recommendations but rather as suggestions.

A more rural way to spend a stay on Chios is in the private rooms let in the medieval villages of the south by the Womens' Agricultural and Tourist Co-operative. Guests stay in the village homes of their hosts and are given opportunities to participate in local events, from festivals to cutting mastic. The telephone number of the office in Pirgi is listed in the Further Information section.

Night-life in Chios is centred around Chios town and at the resort of Karfas, where one can also participate in a wide range of watersports. Apart from the windsurfing and waterskiing, fishing seems to be the most popular recreation; the sea around Chios is said to be particularly productive.

A fortnight of cultural events is held around the island in the last week of July and first week of August. It is mainly centred on Chios town and includes live theatre, music and traditional dancing. On the last Sunday in Lent the boisterous Mostra carnival is held at Thiminia. A similar festival is held on the first Monday in Lent at Olimbi.

Chios Town

Chios town could hardly be described as quaint and charming; it does not possess a beach and reverberates to the sound of cars and motorbikes thundering up the waterfront and through the streets behind. However, this town has a great deal to offer. There is a fine medieval castle, four good museums, an old bazaar and a welcoming atmosphere, all in a town that just brims over with character. Even if Chios town fails to excite, this should pose no problem. It is the transportation hub of Chios and any point on the rest of the island is only a bus journey away.

Most of the activity in Chios town seems to take place along the waterfront, the meeting point of the island's youth. It is a great place to just wander up and down in the evenings, maybe stopping for a meal at one of the tavernas or sipping a *cafe frappe* (iced coffee) at one of the many sidewalk cafés. Most of the travel and shipping agencies can be found here, as can the car rental agencies and, just off the waterfront up Kanari Street, the friendly and very helpful tourist office. At the southern end stands the Chandris, the best hotel in town.

From the tourist office continue inland and arrive at Vounaki Square, spacious and with the statue (to the right) of Bishop Fragiadis, one of the instigators of the 1822 uprising that ended so horrifically. Past the statue is the Porta Maggiore, the arched South Gate through which one enters the well-preserved remains of the medieval castle of Chios and the old town within its walls.

Built on the remains of earlier Macedonian, Roman and Byzantine structures, this Genoese castle remains the principal attraction of Chios town. Its South Gate stretches thickly into the interior, opening out next to a small caged-off room. Here, the rebel Bishop Fragiadis and seventy other of the island's notables were imprisoned during the Turkish rampage through Chios; from here they were subsequently taken out and hanged. Adjacent to this cell, a set of steps lead up to a Byzantine part of the castle. Its rooms now appropriately host the museum of Byzantine antiquities; a small collection of mosaics, frescoes and icons found on Chios, all dating from this era. A beautiful floor mosaic from the fifth century is the museum's showpiece.

After you have viewed the exhibits, the curator will unlock a gate on a path that leads up to the castle's battlements, parts of which have blended in with the old town. A huge cannon, left over from the Turkish occupation, still points out to sea, and the views are good without being truly spectacular. Be careful while wandering around; the battlements have no guard rails and there are a few nasty drops.

Back at the cell of Fragiadis, go around the next corner to an old and crumbling Turkish cemetery. The body of Kari Ali lies beneath the large marble gravestone that dominates all the others. You are now in the old town, a delightful but small mix of narrow streets lined with Genoese and Turkish-style houses, some of these structures dating back to the sixteenth century.

To visit the town's Byzantine museum, return to Voudaki Square and look to the south-west for the mosque in which it is housed. The mosque can be easily identified by the graceful, swirling design of its minaret, giving notice that it was a favourite of the Sultan's. An ornate fountain, where worshippers would ritually wash before prayers, stands in its courtyard, as do most of the exhibits. This is because the museum's interior is currently being renovated and it is unknown when it will re-open.

What can be seen is interesting, though, particularly a collection of gravestones that indicate the cosmopolitan make-up of the population of Chios during the Genoese and Turkish occupations. There are some decorated Roman columns and several old cannons but unfortunately one has to peer through the window to view a copy of the masterpiece by Delacroix that portrayed the massacre on Chios and so arrayed European public opinion against the Turks. The original painting hangs in the Louvre.

A statue of one of the terrors of the Turks, the great Greek Admiral-politician Kanaris, can be seen in the pleasant public gardens behind the main square. Beginning at the Byzantine museum is the bazaar, a curious mixture of wide and narrow streets full of interesting little shops and cafés and reeking with the scent of smoke and spices.

There are two other museums in Chios town, the first to the south of the main square at the Korais library, reportedly the third largest in Greece with 135,000 volumes including the private collection of a local notable, Philip Argentis. He donated the folklore museum to the town; housed above the library, it contains displays of traditional costumes and handicrafts.

The archaeological museum is housed in a modern building inland at the southern end of the town. Exhibiting the finds unearthed on Chios, it features oil-lamps, jugs, vases and headless statues but pride of place goes to a letter from Alexander the Great to the conquered Chiotes in 332BC. Rather severe in tone, it demands that Chios introduce democracy without delay, that all democratic exiles be allowed to return and that the oligarchs who supported the Persians during their war with Alexander be punished. Carved on a large stone slab, the letter is a fascinating piece of history.

Apart from the beaches, the first port of call for most visitors is the monastery of **Nea Moni** (now a convent). It lies 16km (10 miles) inland from Chios town and is considered to be one of the most important Byzantine monasteries surviving in the world today. Its story began when three monks discovered, in a burning bush, an icon of the Panagia (Virgin Mary) that had miraculously been untainted by the fire. In awe of this, they built a small monastery that was later extended and enlarged in 1042 by the exiled Emperor Constantine Monomarchus after the icon prophesied through a monk that he would return to rule Byzantium. The monastery dominated the

*Nea Moni monastery,
flanked by tall cypress
trees*

island from this time onward.

It is set high in the hills, in an area once covered in pines but now barren and scarred from the effects of forest fires and quarrying. It is likely you will have to hire transport or take a taxi to Nea Moni; only one bus a week (on Wednesday) travels there from Chios town, going on to the mountainous medieval village of Anavatos. Its departure time varies according to season; check with the tourist office.

Much of the actual monastic complex is crumbling to ruin but it is still deeply atmospheric. The remains of old chapels, long disused cells, the refectory, the water cistern and the olive press can all be seen. Before visiting the church itself (the sisters supply cloaks for those inappropriately dressed) take a look inside the chapel to the left of the entrance which contains more disturbing evidence of Turkish brutality on Chios.

During the 1822 massacre, many Chiotes fled to Nea Moni for sanctuary in the belief that the Turks would not violate such a holy place. However, the Turks did so and thousands were slaughtered inside its walls. Inside a glass cabinet within the chapel are row upon row of the skulls of the murdered monks, many of them marked with cracks and holes, thus indicating a violent death.

Divided into three sections, the church itself is a treasure trove of Byzantine antiquities and is solemnly decorated. Its beautiful eleventh-century mosaics were a gift from Zoe, wife of the Emperor Monomarchus, and there is a grandfather clock that keeps Byzantine time, with the sun setting and rising at 12 every day. In the third section to the right of the ornate altar acreen is the gold-plated icon of the Virgin Mary, the same one found by the monks in the eleventh century that led to the monastery's founding, and which has incredibly survived through the traumas of the last millennium. North of Nea Moni but only visitable by men, is the monastery of Agii Pateron, founded in honour of the three monks who originally discovered the icon.

Stay on the asphalt road that leads north from Nea Moni and two extraordinary medieval villages are reached, the first being **Avgonima**, whose mostly ruined grey-stone buildings blend in with its barren surroundings. The second is **Anavatos**, precariously perched high on a rocky hill top with a sheer drop to one side, and all but abandoned these days, having only five residents.

Once an important wood-cutting centre (the area was covered in pine trees) under the Turks, Anavatos never recovered from the 1822 massacre. As the Turks burst into the town on that day, the villagers flung themselves off the cliff to plunge to their death below rather than be enslaved, in an event that is known as the Greek Masada. Anavatos has not been populated to any significant degree since.

Southern Chios

The roads south of Chios town are of good quality but together form a rather confusing network which renders any straightforward circuit of the region impossible. A good map — obtainable from the tourist office — will be more than useful and a lot of backtracking will need to be done, particularly on the eastern coast.

Generally speaking, southern Chios can be divided into two rather indistinct halves for purposes of exploration; one that concentrates on the eastern coast as far as Emborio, the other that centres on the Mastichoria region and its wonderful, unique villages.

Heading south towards the eastern coast of Chios, you pass the island's airport before entering the deliciously mellow and rural Kambos plain. This is a productive, citrus-fruit growing region, where abandoned old mansions can often be seen boarded up by the side of the road. There are more of these mansions in the large and attractive and once very rich village of **Kambos**, founded by the Genoans in the fourteenth century.

From Kambos a road leads south-east to **Karfas**, billed as the number one tourist resort of Chios. However, it is not terribly over-developed and instead has rather a half-finished air, with a few hotels already built and others rapidly going up. Anyone who can put up with this is rewarded by its large and beautiful beach of fine golden sand.

Agia Ermioni, just south of Karfas, also has a nice beach and one that is a little less-crowded. From here the asphalt road curves around to the village of **Thiminia**, where prehistoric Mastadon bones have been unearthed, and which is worth visiting on 4 September when it hosts the festival of Agios Ermionis. Unfortunately, this route only has road links with Kambos and so to continue, it is necessary to backtrack to this village and take the Neohori road, which follows a rather convoluted route down the eastern coast to Emborio beach near the southern tip of the island.

Within easy walking distance of Neohori and built high on a hill is the monastery of Agios Minas. Like Nea Moni west of Chios town, this suffered dreadfully during the 1822 massacre. Over 3,000 were slaughtered here and some claim that blood can still be seen on the stones outside. The victims' bodies were dumped down a well but their bones have since been retrieved and are entombed outside the church. Agios Minas is still active today as a convent and the nuns make handicrafts and sell them to their visitors.

From Neohori one can bear south to the medieval village of **Kallimasia**, also known for its handicrafts workshops. The village was hit hard by the 1881 earthquake and yet is quite delightful, all narrow streets and tiny churches. Kallimasia has a nearby beach, Agios Emilianos, where, looking inland to the hills, one can see the first mastic trees.

On the way back to Neohori a minor road bears south leading to Katarraktis, a pleasant little coastal village to the north of the monastery of Taxiarchon, built near the coast on a hill looking out to sea. South of the monastery is Menita, one of the larger mastic growing villages and nearby Flatsia, from where minor roads lead down to two small villages on the south-eastern tip of Chios, Vokargia and Gridia.

Another road from Flatsia leads south and then west to the sandy beach of Komi. From here, via the village of Mproukia, one can head down to the Kalamotis Bay and one of the most famous beaches of Chios, the black pebbles of **Emborio**. There are two beaches here, in fact, separated by a few rocks, and both just beyond the small port from where Chios would export its mastic in medieval times. Indeed, excavations have revealed that Emborio has been inhabited since 3000BC. Its beaches are certainly an unusual sight but the black pebbles are as big as golf balls so those planning a day on the beach here would be advised to bring something soft to lie on.

Back in Kambos, a road (signposted Pirgi) leads into the lush interior of southern Chios, the rolling hills that form the Mastichoria and where the truly medieval character of its villages becomes wonderfully apparent. Some of these villages are absolutely beautiful, as are the Byzantine and Genoese churches that can be seen within them, and there are plenty of opportunities to make detours to the coast for some delightfully secluded beaches. This is a tour that is one of the musts on any visit to Chios.

One kilometre ($^1/_2$ mile) before the village of Vavili is the sandstone and domed church of Panagia Krina-Vavili, a lovely building dating from 1287 and well-worth a stop for the fine frescoes that adorn its interior. The region past Vavili, up to the village of Tholopotami, is known as Sklavia and was popular with the Genoese nobility, many of whom built villas and mansions here. The sorry remains of the castle of Apolichon stand in the area as do some of the old mansions, like the castle dating from the fourteenth century.

Nineteen kilometres (11 miles) from Chios town is the first of the medieval villages, **Armolia**, long renowned for its fine ceramic handicrafts. Here the first signs of the *xysta* appear, decorating some of the exterior walls of the houses and particularly the church of Agii Dimitrios and Nestoras. However, the charming, geometrical black and white designs on show give little hint of what is in store in Pirgi, 4km ($2^1/_2$ miles) south.

There can be little doubt that the medieval village of **Pirgi**, founded by the Genoese in the thirteenth century, is one of the most striking villages in all of Greece. *Xysta* cover almost every one of its buildings. The effect is noticeable as soon as you enter its narrow streets with their tightly packed houses, all paths and alleys leading to the main square, which is a riot of these black and white designs, painstakingly built up over the centuries.

All but one of the buildings — the main church, the café, the shops — are decorated; little wonder that it is called 'the painted village'. Yet it is not paint that produces these designs but the black pebbles of Emborio, only 6km (4 miles) to the south. Some of the pebbles are untouched, others are whitewashed, but all are hammered into the walls to form designs that last as long as the buildings they beautify.

There is just one structure untouched in the square; the fourteenth-century church of Agii Apostolii, entered through an arch created by

A café decorated with xysta *in Pirgi*

the houses that flank it and built in the style of Nea Moni. Its frescoes, painted by the Cretan Cinigos in 1665, cover literally every inch of the interior.

Accommodation is available in Pirgi in the form of rooms to let; these can be booked through the Womens' Agricultural and Tourist Co-operative whose office is the first thing one sees on entering the village (see the Further Information section at the end of the chapter for the telephone number). There is a taverna in the village square.

Soon after leaving Pirgi, a minor road south leads down towards the south coast and to the village of Agios Pantes with its secluded beach. Nearby, to the west, is **Kata Fana** where one can see the scanty remains of a Temple to Apollo, built between the ninth and sixth centuries BC. This was the site of ancient *Fanai*, where, in 412BC, one of the battles of the Peloponnesian Wars was fought between Chios (which had sided with Sparta) and Athens. The road heads back up into the hills from here and rejoins the main road just before **Olimbi** is reached, another of the medieval villages.

Limnos — one of the oldest inhabited islands of the North-East Aegean (ch9)

Surveying the scene from a balcony, Kastellorizo (ch10)

Houses and cypress trees cover the hillside at the port of Gialos, Symi (ch10)

The sleepy atmosphere and crystal-clear water of the Vathi fjord, Kalymnos (ch10)

Mesta is the finest example on Chios of a fortified medieval village, built during the Genoese age as defence against pirates and other unwanted intruders. The village has only one entrance and one exit and its *kentro* (centre) is cunningly hidden by a maze of narrow, roofed-over paths and alleyways. Luckily, the way towards it is well-signposted.

The Greek Tourist Office has declared Mesta a traditional settlement so its appearance will remain unaltered and uncluttered by blocks of rooms to let or hotels. One can find places to stay though, most easily through the tourist office located in the main square.

The square itself is a bright and open-air contrast to the dark and narrow arches of the town's streets. There are several tavernas here, patrolled by an old man wielding an enormous key that opens the door to the twelfth-century church of Taxiarches, huge and breathtakingly decorated, even by the standards of the Greek Orthodox Church. Chandeliers line the ceiling from the door down to the carved wooden altar. The caretaker may also hold the key to the nearby medieval church of Agia Paraskevi. Traditional handicrafts are a popular buy here. Two beautifully quiet and secluded beaches can be reached from Mesta, but only by foot along the mule paths west, at Merikounda and Pasilimani.

The landscape becomes more spartan from Mesta as the road curves around, heading north-east back to the capital. The quiet and friendly medieval village of **Elata** is passed, then Vessa and Agios Georgios Sikousis, before travelling over the Kambos plain into Chios town. Alternatively, though, you could bear north at Vessa for the village of Lithi where a short walk leads down to a fine sandy beach and then on to **Elinta**, also known (but not by many) for its great swimming and good sands.

Depending on the condition of the roads and on the power of your vehicle, it may be possible to climb up towards the abandoned mountain village of Avgonima and from there wind steeply downhill past the monastery of Nea Moni to Chios town. Otherwise, it is a case of doubling back to Vessa, 20km (12 miles) from Chios town.

Northern Chios

Lacking the mastic villages that stayed the hands of the marauding Turks in the south, the north of Chios was the area hit hardest by the 1822 massacre and parts have never properly recovered, many of the villages being all but deserted for much of the year. Add this to the forest fires of the 1980s that robbed the north of its great pine forests and left the landscape mostly wild and barren, and one has a region

A narrow alleyway in the medieval village of Mesta

few tourists venture into. Even its beaches — and most of them are very good — attract few sunbathers, as they are very difficult to reach from Chios town or the resort of Karfas. Yet northern Chios has a great deal to offer and it is well off the beaten track.

Immediately north of Chios town the land is fertile and well-populated — a green and prosperous plain covered in orange trees. Three windmills are passed on the coast just north of the capital (they are ruined but currently undergoing renovation) before reaching **Vrondatos**, 5km (3 miles) away. A pretty and undeveloped little town with an attractive harbour, its beach seems to be patronised mainly by locals and Greek holidaymakers although the large pebbles may prove a little too uncomfortable for some.

Vrondatos is serviced regularly by blue city buses. Just behind the beach, in a lovely spot looking out to sea, is a large and circular-shaped rock with what resembles a seat at its top. Now believed to be the site of an ancient altar, possibly one of the goddess Kiveli, it is claimed that Homer once sat here and lectured his students, who were gathered around beneath him. This explains its name, the Daskalopetra or 'teacher's stone'. Just beyond the stone is the nineteenth century monastery of Panagia Mirtidiotissa, built on a hill looking out to sea.

A quartet of sleepy fishing villages marks the bay of Langada, all of them attractively located on the shoreline and backed by the bare and rocky hills. There are a few rooms to let at Langada, and possibly some at **Pandonkis** but only the latter has any sort of a beach.

The road cuts inland from the bay, skirting the edge of the hills before arriving at the second town of Chios, **Kardamila**. This town is actually divided into two; the upper (*Ano*) and the lower (*Kato*), the latter being 2km (1 mile) away on the coast and commonly known as Marmaro. This is the larger and the prettier, a huge anchor dominating its main square, the gift of one of several wealthy shipowners who were born in Kardamila and have been sturdy benefactors of the town. The upper town lies in a large and fertile plain, an unusual sight in the north.

From the town the road climbs and plunges along the coastline, overlooking first the tiny harbour village of **Nagos**, which has a long and white pebbly beach popular with Greek holidaymakers. In contrast to the barren rocks to the west, Nagos is beautifully green and supported a large settlement in ancient times. Little remains of ancient Nagos, though, with the exception of a temple to Posiedon, the sea-god, at the back of the village near the cliffs. There is a taverna here and a few rooms to let.

Another pebble beach, **Giosonas**, is 1km ($^1/_2$ mile) north and this is a little quieter in season. A local myth claims that Jason and his Argonauts put in here during their quest for the Golden Fleece.

Back at Kardamila, a road leads south-west to the village of **Pitios**, charmingly positioned in the mountains of the interior and another contender for the birthplace of Homer. To the west of Pitios is the sixteenth-century monastery of Moundon, dedicated to John the Baptist.

To travel north from Kardamila is to reach the northern coastline where the road runs west through the villages of Amades and Viki. The latter is the trailhead for the ascent of Mount Pilinio, at 1,300m (4,260ft) high, the highest peak of Chios and named after the temple to Pilineos Jupiter that once stood at its summit.

The road from Viki curves around the foothills of Pilinio to **Kambia**, high in the hills and the base for an excursion into an all but forgotten part of Chios, in the north-west of the island. Yet it is an excursion that must be made either by foot — in which case, allow a full day — or by car, preferably by four-wheel drive vehicle. Mopeds will soon come to grief on the steep and rocky paths. There are no facilities for refreshment en-route.

The path begins 1km ($^1/_2$ mile) before Kambia, descending steadily towards the northern coast through long and empty hills until a pebble beach is reached, pounded by waves. Just above the beach is a small and isolated whitewashed chapel, its interior gaily decorated in green and yellow.

The road climbs onwards from here, still following the northern coastline yet becoming more fertile, until a fork in the road is reached. The path that heads back down to the sea arrives at **Agiasmata**, a tiny little hamlet with hot springs that are claimed to have healing powers and which draw a handful of visitors in season to occupy the few rooms to let that are available.

Continuing north at the fork, one passes through a beautifully lush region, filled with trees and with fine coastal views to the north. The first village is then reached, at **Leptopoda**. This is occupied thinly and then only in the summer. One is unlikely to see any of the residents and it is an eerie place, large yet devastated in parts but with other sectors of the village curiously modern, such as the large and very obviously modern church. Keramos, 3km (2 miles) further on, has a similarly deserted atmosphere. Keep climbing through the pine forests until the shady village of Afrodisia is arrived at, and the asphalt road is only 2km (1 mile) above, running along a mountain ridge and overlooking the rural and rolling hills.

Vrondatos beach is quiet, secluded and rarely visited by foreign tourists

Volissos, the major town of north-west Chios, is 13km (8 miles) south down this road — a gorgeous route offering some of the most beautiful scenery in Chios and with wild flowers covering the roadside. To reach Volissos one has to pass the villages of Halandra and Nea Potomia, where a café off the road to the right provides welcome refreshments. No buses travel along this route.

Volissos is a town that recreates the medieval aura that is prevalent in the villages of southern Chios, although in this case the appeal is further enhanced by the ruins of a Genoese castle standing on top of the hill the town is built on. Beneath the castle, its stone houses — some renovated, some crumbling into ruins — are packed together in cramped streets and alleys centred around a *platia* where there are a couple of small and homely tavernas.

Volissos was the administrative capital of Chios between the two World Wars and, with a population of 300 in the winter, is the busy metropolis of north-west Chios. The town can trace its roots back to the Mycenaean era and is another that claims to be the birthplace of Homer. In the vicinity are some superb beaches, totally unmarred by development.

The closest beaches to Volissos are at **Limnia**, 2km (1 mile) away and a real one-horse town where two tavernas, one at each end of the pretty harbour, account for one-third of all the buildings. Above the taverna at the far end, some rooms to let are available. Limnia has occasional links by caique to the small island of Psara. The beach is a few minutes' walk away up the coast and is sandy, hemmed in by a cove and serviced by a small wooden shack of a café.

Further on up the coast, one travels through the hills, periodically descending towards other coves, all sandy and well out of the reach of the mainstream tourist. After 7km (4 miles) the beach at the monastery of Agia Markella crowns them all, a long stretch of sand with the white walls and domed chapel of the monastery (open to visitors) behind. Those with their own transport may well wish to consider heading further north, to the Cave of Agii Gala ('Holy Milk'), full of stalagmites and stalactites that are said to drip with the milk of the Virgin Mary. A small Byzantine church, the Panagia Agiogala, stands near the entrance to the cave.

South of Limnia there are more good beaches; **Hori**, long, pebbly and less than 1km ($^1/_2$ mile) away, is a nudist beach; and further south, accessible only by car or moped, are the beautiful and secluded sands of Sidirounda and Metohi. From Volissos it is 41km (25 miles) back to Chios town (buses make the journey there and back four times a week) across a mountainous landscape which is sadly barren due to forest fires and tree-felling.

Psara

Psara is a small island; only 9km by 5km (5 miles by 3 miles) and has a spartan and rocky landscape with only a few thorn bushes and fig trees to provide relief. Yet it has been inhabited since the Mycenaean age and, prior to the Greek War of Independence in 1821, supported a population of 30,000, engaged mostly in the island's shipbuilding industry. The 1822 massacre changed this. The people of Psara sent ships to aid the Greek cause and the Turkish Sultan gave orders that it be destroyed.

In the ensuing invasion 90 per cent of the population were slaughtered, an event recorded by the great poet of the day Dionysios Solomos, in his *Destruction of Psara*. Immediately following the devastation, the Greek Admiral Konstantine Kanaris avenged the island of his birth by attacking the flagship of the Turkish fleet and blowing it out of the water, killing its crew and the man who led the invasion, Kari Ali.

Today Psara is a quiet little island, supported by fishing and with a population of about 400, most living around the main town, also called Psara. It draws a few tourists — most come to enjoy its beaches and the peace and quiet that the island offers. Its houses are built on the Cycladic model, whitewashed and squared-off with small yards attached. Rooms to let are available, the nicest ones being in an old church, converted by the Greek Tourist Office into a guest house.

An interesting feature of Psara is that it is said to have no snakes, which is strange as its large neighbour, Chios, was once known as 'Snake Island'. Locals tell a story of how a snake once hid itself in a stack of logs that were being shipped from Chios. The boat docked, the snake crawled out of the logs, slithered about a hundred metres and died.

Psara is linked by boat to Chios town four-times weekly and occasionally to Limnia on the west coast. Visitors may be able to persuade fishermen to take them over to the small island of Andipsara, west of Psara although, being rocky and uninhabited, there is not a great deal to see there.

Inousses

The largest of a group of nine small islands off the north-east coast of Chios, Inousses can lay a good claim to being the richest island in the world. This is the summer home of many of the wealthiest Greek shipping magnates — Stavros Livanos, Kostas Lemos and John Karras (who was born in Kardamila, Chios) — who have built their sumptuous villas here and whose grand yachts grace the island's small harbour. It is a green and attractive island with lots of fine beaches, as one would expect.

Inousses was first settled in the seventeenth century by shepherds from the Kardamila region of Chios, who were attracted to the island by the potential profits to be had in the large numbers of wild goats that lived there. It was considered so insignificant that the Turks ignored it during the 1822 massacre.

Visitors to the island can see the new convent of Evangelismos and stay in one of the two 'D' class hotels. A boat leaves Chios town for Inousses daily at 2pm and returns the following day at 8am, thus necessitating an overnight stay. On Sundays in season there are day-trips here from Chios.

Limnos

A possible excursion from Chios is to Limnos, one of the oldest inhabited islands of the North-East Aegean. It is very rocky and flat and draws very few tourists, Greek or otherwise. This is hardly surprising given that its attractions are less in number than those of its sister islands to the north and south, and that the green uniforms of the Greek army are everywhere.

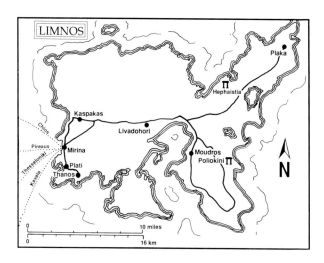

The military bear testimony to the island's strategic importance, guarding as it does the gateway to mainland Greece from the Turkish Dardanelles. Add this to the fact that Limnos is so dry that its water supply is sometimes disconnected at night in the summer, and one has the perfect recipe for scaring off the travel agents and developers. What is left is an island that is very Greek, wonderfully uncommercialised and a good place to stretch out and relax, far from the madding crowds.

Limnos is linked by air daily to both Athens and Thessaloniki and by a rather erratic boat service to and from Lesvos, Pireaus, Chios, Thessaloniki and Kavala. Contrary to what the maps say, there are no connections with the island of Samothraki. To explore Limnos, consider hiring a moped in the capital Mirina; the island's bus service is very poor.

Hephaistos, the god of fire and iron, was exiled to Limnos by Zeus because of his defiance and this unfortunate god was revered by the islanders who named their ancient capital after him. Mythology also relates that Jason and the Argonauts stayed on Limnos during their quest for the Golden Fleece and were well-received by the islanders, who were allegedly all women.

It is only natural that Limnos should figure in the Greek myths for the island can trace its history back a long way. Excavations at Poliokini, at the east of the island, have revealed that it was inhabited back in the Neolithic Age, around 2000BC, and that a settlement existed on the same site through the Minoan and Mycenaean civilisations. In general, however, the ancient past of Limnos is patchy and remains largely unknown. It was a quiet, uneventful place during the Byzantine era, was taken by the Venetians in the thirteenth century, reoccupied by the Byzantines and finally fell to the Turks in 1478. The Turks ruled the island until it became part of the new Greek state in 1912.

It is a lovely sight that greets the visitor arriving by boat at **Mirina**, capital of Limnos, on the western coast of the island. Peering between the masts of the fishing boats, one can see the whitewashed houses of the town curve around the natural harbour to the grand old ruins of a Venetian-Turkish castle, built in the thirteenth century and still dominating the town; its grey stone walls seem like an extension of the bare hills on which it stands. It is an easy walk up to the castle and although little remains of its interior, it has good views of the island.

The town itself is pleasantly uncommercialised, with many of the old wooden-balconied Turkish houses still in place and occupied, but there are a couple of hotels and several rooms to let, usually offered to visitors as they walk off the boat. South of the town there are some fine, long beaches of sand and pebbles, at Plati and Thanos, both with tavernas and some rooms to let.

From Mirina two asphalt roads curve in a half-circle across the island to Moudros Bay. Taking the most northerly road out of town for 8km (5 miles) leads to **Kaspakas**, a quiet and pretty little fishing village with most of its stone houses still intact and the rocky beach of Agios Ioannis nearby. It is hard to imagine that this was the medieval capital of Limnos. The village is also called Zoodochos Pigi ('Fountain of Life'), an apt name as a freshwater spring bubbles beside it, an odd sight on this parched island.

On this northerly route more small villages are passed as you travel across the rocky interior, the scenery lightened by the few vineyards en-route. The southerly route is more direct, going via the large village of Livadohori on its way to Moudros.

Moudros, tucked away in the bay where the ships of the Allied fleet berthed before beginning the assault on Gallipoli in 1915, is not an attractive town, marred by a huge military base. It is from here, though, that a network of minor roads begins, opening up the east of Limnos. Again, there is not a great deal to see, apart from the quiet villages and the wild, serrated coastline. However, **Plaka**, at the north-eastern tip of the island, has the ruins of an ancient city submerged offshore.

Further south, one can see part of the theatre and the agora that belonged to the ancient capital of Hephaistia. Seventeen kilometres (10 miles) due east of Moudros is **Poliokini**, where the impressive walls of this 2000BC settlement can still be seen.

Further Information
— Chios —

Places of Interest

Chios town
Archaeological Museum
Open: 9.30am-2.30pm.
Closed Tuesdays and Sundays.

Byzantine Museum
Open: Tuesday to Sunday 9am-2pm.

Folklore Museum
Open: 5-7pm daily.

Museum of Byzantine Antiquities
The castle
Open: Monday to Saturday 10am-1pm.

Tourist Office
1 Kanaris Street
☎ (0271) 24217
Open: Monday to Friday 7am-2.30pm, Saturday 9.30am-1.30pm, Sunday 10am-1pm.
May also be open evenings, during the summer.

Nea Moni
Monastery
Open: daily, dawn to dusk.
Closed 1-4pm.

Pirgi
Church of Agii Apostolii
Open: 10am-2pm.
Closed Mondays and Fridays.

Accommodation Possibilities

Chios town
Chandris Hotel (B)
☎ (0271) 25761

Diana (C)
☎ (0271) 25993

Giannis (Pension)
☎ (0271) 27433

Kambos
Perivoli (P)
☎ (0271) 31513

Kardamila
Kardamila (B)
☎ (0271) 22378

Mesta
Information on accommodation
☎ (0271) 76319

Pipidis
(operated by Tourist Office)
☎ (0271) 76319
Lida (Pension)
☎ (0271) 76217

Pirgi
Womens' Agricultural and Tourist Co-operative
☎ (0271) 72496

PSARA
Information on accommodation
☎ 0272 61293

10 • Island Hopping in the Dodecanese

Introduction

Scattered across the South Aegean Sea, with many hugging the coastline of Western Turkey, are the islands of the Dodecanese. Literally translated, the name means 'twelve islands' although there are in fact sixteen inhabited islands in total, each with their own characteristics, peculiarities and personality. However, they are all bound together by a common heritage that has been turbulent, violent and marked by foreign powers' domination. Indeed, these islands only officially became part of Greece in 1948; unofficially they have always been Greek.

The chain covers a large expanse of ocean, from tiny Agathonissi in the north to isolated Kastellorizo in the south, from rocky Astipalea in the west to the flagship island of Rhodes in the east. Yet in season, and even accounting for changeable weather conditions that can rapidly turn smooth seas choppy and thus frustrate ferry schedules, getting from one to the other is a relatively simple affair.

Distances are short, particularly along the islands that run alongside the Turkish coast, and passenger ferries and private excursion boats operate regularly. These small boats are an excellent alternative to the huge ferries; they normally shuttle day-trippers to islands near their own but one-way tickets are available and the boats usually run daily. Destinations, departure times and prices for these boats are advertised each night along the main harbour of each island. However, the boats tend to run only in season — between May and September — and outside of these months they are very few and far between. Also, regular ferry services between the islands may drop to one per week. On the islands, many of the facilities taken for granted in the summer — accommodation, public transport and tavernas — close down in winter. For these reasons, as well as for the wonderful climate, it is best to visit the Dodecanese in season.

251

Of all the islands in the group, Rhodes and Kos are the best-known and with very good reason. Both are a travel agent's dream — beautiful and intriguing with fine museums, glorious beaches and international airports. However, they most certainly are not off the beaten track and so neither is included here, except when serving as a transportation hub to the other islands.

Much of what can be found on Rhodes and Kos can be found on many of the smaller, less-visited islands and a lot more besides; a magnificently imposing monastery on the Holy Island of Patmos, a dormant volcano on Nissiros and a truly timeless village on Karpathos are all good examples.

From Samos, technically a North-East Aegean island but one only a 2 hour boat journey from Patmos, a day-trip can be made to Ephesus. This, the best-preserved of all the cities of Ancient Greece, ironically now lies in Turkey. However, each island boasts remnants of the region's history and so to fully appreciate the attractions of the Dodecanese, a little background knowledge of the past is needed.

Some of the islands of the Dodecanese were deemed worthy of a mention by Homer in *The Iliad* for having sent ships and troops to the siege of Troy, that 10 year venture by King Menelaus of Sparta to rescue his wife Helen from within its walls. Apart from a few bleak centuries of rule by the northern Dorians, the islands prospered both materially and intellectually during ancient times.

Kos was the leading island of the group, its most famous son being the great Hippocrates whose famous oath for medical practitioners is still sworn today. The descendants of Ptolemy of Egypt, an ex-general of Alexander the Great, ruled the islands briefly until around 160BC when the mighty Roman Empire swallowed up the region.

By the fourth century, Rome had been usurped by the Byzantines whose rule in the Dodecanese continued undisturbed until the eleventh century. Then several Crusaders en-route to the Holy Land ended their journey at the Dodecanese and began to fortify their own little fiefdoms in parts of the islands.

By this time, the Byzantine Empire was on the point of collapse and a group of Genoese pirates were quick to take advantage, gaining control of the Dodecanese. They sold the islands in 1309 to a privileged band of Crusader knights, the Knights of St John, who had fled the Holy Land in 1291 at the fall of their capital, Acre, to the Ottomans.

Most of the castles seen in the Dodecanese today — and almost every island has one — were either constructed or renovated by the Knights. Their rule lasted for over 200 years until Suleiman the

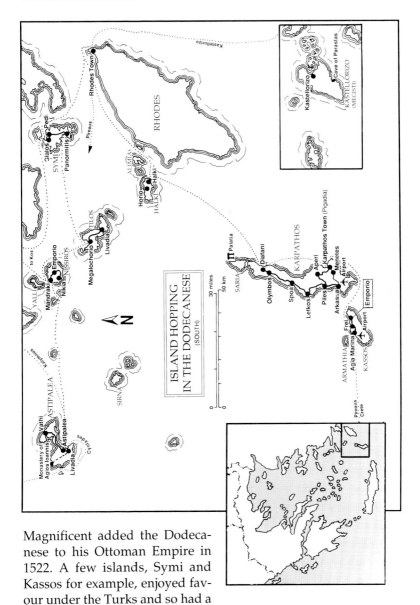

Magnificent added the Dodecanese to his Ottoman Empire in
1522. A few islands, Symi and
Kassos for example, enjoyed favour under the Turks and so had a
consequent degree of autonomy. However, the participation of the
islands in the Greek War of Independence (1821-27) only incited the
Turks to commit atrocities to keep the islands under their control.
Over 7,000 men were killed on Kassos alone.

The defeat of the Ottomans in the 1912 Balkan War saw off the
Turks in the Dodecanese. The Turks, though, were replaced by the

Fascist Italians. The Italians did not neglect the Dodecanese in the way the Turks had done and a lot of money was invested in public buildings and archaeological excavations. Their attempts to stamp out the Greek language and culture, however, were loathed by the populace. Many of the blue and white houses, stairways and churches seen on the smaller Dodecanese islands were painted in defiance of this policy — blue and white being the colour of the Greek national flag.

When the Italians switched sides during World War II, the Germans arrived, only to be driven out by British forces. At the war's conclusion, there was never any doubt that these Greek islands would at last become part of modern Greece and a treaty signed in March 1948 on the small island of Symi, made it official.

Once on the islands, finding places to sleep and to eat should rarely pose a problem. All have hotels (although Luxury and 'A' class establishments can only be found on Rhodes and Kos) but a very popular option is to stay in private rooms. On most of the islands, room-owners approach new arrivals as they clamber off the boat with offers of rooms that are usually clean and inexpensive. Just beware of being driven out to a place that is miles from where you want to be. Prices are often negotiable, particularly if you are staying 3 nights or more.

Where there are hotels and rooms to let, there are also tavernas. Waterfronts are often lined with restaurants serving a variety of international cuisine. However, for authentic Greek eating, look out for the small, menu-less tavernas that cater for locals where one can visit the kitchen and look in the pots to see what is on offer. In the Dodecanese, as in most of the island groups, seafood is the standard fare.

Transport on the islands can be a problem if one relies on public bus services which, if they exist at all, are usually very infrequent. Hiring one's own transport is best, either a car, motorbike or moped. Be aware that in the case of the latter two, insurance is often third-party only and crash helmets are rarely supplied. Bicycles can be rented very cheaply on the island of Leros and hitch-hiking is popular among the very budget conscious. Some of the Dodecanese islands are very small; just walking between villages can be very pleasurable.

Karpathos

It is quite extraordinary that the long and slender island of Karpathos draws as few tourists as it does. It contains a little bit of everything for everybody; from lovely beaches, to deserted rambles, to ancient but living villages. The number of visitors have certainly increased in recent years, as have the relevant facilities, but Karpathos still has a long way to go before rivalling the major tourist meccas of Rhodes and Crete which it lies halfway between.

Two ports service Karpathos — Diafani in the north and Pigadia (commonly called **Karpathos town**) in the south. The latter is a busy and modern town — the island's capital — and endowed with plenty of hotels and tavernas, making it the ideal base from which to explore the south of the island. There is a sandy beach here, worth a visit for a swim and for a look at the ancient basilica of Agia Fotini that dates back 15 centuries. Only recently discovered, its remains stand enclosed on the beach under shady trees. The bus service that connects Karpathos town to the rest of the island is at best infrequent so, to see Karpathos properly, rent a car or motorbike.

Despite the stony and desolate appearance of the south, most of the beaches are sandy and inviting with **Ammopi**, 7km (4 miles) south of Karpathos town, being the most popular. The village has several rooms to let. For some seclusion, head south along the sand. By heading back inland, the turn-off for the airport, positioned at the southern tip of the island, is passed before reaching the village of **Menetes** with its large and imposing church and tiny folk museum.

The same road runs on to **Arkassa** on the western coast. There are good beaches here and several rooms to let for those who wish to spend a few days stretched out on the sand. If sunbathing gets a little tedious, there are always the ancient ruins of ancient Arkassa to visit. The crumbled walls south-west of the town date back 30 centuries and the ruined Byzantine church on the shore has bright floor mosaics, visible if you brush away the sand.

North of Karpathos town, but still very much in the south of the island, the landscape becomes lusher and more mountainous as the highest point on Karpathos, Mount Kalilimni (1,188m, 3,900ft) is neared. The region shelters some lovely villages such as **Aperi** which stands above two quiet beaches and was once the old capital of the island. Its cathedral shelters an icon of the Virgin Mary which has allegedly miraculous powers.

From the village of Piles on the western coast, a road runs up to the beautiful retreat of **Lefkos** with its quite sandy beach hemmed in by trees. North-east are the villages of Mesochorio and Spoa, the former nestled in the mountains, the latter with a nearby beach and the best starting-off point for the long trek to the north.

The north of Karpathos could easily be another island, it certainly seems to exist in another age. Connected to the south only by a dirt track that squirms its way snake-like through Mount Kalilimni, this region has, until very recently, been almost totally shut off from the outside world. Consequently, an ancient way of life is led by many, most noticeably in the timeless village of Olymbos.

Getting to the north can be easy or a struggle, depending on taste. It is possible to make the 6 hour trek from Spoa to Olymbos, passing countryside that was unfortunately devastated by a 1983 forest fire that destroyed the pines. Taxis also make the long and expensive journey. The easiest route is by sea, either by passenger ferry en route to Rhodes or one of the excursion caiques that make the trip daily in season to the port of **Diafani**. Rooms to let are available here and a stony but pleasant beach is a half hour walk to the north.

From Diafani you can walk or take the minibus that meets the excursion boats to the village of **Olymbos**, high in the mountains. Great views over the western coast of Karpathos and tiny houses beautifully decorated with bright paintings and ornate plaster designs are only the most obvious attractions of this attractive village. The real appeal lies in the lifestyle its residents lead, one that has barely altered in centuries.

The bakery has not yet reached Olymbos and bread is still baked in outdoor stone ovens from wheat that is still ground by windmill. It is baked by women, who, dressed in their traditional costumes of white shirt, patterned apron and red goatskin boots, seem to dominate the village and not just because most of the men work outside the town or island, sending their money home. For property inheritance is matrilineal here, with wealth being passed on to the eldest daughter rather than the eldest son. The men that remain take a back seat while still retaining the *kafenion* as their customary preserve. Even the local dialect has a venerable touch, using some words that were last heard in the rest of Greece 25 centuries ago.

Traditional feasts and weddings are a sight to behold at Olymbos and it is a lucky visitor who turns up on the day of one. The festival of the Assumption of the Virgin Mary on 15 August is celebrated with good food and traditional music and dancing. Be warned that accommodation in the several pensions may be hard to find at this time.

The rest of the north is sparsely inhabited and what cultivatable land exists is being farmed by those from Olymbos. Between 27 August and 29 August, though, a large and happy festival takes place in celebration of Agios Ioannis, held in a chapel of the same name at Vrugunda, north of Olymbos. Those who wish to attend the full 2 day festivities should bring a sleeping bag — there is no available accommodation and participants sleep under the stars.

Further north still, day-trips can be made from Diafani to the northern islet of **Saria**. Now deserted, several ruined villages can be seen including Palatia, built as a base for pirates during the Byzantine era.

Kassos

First impressions can always be deceiving but this is particularly so in the case of Kassos. Constantly buffeted by stormy seas, this austere limestone rock of an island appears to offer little more than sheer cliffs and a stony, scrubby landscape. Yet, for the right person, Kassos is the ideal retreat; there are several beaches, a welcoming population and hardly a tourist in sight. For this is the least visited island in the southern Dodecanese.

The bulk of the 1,000 residents of Kassos live in the central section of the island — the extremities are virtually deserted — and it is here that the small fishing town of **Frei** is located. It is the island's capital and is built around the blue bay of Bouka. Frei is the most convenient base for a stay on Kassos with a couple of hotels, money-changing facilities and an airport with flights to Rhodes, Karpathos and Sitia (Eastern Crete) that is only a 15 minute walk away. Near the airport is Ammoudia, the sandy town beach. Frei is connected by bus or by a short walk to Emporio, its neighbouring port up the coast.

Inland, and again within easy walking distance, are several small and photogenic villages; one of them **Agia Marina**, being 2km (1 mile) from the main 'attraction' of Kassos, the stalactite and stalagmite-filled cave of Selai. South of the village of Poli is the monastery of Agios Memas, dedicated to the patron saint of shepherds.

Further south, at the end of a green and quiet valley, is the beautifully secluded beach of Helathros. More good swimming is to be found on **Armathia**, a small islet linked by caique to Frei.

In the early part of the nineteenth century, Kassos was a relatively prosperous island that enjoyed a good degree of autonomy under its Turkish overlords. However, the War of Independence (1821-27) put an end to that and dealt Kassos a blow from which it never really recovered.

In July 1824, a massive force led by Ibrahim Pasha of Egypt set sail from Alexandria in aid of the beleagured Turks. The first island they encountered was Kassos and, in the ensuing slaughter, 7,000 Kassiot men died and their women and children were taken into slavery. Every 7 June, an all-night ceremony is held in memory of that terrible event. A happier festival, with music and dancing, is held every 17 July in the village of Agia Marina in honour of the saint of the same name.

Kastellorizo (Megisti)

Kastellorizo (Megisti) is not ideally positioned for the island hopper. Geographically, it is about as far off the beaten track as one can get in Greece. The island is over 300 nautical miles from Pireaus and 6 hours sailing over sometimes choppy waters from its nearest Greek neighbour, Rhodes. In addition, as it is impossible to travel further south in Greece from here, to visit is a long hop from Rhodes and a long hop back again. However, Turkish Kas is only a nautical mile away and this would be the best jumping-off spot to visit Kastellorizo from. Unfortunately, the obduracy of the Greek and Turkish governments occasionally renders the crossing impossible.

Kastellorizo is connected to Athens by air but the island has few visitors. Few residents (roughly 200) live here, supported mainly by the remittances sent home by the many who have left.

The 'Megisti' in the island's name refers to 'big' or 'maximum', quite a misnomer when one considers that its land mass is only 3km by 7km (2 miles by 4 miles). Yet Kastellorizo is larger than the small, uninhabited islands that surround it, hence the addition to its name. Prior to World War I, it was a prosperous trading post for the Greek cities of Asia Minor but the Italian occupation, an earthquake in 1927 and an ammunition dump explosion that levelled half of the island's homes during World War II, all hastened a steady decline. Today it is quiet and restful with no beaches as such but plenty of opportunities to swim in clear water off the rocks. There is a hotel and there are some private rooms to let.

Kastellorizo is also the name of the island's only town, a town whose former grandeur is evident in the stately but now deserted mansions that stand near the waterfront. Next to the old mosque there is a small museum of local history. Dominating the area and built by the Knights of St John, is the ruined Kastello Rosso (the 'red castle' from which the island derives its name).

Two sites outside the town are worth a visit — the church of Agia Konstantinos and Helena, whose granite pillars once shored up a temple to Apollo in Anatolia; and the Paleokastro, south-west of the town and the site of an Hellenic fortress-style settlement. From the harbour, a caique can be hired to make the short journey to the eastern coast to view the Cave of Parastas, crammed with stalactites reflecting off the multi-tinted blues of the water.

Halki

This is a marvellous island on which to simply relax and do nothing. Its 40km² (15sq miles) of limestone rock have little to entice the mainstream tourist — no graceful acropolis, no green valleys and mountains, not even a small museum. However, those seeking to 'get away from it all', could not find a better place.

Halki's sponge-fishers made the island a prosperous one in the last century but disease struck down the region's sponges with the result that now only 400 people live on the island, mostly in the port and capital of **Nimporio** (also called Halki). Built around the bay, its whitewashed houses are dwarfed by the church of Agios Nikolaos. Accommodation is available in the form of a few waterfront tavernas and several rooms to let. The nearest beach is a 15 minute walk away along 'Tarpon Springs Boulevard'. This is hardly the most common Greek street name; the paved road was financed by Halki expatriots living in Florida. The beach itself is pleasant, sandy and very small.

Secluded coves can be found along the island's coastline and are reached by caique from the harbour. Caiques also make the crossing to Alimia, a green and quiet islet to the east of Halki with several beaches. Thirty minutes walk inland leads to **Horio**, the old capital of Halki but now deserted. The ruins of the castle of the Knights of St John are here and nearby is the church of Stavros, host to a large festival on 14 September.

In 1983, the United Nations declared Halki an Island of Peace and Friendship of Young People of All Nations, a cumbersome name for a cumbersome project that collapsed under the weight of its own bureaucracy. The plan was for Halki to host an annual youth conference, converting old mansions into guest houses and constructing a hotel for delegates.

The Halkian economy benefited accordingly and tourism increased. However, frequent disruptions led to the project's cancellation and islanders have decided to encourage tourism by their own efforts; bit by bit, they are succeeding.

Tilos

This is another small island, sandwiched between Halki and Nissiros in the southern Dodecanese. It is one of those islands where relaxation is the best form of recreation. The 500 residents of Tilos live life at an unhurried pace — motor vehicles are few and far between and the most common forms of transport are the caique and the donkey. Although day-trippers from Rhodes and Kos sometimes disturb the calm, very few visitors stay one night or more. Those that do, discover a well-watered, pleasingly unspoilt island with several beaches and, as public transport is non-existent, some good opportunities for walking.

The island's port is at **Livadia**, a small town with a few restaurants, some rooms to let and a couple of hotels to cater for visitors. It boasts a long, pebbly beach. It is probably better to stay here than in the main town of **Megalochorio** ('big town') which has only the barest tourist facilities — a few rooms to let and a couple of restaurants that only open in the evening. The name is at best misleading — this is a small village built on the site of ancient Tilos; the walls near the ruined Venetian castle date back 30 centuries and finds from the area can be seen in the tiny local museum.

A forty minute walk south leads to the beach at Eristas, which is wide and claimed to be the island's finest. West of the town is the pleasant beach of Agios Antonios. A path also leads here from Livadia but allow at least 90 minutes for the walk. In a cave between Livadia and Megalochorio some of the bones of the woolly mammoths that used to live around Tilos were recently discovered.

Creature comforts are sometimes difficult to find on Tilos — there are no luxury hotels and, despite its abundance of water, very little in the way of fresh food. Out of season, it is best to bring a few provisions along. If arriving over a weekend, be sure to have enough drachmas for a few days' survival; the post office (open Monday to Friday 7.30am-2.30pm) is the only place where money can be changed.

Symi

Symi is one of the loveliest islands in the Dodecanese and by now would almost certainly be a mini-Rhodes if the island was not hindered by one factor — a severe lack of fresh water. Being so dry, rocky and parched, it is simply unable to supply the vast amounts of water that a string of high-class hotels would require. Due to this, most of the visitors to Symi come over on day trips from Rhodes, a 90 minute journey, thus making the island a bustling place during the day. However, by late afternoon, the excursion boats begin to chug away and Symi returns to the Symians and the handful of visitors who stay overnight here to enjoy the peace and calm.

The island has only 2,500 inhabitants who mostly derive their income from the day-trippers, a far cry from the heady days of the past when Symi was the most important island of the Dodecanese after Rhodes. Its importance was based around its shipbuilding

The ornate tower of
Panormitis monastery,
Symi

skills, for which it has been famed since the days of the Trojan War;
the rapid wooden vessels produced here were favoured by the
Knights of St John and the Turks.

Sponge-diving was also a prime money-spinner for the Symians,
who paid their taxes to the Turks in sponges. In time the island was
granted a high level of autonomy by the Ottomans and the island
flourished, its tiny mass accommodating up to 30,000 inhabitants.

The advent of the steamship and the decline in the sponge industry, as profitable beds became diseased, caused a drastic drop in the
island's fortunes and the splendid mansions around the main port of
Gialos are now in a sad state of dilapidation. Yet the island's beauty
is unscarred and its residents are welcoming, particularly to those
who stay a few days.

The port and old ship-building centre of **Gialos** is a fine introduction to Symi; built around a deep blue bay, its houses painted
with cheerful splashes of colour. There are more than a few signs of
commercialism, though, as you alight from the boat; photographers

happily snap away at new arrivals and waiters steer people towards empty seats. One restaurant that is worth a look is Les Katerinettes, on the waterfront — it was here in March 1948 that the treaty giving the Dodecanese to Greece was signed. There are two hotels and several rooms to let but ensure that running water is available before agreeing to a room.

To discover more of the character of Symi, walk around the harbour and ascend the steep steps to the old capital of **Horio**, virtually untouched by tourism and a wonderful place to wander amongst small white terraced houses and meandering, unmarked streets.

At the top of the village are many shattered houses, the result of an ammunition dump explosion during World War II. There are several churches, a museum exhibiting local archaeological finds and, at the top of the town, a ruined Byzantine fortress. The views from any part of Horio are gorgeous.

Sheltered in the south of the island at the centre of a stunning horseshoe of a bay, is the monastery of Panormitis, named after the patron saint of Symi. All excursion boats from Rhodes stop here, despite the fact that without its impressive bell-tower, the actual structure has more in common with a penitentiary. However, the chapel is richly decorated, featuring gold incense pots dangling from the ceiling and providing a dash of colour against the charred and fading frescoes, blackened by flickering candles.

Just behind the chapel, in a shady courtyard, is a museum. This is a delightful mish-mash of goodies including a grandfather clock, sponges, swords, ivory tusks and, for reasons perhaps best-known to the monks, a stuffed crocodile. Basic but inexpensive accommodation is available at the monastery and there is a small taverna at the end of the bay past a tiny sandy beach. Panormitis is linked by road to Gialos.

As can only be expected from such a rocky island, Symi's beaches are of the pebbly variety. Nearest to Gialos, a 15 minute walk north, is Nos beach; keep on the same road for 30 minutes to reach the beach at Emporio, which is nothing very special.

Pedi, 3km (2 miles) east of Gialos, is a surprisingly green village with a beach and a few rooms to let and more swimming is to be had at Agios Nikolaos, 20 minutes away on foot. Further afield, accessible only by walking or by boat, are the caves at Agia Marina and Agios Vassilios. At the very west of Symi, the monastery of Agios Emilianos stands adjacent to a pleasant bay.

Nissiros

Very few tourists stay overnight on the lush island of Nissiros, but in season a fair few day-trippers make the 90 minute crossing from Kos and with good reason. For Nissiros boasts a geological sight unique to the region — a large, and thankfully dormant volcano.

The volcano is named after the Titan Polyvates, who features heavily in the mythology of Nissiros. Legend has it that Polyvates, weakening in battle with the sea-god Poseidon, fled, only to be squarely struck by a huge rock the fearsome Poseidon had torn from Kos and flung after him. The rock pinned Polyvates to the sea-bed and became known as Nissiros while the periodic groans and grumbles of the volcano are said to be those of the hapless Titan, trying to squeeze out of his watery prison.

Nissiros itself has a charming and reasonably prosperous air, its population of 1,300 (down from 12,000 in the fifteenth century) deriving its income from the farming of citrus fruits and olives, fishing and from quarrying pumice on the nearby islet of Yalli.

As with many small Greek isles, it has been hit hard by the emigration of many residents to Australia and the USA but the remittances sent home by ex-patriots provide a welcome boost to the island's economy.

Cosy **Mandraki**, capital of Nissiros, is a good introduction to the island. Built on flat ground rather than the more favoured hill-side locations, the whitewashed houses and very narrow streets on the waterfront give way to a more typically modern European residential area as one moves inland and large detached houses with gardens can be seen. There are several hotels of varying standards and more than a few tavernas to cater for day-trippers, most of which are sited on the water's edge.

At the far end of town away from the harbour, on a high rock peering out to sea, is the monastery of Panagia Spiliana. Whitewashed steps lead up to the entrance before the visitor descends into a chapel, painstakingly hewn out of the rock. A 'miraculous' icon of the Panagia hangs here, dripping with silver plates that each depict a part of the body and were placed there by worshippers praying for the relief of a specific ailment. The monastery was built on the site of an old Venetian castle, ruins of which stand just before the entrance.

Further down the coast are the impressive ruins of the Paleokastro, an ancient castle first constructed around 500BC. By scrambling over the rocks at the foot of Panagia Spiliana, a black pebble beach is reached. The sea here can get a little choppy and is not really suitable for children.

Nine hundred Nissirians live in the capital, the remaining 400 being split between the villages of Pali, Emporio and Nikia, which are all linked by road from Mandraki. The first landmark on this road are the hot spas at **Loutra**, now deserted but with a sandy beach nearby. Pali, on the northern tip of Nissiros, boasts the long beach of Lies and has several rooms available for visitors. The road cuts inland here to **Emporio**, now inhabited by only five families but offering good views of the volcano.

Further on, located at a height from which the island of Tilos is easily visible, is **Nikia**. The large overhanging rock that dangles nearby is named Calacana after a wise old lady of the village. From here it is an hour's walk to the Polyvates volcano. Usually, however, it is not necessary to walk. A local travel agency bus shuttles between Mandraki and the edge of the crater daily in season, its frequency and departure times dependent on the amount of day-trippers on the island.

Travelling by road, you can see the landscape change from a soothing green to a stark and dour desert brown. This is perhaps one of the most forbidding regions of Greece. A powerful wind howls across the shadeless, featureless plain, swirling up great clouds of sand and dust.

It is a steep but easy descent from the rim of the crater into the volcano proper, where you can wander over the soft yellowy-brown surface. Do not worry about possible eruptions — the last one was on 4 May 1873 and the villagers, who had been expecting volcanic activity, had time to dig channels in the rock to divert the lava back into the crater. A wooden hut nearby sells souvenirs, snacks and drinks.

Those who fancy the long walk back to Mandraki can take an alternative route to the road; a series of donkey tracks that pass the monastery of Stavros. The bus, however, returns to Mandraki 50 minutes after its arrival at the crater.

Astipalea

Dumbell-shaped Astipalea is on the doorstep of the Cyclades and those who know that group of islands will spot similarities, particularly architecturally. Also known as Fish Island (Icthyoessa), its income has long been centred around this industry although recent attempts have been made to entice tourists to its beaches.

Astipalea achieved a certain notoriety in the days of Ancient Greece thanks to a boxer called Kleomedes who competed at Olympia and was victorious, only to be stripped of his laurels for killing

Whitewashed houses in Astipalea town

his opponent. The enraged pugilist returned home and, in a fit of frenzy, demolished the local schoolhouse, killing all those within. It is said that some of the islanders have inherited the temper of Kleomedes but this is hardly fair. It is difficult to get to Astipalea from the rest of the Dodecanese but the island does have its attractions.

The capital and main port, called **Astipalea town**, is composed of row upon row of narrow streets and squared-off, whitewashed houses that lead up steeply to an impressive castle, the work of the Byzantines and the Venetians. Just below the castle is the church of Panagia Portaitissa, worth putting on the itinerary for its delicately carved wooden shrine. The town has a small beach and a selection of small hotels and rooms to let.

Thirty minutes easy walking south over green arable countryside leads to **Livadia**, which boasts a lovely and popular beach with the usual rows of restaurants on the waterfront; rooms to let are available. Further down the coast are the quieter beaches of Tzanaki (unofficially nudist) and Agios Konstantinos.

There is a very limited bus service on Astipalea for travel to the island's extremities, so ask about caiques at the harbour. Walking is often a rewarding option, particularly out to the monastery of Agios Ioannis on the western coast. Trekkers who make the 2 hour journey can take a refreshing dip in pools near the monastery before heading back.

Crossing the natural bridge that connects east and west Astipalea, the villages of Maltelana and Analipsi are passed before reaching **Vathi** with its deep and narrow harbour. Stalactites and stalagmites can be viewed by torchlight at two caves in the village's vicinity — they can be reached either by foot or by caique.

Kalymnos

The craggy island of Kalymnos is one of the more prosperous of the Dodecanese chain but its inhabitants have had to work hard for their wealth. Its infertile soil supports only a relatively minimal amount of agriculture, so islanders farm the sea for sponges.

Sponge-diving is an extremely hazardous occupation, even today when the wet suit and aqualung have long replaced the terrifyingly cumbersome diving suits that were once worn. However, the technique for picking and processing this half-animal, half-plant remains essentially the same. Plucked from deep waters, the sponge is beaten until a black, milky substance squirts out, thus leaving it hard, coarse and black. It is then dipped in both potassium permanganate and

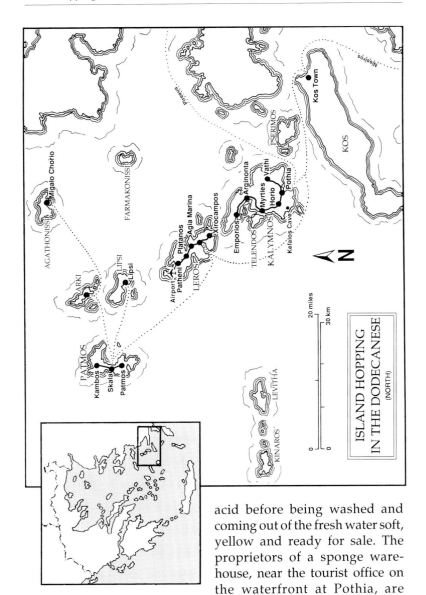

ISLAND HOPPING
IN THE DODECANESE
(NORTH)

acid before being washed and coming out of the fresh water soft, yellow and ready for sale. The proprietors of a sponge warehouse, near the tourist office on the waterfront at Pothia, are happy to demonstrate the process.

The divers' happiest hunting ground was the North African coast until disease struck down the sponges in this area and sent the industry at Kalymnos spiralling downwards. Now it is on the upsurge again, with over forty boats leaving annually for 4 months of the year to dive in Greek, Spanish and Italian waters. Celebrations

Boats arriving at the island of Kalymnos, famed for its sponge-divers

and festivities mark their departure the week after Easter — a good time to be on Kalymnos.

With a little imagination, Kalymnos geographically resembles a miniature United Kingdom, with the tiny islet of Telendos representing its Northern Ireland and Eire. Strangely enough, **Pothia**, the capital and second largest town in the Dodecanese is located just about where London would be and, in terms of relative activity, certainly rivals its larger counterpart. Motorbikes roar ceaselessly down a seemingly endless waterfront and shops and restaurants spill out onto the pavement. This is not everyone's idea of an idyllic island town but certainly one with its own appeal and character.

The waterfront is dotted with sculptures by two local artists — they include a mermaid, the sea-god Poseidon and a tall column dedicated to sponge-divers. There is also a small museum and, further back from the harbour, a network of narrow streets and alleyways that make getting lost almost a pleasurable experience.

The town is sandwiched between two large and impressive churches and, on a hill overlooking Pothia, is the monastery of Agios Pantes, open to appropriately dressed visitors, i.e. no shorts or bare shoulders. The nearest beach is 2km (1 mile) away at Therma, past some hot springs that reputedly have healing properties.

In season, an excursion boat leaves Pothia for the Kephalos Cave

Pleasure boats moored in the picturesque Vathi fjord

at the south of the island, an ancient shrine to Zeus filled with stalactites and stalagmites. Locals claim that it is possible to walk across the island to the cave from Pothia but one look at the rocky, unpathed mountain that must be cleared to reach there, should be enough to send all but the foolhardy scrambling for the boat.

One of the most beautiful spots on Kalymnos is the **Vathi fjord**, a 30 minute drive north of Pothia. The road passes dour landscapes but does overlook beautifully deserted beaches (accessible only by a downhill scramble) before breaking into a green, citrus-tree filled valley that runs down to the fjord with its small fishing boats and crystal-clear water. Swimming is possible here — most bathers head for the Cave of Daskaleios, 100m (110yd) out and featuring more stalactites and stalagmites. Keep a wary eye open for sea urchins though; their spikes can leave victims hopping around in pain for days. Vathi has a small hotel and two tavernas, catering for visitors who want peace and quiet, in a lovely setting where there is absolutely nothing to do.

The western coast of Kalymnos has the best beaches (although none are outstanding) and consequently has more facilities for tourists. Daily buses run regularly out to this area so its better not to walk; it is a long way made worse by the lack of pavements and the intensity of traffic.

The road west out of Pothia passes three disused windmills and the devastated Pera Kastro, a fortress built by the Knights of St John, before **Horio** is reached. This was the old capital of Kalymnos and is pleasantly whitewashed without offering any incentives to stop and linger. A kilometre ($^1/_2$ mile) further west is a ruined Byzantine church, the church of Christ of Jerusalem, built from stones taken from a 400BC temple to Apollo.

The road lurches upwards, then heads down to the coast. A succession of resorts are passed, the beaches being either of grey sand or pebbles — Kantouni, popular and busy; Plati Gialos, less so, and Massouri and Myrties. It is from Myrties that small boats make the 10 minute crossing to the islet of Telendos.

Telendos formed part of Kalymnos until 554BC when a shattering earthquake sheared it away from the main body of the island. Geographically, therefore, it is very similar to its larger neighbour — sparse and rocky but possessing some quiet beaches and several tavernas and guest houses. The largest beach is to the left of the harbour as you enter, reached by passing through a small village and descending steeply. To the right of the harbour the remains of an early Christian church mark the beginning of a string of pebbly beaches; the last one is reserved for nudists. To reach the Byzantine monastery of St Constantine, climb uphill just before this beach.

The north of Kalymnos is practically deserted save for the beaches at Arginonta and Emporios, popular among sunbathers seeking solitude. Hikers in this region will find small goat paths and lovely views of both the coastline, and, looking to the extreme north, of Leros.

A popular destination for day-trippers from both Kalymnos and Kos is the tiny island of **Pserimos**, about 1 hour's sailing from either direction. Outside of the one small settlement are a few quiet and secluded coves for bathing but the main beach near the port is packed in season with sun-seekers on the sand. Having said this, it is a quiet place to spend the night — private rooms are available for let and good fresh fish can be had in the tavernas. There is a good chance that all of the island's accommodation will be snapped up around 15 August, the Feast of the Assumption of the Virgin Mary, for which Pserimos hosts a large festival.

Leros

With a coastline as serrated as a circular saw, Leros has had its greatest natural asset well-exploited over the years — four deep harbours in which whole fleets can shelter. The Phoenicians were among the first to dock their boats here in around 1500BC and, at

Agia Marina, Leros

various stages over the last 70 years, Leros has accommodated the warships of Italy, Germany and Great Britain.

In recent years the island has had to struggle hard against some bleak associations. Not only was it to Leros that political opponents of the Greek military dictatorship of 1967 to 1974 were exiled, but the island is also the base for three psychiatric hospitals incarcerating the extremely disturbed. A recent attempt by the municipality of Leros to encourage tourism suffered a severe setback when accusations of cruelty and neglect to patients in these hospitals were published in a British newspaper, an accusation denied vigorously and angrily by the islanders.

The stigma thus attached to Leros means that it will never become a Rhodes or a Kos but the visitors that do set foot on the island will find it soft and green with beautifully green panoramas, pleasant beaches and a welcoming population. The institutions do provide a constant source of income for its inhabitants; the mass emigration that has affected many of the islands in the Dodecanese has not hit Leros too hard.

A map of Leros shows the island to be divided into three distinct chunks, the busiest being the middle portion, hemmed in as it is by the bays of Panteli, Alinda, Lakki and Gournas. The towns in this region all seem to blend into each other but centrally located

Platanos is the capital, built around an inviting *platia*. Just off the *platia*, opposite the whitewashed church, is the small Antonello museum featuring the bits and pieces that belonged to the powerful nineteenth-century Lerian family of the same name. It is run by descendants of the family and is lovingly presented.

From Platanos it is only a short walk up to the well-preserved Byzantine castle, a structure that dominates Leros. Reach the path by turning right out of the *platia* and then taking the second left, passing houses for the first half of the walk. Once there, large chunks of the island are spectacularly revealed below and a head-scratching few minutes can be spent poring over a map trying to work out which bay is which. The Byzantines, the Knights of St John, the Venetians and the Italian and German armies all used the castle as a look-out post, as do the Greek army today. The result of this is that photographs are forbidden.

Of the two churches built within the walls, the Kyra Kastro houses a miraculous icon of the Panagia (the Virgin Mary) that kept mysteriously finding its way to the castle's ammunition room, despite being repeatedly hung in the main church at Leros. The ammunition room was converted into a church and the icon hangs there, supposedly at peace.

The main port of Leros is at **Lakki**, 3km (2 miles) downhill from Platanos and the most obvious remnant of the Italian presence on the island. The grand, tall buildings either side of wide streets and pavements look oddly out of place on a Greek island; the occupiers presumably built them to show Lerians how wonderful Italian Fascist architecture was. Yet it has several small but leafy parks away from the harbour and manages to conjure up an almost eerie charm.

There are two monuments that are worth a look. One is to a Lieutenant Staphylos who died heroically in 1956 trying to rescue five children who had fallen down a well. The other is to the seamen of the Greek warship *Queen Olga*, sunk by German dive-bombers whilst in dock at Lakki in September 1943, having just completed a series of patrols in the Aegean.

There are several hotels and tavernas and a beach west of the town at Koulouki. If leaving Leros by boat from Lakki, be sure to find out where your vessel docks — the harbour here is huge.

Back in Platanos it is never very far to a beach, whether by walking or hiring transport in the form of a moped or bicycle. Agia Marina is the most popular but Panteli is nearer the capital and Alinda is larger. Two other beaches are at Vromolithos, south of Panteli, and Gournas, past Alinda.

Alinda hosts an annual wine festival (unfortunately there is no exact date for this — either July or August). It is a traditional celebration that had petered out before being restored in the mid 1980s. All the wine is locally produced and free of charge. Again at Alinda, on an unspecified Sunday in August, a sports day is held with competitions for swimming, cycling, running etc. It is very much a family event and open to all.

At the southern tip of Leros lies the small and quiet fishing village of **Xirocampos** where a couple of tavernas, a campsite and private rooms cater for those seeking a few days relaxation on the pebbly beach. Nearby are the ruins of an early Byzantine church, whose floor mosaics date back to the reign of the Emperor Justinian.

At the far northern end of the island, **Patheni** has an army base, an airport and precious little else. Those who like their religious festivals wild and happy may care to visit Leros for the Assumption of the Virgin Mary. This takes places on 15 August and is a national holiday throughout Greece. After the church service a great party is held with live music, food and dancing in the streets.

Patmos

Visitors docking at Skala, capital of Patmos, are greeted by a rather severe sign: 'This is a Holy Island. Therefore, nudism and improper dress is forbidden!'. Well, nobody actually wanders the rolling hills of Patmos naked but the sign does serve as an immediate introduction to the never-ending conflict on this island. It is a conflict between the interests of the church and those of tourism and one that has had the welcome effect of keeping Patmos away from the top of European travel agents' lists of package holiday destinations. For this is a beautiful Greek isle with whitewashed villages, sandy beaches and an enchanting aura — essentially, it is a quiet, soothing place.

The Greek Orthodox Church have every reason for maintaining this serenity. It is certainly appropriate that Patmos is a holy island as it was to here that St John the Theologian, one of the Twelve Disciples of Christ, was exiled in AD95. Indeed, it was here, in a cave overlooking the bay at Skala, that he received his stark vision of the Apocalypse that was duly recorded in Revelations, the final book of the New Testament.

Nearly 1,000 years later a monastery was erected near this cave and is still in operation today, its fortress-like structure dominating Patmos and still retaining a powerful voice on the island that it ruled for nearly 700 years. In recent years the monks have been vociferous in keeping the brakes on tourism — plans to build an international airport here have been shelved — and in portraying a visit to Patmos as a spiritual as much as a physical experience.

Skala is the only commercially developed town on the island and sports the usual rows of small supermarkets, travel agents and restaurants. A pleasant sandy beach, patronised mainly by Greek families, is a 5 minute walk away from the harbour, near the remains of a church where St John would bless and baptise converts to Christianity. There is plenty of accommodation both in hotels and in private rooms. Skala is a pretty but very functional town and visitors soon make the journey up the steep hill to the whitewashed village of Hora and, above that, the monastery of St John the Theologian.

A bus regularly rumbles up this hill but to walk is more rewarding by far, providing excellent views of the narrow 'waist' of Patmos. From the harbour walk directly up the town, take the main road on the left and after 20 minutes a sign points to the small monastery of the Apocalypse, an immaculately maintained structure built around the cave in which St John received the revelations, dictating them to his follower Prochoros.

The cave itself, known as the 'Sacred Grotto of the Revelation', is open to visitors and is entrancing in its simplicity. Silver plating on the walls marks the places where the elderly disciple supposedly rested his head while sleeping and his hands while praying.

From the grotto it is another 15 minutes to **Hora**, the old capital of Patmos and a town that would happily feature on any picture post-card from Greece. Quiet and calm, its cobbled streets and tightly packed houses make for pleasant meanderings. Its commanding views over the sea meant that, in earlier times, pirates and raiders could be spotted from afar. There is a very limited number of rooms to let.

Hora boasts over twenty churches and chapels — unfortunately these are usually locked and locating the caretaker who holds the keys can be a time-consuming and often futile task. However, do not let this worry you as everything pales before the monastery of St John the Theologian in terms of sheer ecclesiastical magnificence.

The appearance of the monastery leaves you wondering whether this is actually a holy place of worship. With massive fortifications and towering look-out posts, all built by successive generations of monks to guard against raiders from Asia Minor, it looks more like a castle. The entrance twists its way through the thick stone walls until a bright and airy courtyard is reached, its left wall adorned with a colourful display of seventeenth-century frescoes.

Two frescoes in particular deserve a closer look, one depicting the ghastly demise of St John (buried alive at his own request), the other relating a battle of miracles between St John and Kynops, a local wizard of the age. St John ended their dual rather abruptly by the simple and quick expedient of turning the unfortunate Kynops into a large rock and casting him into the sea where 'he' has remained ever since, easily visible from the shore. To the right of the courtyard a discreet gift shop sells postcards and detailed guide books.

A door in the frescoed wall leads to the main chapel; cool and dark and filled with mysterious icons, dangling incense pots and some stupendous wood carvings, most notably the altar screen. A silver casket to the right contains the remains of the Blessed Christodoulos, who founded the monastery in 1088 after obtaining the favour and funding of Byzantine Emperor Comenmos. Pass through the side door of the chapel to the monks' bleak refectory.

Returning to the courtyard, a corridor leads to a museum. The Byzantine artefacts housed here — mitres, icons, bibles and parchments dating back to the sixth century — are priceless. So, for many people, are the icons and wood engravings on the second floor of the museum. They are the work of the resident monks and command prices of up to a cool £400 ($600).

After such an intense infusion of Byzantine culture a swim may be needed to clear the head and the keen bather is certainly spoilt for choice. To the north of the island are the beaches of Kampos and Lampi, sandy and pebbly respectively, and at the extreme south, Psiliammos, considered by many to be the island's finest. All of these can be reached on foot over dirt tracks but it is a hard slog.

A far better idea is to take one of the fishing boats that are pressed into service every season as excursion boats for day-trippers. All boats advertise their destinations on the waterfront at Skala every night and leave between 9 and 10am in the morning, returning in the late afternoon.

Closer to Skala there are a couple of very pleasant beaches. Sandy Grikou, south of town and reached by bus from Skala or Hora; and long and shady Moloi beach, a 40 minute walk north of Skala. Follow the signs to the campsite nearby.

At Moloi the notices prohibiting nudism and topless bathing are blithely ignored. The church, unenthusiastic about disrobed bathers but willing to compromise in the conflict of Patmos, tends to turn a blind eye.

Lipsi

The small and green island of Lipsi is linked by ferry with both Leros and Patmos and is a popular day-trip from the latter. Some claim it to be the island where the beautiful nymph Calypso held the heroic Odysseus captive for 10 years, a tale related by Homer in *The Odyssey*. As Lipsi is often referred to as Lipso, the name itself lends some credibility to the legend.

If this was the isle referred to by Homer, Odysseus could at least have comforted himself with the fact that there are many worse places to be held prisoner. Lipsi is an enchanting place and the beaches here are gorgeous. They are, however, no secret to travel agents in Patmos and in season at least one excursion boat a day makes the hour-long crossing.

Of the beaches, Plati Gialos is the finest; sandy with beautifully blue and shallow water. To get there, take one of the small 'taxi-trucks' that regularly leave from the town. Alternatively, you can walk — turn left out of town and keep going for 1 hour.

Nearer to the port are the white pebbles of Choklakora and, further on, is Katsadia, said by some to rival Plati Gialos in beauty. Small and deserted strips of sand appear everywhere around the coastline; just walk to find them; nothing is too far away on Lipsi.

The only town, in Greek island fashion also called Lipsi, has its own pleasant but often crowded beach. Visitors are well catered for; accommodation is available in the hotel Kalypso (which has money-changing facilities) or in private rooms. There are also plenty of tavernas, all of which have fresh fish featuring prominently on the menu.

The main section of town stands above the harbour, centred around a *platia* that numbers among its buildings the Nikiforeion ecclesiastical folk museum which is, as the title suggests, a folk museum with a religious slant. The church has influence on Lipsi — the monastery of St John the Theologian on Patmos owned the island for nearly 600 years and still has property rights here. There are forty-four churches and chapels dotted around the hills. One of these, the Madonna of Charos, a short walk out of Lipsi town, hosts the island's largest festival on 24 August; the dried flowers kept inside the chapel are said to miraculously return to life on this day.

The Tiny Islands

The tiny islands of Arki, Marathi and Agathonissi are loosely clumped together in a group with Patmos to the west, Lipsi to the south and the North-East Aegean island of Samos to the north. None of them hold any awe-inspiring sights or glorious attractions for the visitor; what they offer is pleasant swimming, some fine beaches and peace and quiet. Ferry connections between the islands can be rather sporadic, though, particularly in the off-season when services may well be down to one per week. Those with a fixed flight date out of Greece and who plan to visit the islands towards the end of a vacation ought to bear this in mind.

Agathonissi only has a handful of residents living in the two villages of Migallo Chorio and Mikro Chorio ('big town and little town'). It caters gamely for the few guests that arrive here, with a pension and several tavernas. Even in season, only one ferry per week docks here and so for many it will be just a little bit too far off the beaten track.

Arki, flanked by the small islet of **Marathi**, is a little closer to civilisation and therefore draws excursion boats several times a week from Patmos, usually to swim at Marathi's lovely beach. Arki is small and unspoiled but those that visit will have to do without some of life's 'essentials' — electricity, for example.

Further Information

— The Islands of the Dodecanese —

ASTIPALEA

Connections
Four times a week with Pireaus, twice a week to Kos, Kalymnos and Rhodes.

HALKI

Connections
Daily in season, a caique from Kameros Skala (Rhodes). Otherwise, three times a week with Rhodes, Kassos, Karpathos and Crete. Weekly to Pireaus. Occasional caique to Tilos. Nearest airport — Rhodes.

KALYMNOS

Connections
Daily to Pireaus, Kos, Leros and Patmos. Weekly to Crete, Kassos, Karpathos, Symi, Tilos, Halki, Nissiros. Nearest airport — Leros.

Tourist Office
On the waterfront, near the Poseidon statue.
☎ 0243 29310
Open: daily 7.30am-7pm.

Pothia
Folk Museum
Open: daily 10am-2pm.
Closed Monday and Tuesday.

KARPATHOS

Connections

Three times a week with Rhodes and Pireaus; three times a week to Crete. Four times a week with Kassos. Airport — daily flights to Athens and Rhodes. Weekend flights to Kassos.

Menetes

Folk Museum
Ask locals for the key.
No regular opening hours.

KASSOS

Connections

Twice weekly with Pireaus. Four times a week with Rhodes and Karpathos. Three times a week with Crete. Airport — daily flights to Rhodes and twice weekly to Sitia (Crete) and Karpathos.

KASTELLORIZO (MEGISTI)

Kastellorizo town

Museum of Local History
Next to mosque
Open: 8.30am-2.30pm.
Closed Tuesday.

LEROS

Connections

Daily flights to Athens, three times a week to Kos. By sea, daily to Pireaus, Rhodes, Kos, Kalymnos, Patmos. Excursion boats daily in season to Lipsi. Weekly to Samos.

Platanos

Antonello Museum
Off the main square
Open: 10am-12.30pm, 6-8.30pm.

LIPSI

Connections

Weekly with other Dodecanese islands. In season, daily excursion boats from Leros, Patmos and Kalymnos.
Nearest airport — Leros.

Lipsi town

Nikiforeion Ecclesiastical Folk Museum.
Main square
Open: daily, Monday to Friday 9.30am-1.30pm and 4-8pm; weekends 10am-2pm.

NISSIROS

Connections

In season, daily excursion boats from Kos. Three times a week with Pireaus. Weekly link with the rest of the Dodecanese.
Nearest airport — Kos.

PATMOS

Connections

Daily to Pireaus, Kalymnos, Kos, Leros and Rhodes. Seasonal excursion boats to Pythagorion (Samos) and Lipsi. Once a week to Arki, Agathonissi, Nissiros, Tilos, Symi. No airport — nearest airport — Leros.

Skala

Tourist Office
Off the main square, right as you face the harbour.
☎ 0247 31303
Open: daily in season, 9am-2pm.

Hora

Monastery of St John the Theologian
Open: Monday, Friday and Saturday 8am-2pm; Tuesday and Thursday 8am-1pm, 4-6pm; Wednesday

8am-2pm, 5.30-7pm; Sunday 8am-12noon, 4-6pm.

SYMI

Connections
In season, daily excursion boats from Rhodes. Twice weekly with the rest of the Dodecanese. Nearest airport — Rhodes.

Horio
Museum of memorabilia
At Panormitis Monastery
Open: daily 10am-2pm, closed Saturday and Monday.
Open: when the excursion boats arrive.

TILOS

Connections
In season, regular excursion boats from Rhodes. Twice weekly with Pireaus. Weekly with other Dodecanese islands.
Nearest airport — Rhodes.

THE TINY ISLANDS

Connections
Agathonissi and Arki linked weekly with the rest of the Dodecanese. Frequent excursion boats in season to Arki and Marathi from Patmos.

TOURIST OFFICES

Rhodes
5 Archbishop Makarios and Papagou Streets
☎ 0241 23655/23255

Kos
The waterfront, Kos town
☎ 0242 28724

These are the two main offices serving the Dodecanese. Few of the islands covered here have a tourist office. For other information try either the police (*Asteemonia* in Greek), local travel agents or the town hall in the island's capital. The town halls are usually in the main square and are open Monday to Friday 8am-2pm.

Index

Note: All the main islands are in bold and their places of interest are indexed under them accordingly. All other entries refer to places on the mainland or minor islands.

ACCOMMODATION AND EATING OUT

In some cases accommodation and restaurants may be not as widely available as in more popular areas. Similarly, it is often possible to obtain meals in a local inn. These can frequently be a preferred option on account of cheapness, a chance to try a local dish and mix with local people.

Currency and Credit Cards

The Greek unit of currency is the *drachma* (dx or drx), available most commonly in notes of 5,000, 1,000, 500, 100 and 50 and coins of 50, 20, 10, 5, 2 and 1. Outside the main tourist centres, the 5,000 drx note can sometimes be difficult to dispose of — vendors never seem to have enough change — so when changing money, ask specifically for 1,000 drx and 500 drx notes instead. Another good tip for those heading off the beaten track is the change more money for the trip than one actually needs: although almost every town of any size has a bank, very few of the smaller villages are so blessed.

Changing money at a bank is an easy, if somewhat lengthy process thanks mainly to the practice of having to complete the paperwork at one counter, and then collect the cash at another. Travellers Cheques and hard currencies are accepted by all banks, the larger post offices, many of the more upmarket hotels and, in the well-visited areas, by some restaurants and shops too. Rates of exchange in the hotels though, will invariably be very poor. Eurocheques are valid at the banks, as are cash advances by credit card, although the latter requires a minimum change limit of £60 ($90). Note that the Commercial Bank handles Visa holders while the National Bank caters for Access/Mastercard customers. It should be remembered that in rural areas the use of credit cards may be infrequent or even non-existent. Note too that the vast majority of filling stations are loathe to accept any form of credit card and in all probability, will insist on cash. Bank opening hours are 8am-2pm Monday to Thursday, 8am-1.30pm Fridays.

Those entering Greece with more than US$1,000 in hard currency should declare this to the port authorities on arrival, or risk the imposition of fines or confiscation. There is no limit on gold or gold coins.

Importation of the *drachma* is limited to 100,000.

Greece also has controls on the export of currency. Tourists can take out up to 20,000 drx plus foreign currencies up to the value of US$1,000. Higher amounts are allowed if there has been an import declaration. Those seeking further clarification of these currency import/export regulations should contact their nearest Greek Tourist Office.

Eating Out

Generally speaking, fine cuisine is not one of the great delights of Greece and those visitors who never venture beyond the established tourist spots are particularly liable to disappointment. There are some noble exceptions of course, but the 'international' restaurants of the resorts, usually called 'Zorba's' or 'Apollo's' or something equally pseudo-Greek, do have a sad tendency to offer fare that is either dull, stodgy, overpriced or quite possibly, all three. Those who intend to travel off the beaten track however, can look forward to far more satisfying culinary experiences. In the less visited regions, a restaurant may lack the glitz and cosmopolitanism of its counterparts in the resorts — indeed, some may look distinctly down at heel — but the food will be consistently of a higher standard, and more reasonably priced: local restauranteers, after all, have to put up with the demands of a highly critical local clientele. One can also be sure that, for better or worse, the eatery in which one dines will at least be authentically Greek. Yet eating in the rarely frequented regions can, for the uninitiated, at first be a confusing experience so, to help ease matters, here follows a step by step guide to eating out when off the beaten track in Greece.

First, one has to decide when to dine. Although as a rule, Greeks tend to eat late — around 2.30pm for the midday meal, between 9pm and 10pm in the evening — some restaurants in the smaller towns and the villages will open early in the morning, and then close when all the food that was prepared that morning, and kept warm throughout the day, has been sold — at around 7pm. Watch out for this to avoid late evening hunger. In the larger towns and the cities, it is possible to get a meal at any time up to midnight and often beyond.

Secondly, there is the question of recognising a restaurant, as in the out-of-the-way areas, they do not advertise themselves in English. Consequently, one has to be familiar with the Greek terminology and the signs *estiatorio* and *taverna* are the ones to look out for. An *estiatorio* is usually a no-frills, workers-type eatery, selling a selection of stews, macaroni, soups and so on from steam warmed hot trays. It is likely to be cheap, cheerful and possibly scruffy but do not worry about that. One never judges by appearances when off the beaten track in Greece. A *taverna* is a step up from this, with various fish and meat dishes grilled to order and always a good selection of salads and wines. The sign *kafenion*, which the visitor will see plenty of, does not denote 'café' or 'restaurant' as one may expect. Rather, it is the Greek equivalent of the English pub or American bar.

The *estiatorio* is by far the most common of eateries in the out of the way areas, so let us assume you have found one open and have entered it. It will be clean enough, with tables well wiped and a floor that has been brushed at least once that day. To one side will be the steamer, filled with stainless-steel trays of hot food and attended by a ladle-wielding chef. The idea is that you examine what is on offer and tell the chef, whereupon he will spoon the dish or dishes you order onto plates and have it brought to you at your table. If you and the chef have a common language, then this will be no problem. If you are prepared to just point and hope, then that is no problem either. But if you want to know exactly what it is that you are ordering, and there is a language barrier, then that is when difficulties can occur.

Asking for a menu will not be much help. If the *estiatorio* has one — and that is a definite 'if', then it will be in Greek. As such, it is worth knowing the Greek names for the most common dishes on offer always, of course, prefacing your request with *paragalo* (please) — the Greeks are a polite people, with plenty of patience for children and the elderly.

Dolmardes — stuffed vine leaves

Makaronia — macaroni

Patates — potatoes/french fries

Tomates yemistas — stuffed tomatoes

Melitzanes yemistas — stuffed aubergine

Fassolia — beans

Moussaka — eggplant/potato/ground meat

Pastitsio — noodles and ground meat

Spanaki — spinach

Horiatia — Greek salad (tomatoes, cucumber, feta cheese) can be improved by tossing it with a 1:3 measure of vinegar: oil, adding salt and pepper to taste.

Whatever dishes you order they will all arrive at the same time, all be luke warm and all be drenched in olive oil which is how the Greeks like it. Besides, one can get used to food that is served in this manner, particularly the olive oil which, after all, is easier to digest than other oils. Mop it up with the bread which will have been heaped upon your table, and it tastes delicious. Do not expect a side plate for the bread, incidentally — a paper napkin is used instead — and do not expect the bread to be anything other than thick, white and crusty — wonderful when fresh but, like baked cardboard when not. To accompany the meal one can always ask for soft, fizzy drinks or *nero* (water) but a request for beer or wine may well be met with an upward inclination of the head and a sorrowful *oki* (no).

Ordering food in a *taverna* can also be quite an experience. Immediately upon arriving, expect to be whisked into the kitchen so that you may inspect the delights on offer that day. A fridge door will be flung open and trays of glistening meat revealed. Which piece would you like? This one? Or that one? You do not want meat? No problem. See this fish! And another fridge will be open and a fish hoisted out with a flourish. Then another. And another. If you choose one — and there is really no obligation — it will be fried on the spot to order. Just remember that you pay by the kilo and not by the fish so it is worth asking for an estimate beforehand of how much an individual portion will cost. You can try to haggle the restauranteer down in price but do not expect too much success. Fish, is one of the more costlier foods in Greece due to fishing methods used in the past that have led to the seas being overfarmed.

One of the more pleasing aspects of the *taverna* is its selection of *mezes* or starters, several of which come in the form of dips. You can try *tzatziki* (yoghurt, cucumber and garlic), *melitzano-salata* (eggplant dip) or whatever else catches the eye. Taken together, with a plentiful supply of bread, the *mezes* can form a very tasty meal in themselves. There is also often a good selection of salads on offer, and a choice of beers and wines.

Yet whether in an *estiatorio* or a *taverna*, the customer is likely to be disappointed when it comes to dessert. A few pieces of fresh fruit may be available, or if you are lucky some ice cream, but all told it is probably better to settle the bill at this point and go in search of a *zacharoplastio*. Any medium-sized town will have several of these bright, clean, pleasant cafés which serve tea, coffee and enticing, gooey, hopelessly calorific sweets such as honey-drenched *baklava*.

Paying the bill, occasionally the source of an evening-spoiling argument in the restaurants of the tourist resorts, should pose no problem when off the beaten track. Slipping the odd extra item or two and other tricks like that are rarely even contemplated in the out of the way area. You may find that a small sum — 100 *drachmas* or so — has mysteriously appeared on the bill but do not worry about that: it will be for the bread which you get whether you want it or not. It is the same for the locals. Pay the bill in cash, Greek *drachmas* (not US dollars or English pounds) and leave the credit card in the pocket or purse; except in very few instances, it will not be accepted. Tipping is not compulsory but if you have been served by a young boy and you are reasonably happy with his service, it is nice to leave a few coins: tips may well be all he earns.

Snacks are big news in Greece. The most popular of fast foods is still the *souvlaki* — pieces of grilled meat, served with chips and salad and wrapped in pita bread — but *tost* is catching up fast. *Tost* stalls and shops are everywhere, selling toasted sandwiches with a quite bewildering choice of fillings. Then there is *tiropitta* and *spanakopitta*, cheese and spinach pies respectively, very tasty and very cheap. One can also get pizza and, particularly in Thrace, doner kebab.

Breakfast is not a meal that the Greeks attach a great deal of importance to and when off the beaten track, finding a restaurant that serves
it can be a problem. If you are staying in a hotel that supplies breakfast
then you will have no worries beyond the quality of what may be
supplied — white bread, an egg, jam, a few slices of processed cheese
and ham and tea or coffee is what most hoteliers seem to believe their
guests enjoy for breakfast. Alternatively, one can buy and make ones
own breakfast. Look out for a *fornio* (bakery) to supply the fresh bread,
buy jam and sumptious Greek *yiorte* (yoghurt) at a local shop, finish it off
with tea or coffee at a nearby *zacharoplastio* and you have a meal to set you
up for the day.

Retsina, a pine-resinated wine that could be termed as the national
drink, may well make you shudder after the first sip. Yet persevere: once
the taste has been acquired it can be loved and there is no better liquid
companion than this for staring out onto a gentle sea on a clear moonlit
night. The more conventional wines can be pretty good as well; the
brands from Samos and Patras particularly so. Amstel is the most common brand of beer and is perfectly acceptable, as is *metaxa*, the fiery
Greek brandy. A wide variety of soft drinks is available, as is tea (served
without milk) and coffee. Greek coffee will either be of the thick, Turkish
variety (ask for it *me gala* if you want milk) or instant, in which case it is
referred to as *nes. Nes* can often be best enjoyed served iced in a glass,
which the Greeks call *cafe frappe*. Otherwise, one can stick to water.
Greece's tap water is safe to drink and in many of the off the beaten track
areas, where the water runs down from mountains high, it may well be
the sweetest you have ever tasted.

Telephone Services

The easiest and cheapest way to place an international telephone call
from Greece is to use the services of the OTE (Organismos Tilie-
pikinonion tis Elladhos), the national telecommunications agency. Most
towns have an office of the OTE, identifiable by a yellow sign and usually
located next to the town's main post office. Once inside the OTE office,
choose one of the telephone booths (the international booths are all
marked accordingly), check that the meter inside is set to zero (if it is not,
ask the clerk at the counter to reset it), dial and make your call. As you
speak, the meter will clock up the cost of the call in *drachmas*. When you
have finished go to the counter, give the clerk your booth number and
pay.

To make a collect or reverse charge call from the OTE, first visit the
counter clerk. You will be given a form to fill out which you then return
to the clerk, who calls the international switchboard. When the connection is made, you will be beckoned to the appropriate booth. How long

this takes depends on how busy the operator at the international switchboard is; sometimes, the wait can be an hour or more.

Some public telephone booths (those marked with an orange strip at the top and the word 'international') can be used for international calls. The booths only accept low denomination coins though, and a series of rapid bleeps will continually disrupt your conversation, reminding you that the machine requires re-feeding. So frequent are the 'bleeps' that a dropped or fumbled coin can easily lead to the connection being broken: use the OTE instead. For local calls however, the public booths are easy to use and very cheap.

One can also telephone abroad from a *periptero*, those small kiosks that sell newspapers, sweets, cigarettes, etc and which can be found on almost every Greek street. Use the *periptero's* telephone by all means (although it makes sense to find one located away from a loud and busy street) but be aware of one significant drawback: only the owner of the *periptero* will have sight of the call cost meter meaning in effect that he can charge you whatever price he feels like charging. Finally, one can place an international telephone call from your room at the more upmarket hotels. Like the *periptero* though, the hotel is liable to charge prices that are over and above the government norm.

Those who have access to a private phone can dial direct internationally: 00 first, then the country and area code. To make a reverse charge call from a private phone, dial 161 for the international operator. When making an international call, remember to delete the first number of the area code when dialling.

To telephone Greece, the international code to add is: from the USA and Canada: 011 30; from the UK: 010 30; from Australia: 0011 30.

Tourist Information Offices

UK and Ireland
4 Conduit Street
London W1R 0DJ
☎ 071 734 5997

Australia
51-57 Pitt Street
Sydney NSW 2000
☎ 241 1663/4

Canada
1233 Rue de la Montagne
Montreal
Quebec H36 1Z2
☎ 871 1535

1300 Bay Street
Toronto
Ontario M5R 3K8
☎ 968 2220

USA
645 Fifth Avenue
Olympic Tower (5th Floor)
New York NY10022
☎ 421 57777

168 North Michigan Avenue
Chicago
Illinois 60601
☎ 728 1084

611 West Sixth Street
Suite 2198
Los Angeles
California 90017
☎ 626 696

For tourist information when in Greece, contact the nearest office of the EOT (Ellinikos Organismos Tourismou, the National Tourist Organisation of Greece). Each office will have details of information on items such as bus, train and ferry times, accommodation lists, local curiosities, left luggage storage, and so on. For the addresses, telephone numbers and hours of opening of the offices relevant to the areas covered in this book see the Further Information section at the end of each chapter.

Accommodation and Eating Out

※※※ Expensive
※※ Moderate
※ Inexpensive

Chapter 1 •
Western and Central Crete

Agia Roumeli
Hotel Agia Roumeli ※※
Agia Roumeli
☎ 0825 25657/91293

Georgiopolis
Manos Beach Hotel ※
Georgiopolis
☎ 0825 2200

Hania
Hotel Porto Veneziano ※※
Aktienosseos Old Harbour
Hania
☎ 0821 29311-3

Doma Hotel ※※
124 El Venizelou St
Hania
☎ 0821 21772-3

El Greco Hotel ※
49 Theotokopoulou St
Hania
☎ 0821 22411/21829

Panorama Hotel ※※※
Cato Galatas
Hania
☎ 0821 20092/20467

Iraklion
Hotel Daedalos ※※※
Daedalos St
Iraklion
☎ 081 224 391

Kastelli
Helena Beach Hotel ※※
Kastelli
☎ 0822 23300

Hotel Peli ※
Kastelli
☎ 0822 22343

Maleme
Maleme Chandris ※※※
☎ 0821 61221-5

Paleohora
Hotel Polydoros ※
Paleohora
☎ 0823 41068

Sougia
Pikilassos Pension ※※
Sougia
☎ 0823 51242

Zaros
Hotel Idi ※
Zaros
☎ 0894 31302

Chapter 2 •
Southern Peloponnese

Aeropolis
Kapetanakos Tower (NTOG Traditional
 Guest House) ❊❊
Aeropolis
☎ 0733 51233

Gythion
Pantheon Hotel ❊
Gythion
☎ 0733 22284

Kirparissia
Ionion Hotel ❊
Kirparissia
☎ 0761 22511/2

Koroni
Auberge de la Place Pension ❊
Koroni
☎ 0725 22401

Kythera
Keti Pension ❊❊
Kythera Town
☎ 0733 31318

Messini
Drossia Hotel ❊
Messini
☎ 0722 31544

Methoni
Alex Hotel ❊
Methoni
☎ 0723 31239

Monemvassia
Malvasia Hotel (NTOG Traditional
 Guest House) ❊❊
Monemvassia
☎ 0732 61435

Pylos
Karalis Hotel ❊❊
Pylos
☎ 0723 22960

Sparta
Panhellion Hotel ❊
Sparta
☎ 0731 28031

Vathia
NTOG Traditional Guest House ❊❊
Vathia
☎ 0733 54229

Chapter 3 •
The Ionian Islands and the
North-West Peloponnese

Cephalonia
Hotel Perikles ❊❊
Sami
☎ 0674 22780

Xenia Hotel ❊❊
Argostoli
Cephalonia
☎ (0671) 22233

Panormos Pension ❊❊
Fiskardo
Cephalonia
☎ (0674) 51340

Ithaca
Pension Odysseus ❊❊
Vathi
Ithaca
☎ 0674 32381

Nostos Hotel ❊
Frikies
☎ 0674 31644

Kalavrita
Filoxenia Hotel ❊❊
Kalavrita
☎ 0692 22422

Loutra Killini
Xenia Hotel ❊❊❊
Loutra Killini
☎ 0623 96270/2

Olympia
Amalia Hotel ❊❊❊
Olympia
☎ 0624) 22190/1

Olympic Torch Hotel ✳
Olympia
☎ 0624 22668

Patras
Astir Hotel ✳✳✳
16 Agiou Andreou St
Patras
☎ 061 276 311

Galaxy Hotel ✳✳
16 Agiou Nikolaou St
Patras
☎ 061 278 815

Pirgos
Letrina Hotel ✳
Pirgos
☎ 0621 23644

Zakynthos
Strada Marina Hotel ✳✳
Zante
☎ 0695 22761

Zante Park Hotel ✳✳✳
Laganas
☎ 0695 51948

Chapter 4 •
Mount Pelion and the Sporades

Alonissos
Galaxy Hotel ✳
Patitiri
☎ 0424 65251/65263

Evia
Chryssi Akti Hotel ✳✳
Eretria
Evia
☎ 0221 61012

Hotel Beis ✳
Paralia Kimi
☎ 0222 22604

Avra Hotel ✳✳✳
Edipsos
☎ 0226 22226

Pelion
NTOG Traditional Guest House ✳✳
Vizitsa
☎ 0423 86373

NTOG Traditional Guest House ✳✳
Makrinitsa
☎ 0421 99250

NTOG Traditional Guest House ✳✳
Milies
☎ 0423 86373

Skopelos
Hotel Amalia ✳✳
Skopelos Town
☎ 0424 22688

Rigas Pension ✳✳
Staphylos
☎ 0424 22618

Hotel Avra ✳
Glossa
☎ 0424 33550

Skyros
Xenia Hotel ✳✳
Magasia
☎ 0222 91209

Volos
Park Hotel ✳
Volos
☎ 0421 36511-5

Chapter 5 •
Epirus and Lefkada

Arta
Hotel Kronos ✳
Arta
☎ 0681 22211-3

Igoumenitsa
Xenia Motel ✳✳
Igoumenitsa
☎ 0665 22282

Ioannina
Palladion Hotel ✳✳
☎ 0651 25856-9

Xenia Hotel ✳✳
Ioannina
☎ 0651 25087-9

Lefkada
Apollon Hotel ✴✴
Lefkada Town
☎ 0645 31122

Ponti Beach Hotel ✴✴
Vassiliki
☎ 0645 31572

Hotel Odyssia ✴✴
Agios Nikitas
☎ 0645 99366

Monodendri
Vikos Pension ✴✴
Monodendri
☎ 0653 61232

Megallo Papingo
Papingo Pension (NTOG Traditional
      Guest House) ✴✴
Megallo Papingo
☎ 0653 41088

Parga
Lichnos Beach Hotel ✴
Parga
☎ 0684 31293

Paxos
Paxos Beach Hotel ✴✴
Gaios
☎ 0662 31211

Preveza
Dioni Hotel ✴
Preveza
☎ 0682 22269

Chapter 6 •
Northern Thessaly and
Southern Macedonia

Grevena
Milionis Hotel ✴
☎ 0462 23223

Kalambaka
Motel Divani ✴✴✴
Kalambaka
☎ 0432 22330

Galaxy Hotel ✴
Kalambaka
☎ 0432 23233

Kozani
Xenia Hotel ✴✴
Kozani
☎ 0461 30484

Larissa
Divani Palace ✴✴✴
Larissa
☎ 041 252 791-4

Metsovo
Diasselo Hotel ✴✴✴
Metsovo
☎ 0656 41719

Olympic Hotel ✴
Metsovo
☎ 0656 41337

Platamonas
Platamon Beach Hotel ✴✴
Platamonas
☎ 0352 41212

Siatista
Arhontiko Hotel ✴
Siatista
☎ 0465 21298

Trikala
Achillion Hotel ✴✴
Trikala
☎ 0431 28192

Chapter 7 •
Western Macedonia

Edessa
Kataraktes Hotel ✴✴
Edessa
☎ 0381 22300

Xenia Hotel ✴✴
Edessa
☎ 0381 22221

Florina
King Alexander Hotel ✴✴
Florina
☎ 0385 23501-3

Antigone Hotel ✻
Florina
0385 23180

Kastoria
Hotel Xenia du Lac ✻✻✻
Kastoria
☎ 0467 22565

Tsamis Hotel ✻✻
Kastoria
☎ 0467 43334

Naoussa
Vermion Hotel ✻✻
Naoussa
☎ 0332 23013

Thessaloniki
Makedonia Palace ✻✻✻
Leoforos Megalou Alexandrou
Thessaloniki
☎ 031 837 520

Capitol Hotel ✻✻✻
8 Monastiriou St
Thessaloniki
☎ 031 516 221

Palace Hotel ✻✻
12 Tsimiski St
Thessaloniki
☎ 031 270 505

Hotel Grand Bretagne ✻
46 Egnatia St
Thessaloniki ☎ 031 530 735

Veria
Makedonia Hotel ✻✻
Veria
☎ 0331 66902

Chapter 8 •
Eastern Macedonia and Thrace

Alexandropoulis
Alexander Beach Hotel ✻✻
Alexandropoulis
☎ 0551 29250-3

Didimotiho
Plotini Hotel ✻✻
Didimotiho
☎ 0553 23400

Kavala
Blue Bay Hotel ✻✻
Kavala
☎ 051 227 441-4

Galaxy Hotel ✻✻
Kavala
☎ 051 224 521

Komotini
Orpheus Hotel ✻✻
Komotini
☎ 0531 26701-5

Nea Moudania
Hotel Kouvraki ✻
Nea Moudania
☎ 0373 91292

Ouranopolis
Eagle's Palace ✻✻✻
Ouranopolis
☎ 0377 22747/8

Samothraki
Hotel Aeolos ✻✻
Kamariotissa
☎ 0551 41595

Thassos
Hotel Amfipolis ✻✻✻
Limenas
☎ 0593 23101-4

Menel Hotel ✻
Limenaria
☎ 0593 51396

Xanthi
Motel Natassa ✻✻
☎ 0541 25111-3

Hotel Democritus ✻
Xanthi
0541 25111-3

Chapter 9 •
Chios

Chios Town
Chios Chandris Hotel ✻✻
Eyg Chandris St
☎ 0271 25761

Diana Hotel ✳
92 Eleftheriou Venizelou St
Chios Town
☎ 0271 25993

Emborio
Menis Hotel ✳
Emborio
☎ 0271 25352

Kardamyla
Hotel Kardamyla ✳✳
Kardamyla
☎ 0271 22706

Karfas
Golden Sands Hotel ✳✳✳
Karfas
☎ 0271 32080-1

Hotel Pantheon ✳
Karfas
☎ 0271 32060

Limnos
Akti Myrini Hotel ✳✳✳✳
Mirini
☎ 0254 22681

Mesta
Pipidis (NTOG Traditional Guest
    House) ✳✳
Mesta
☎ 0271 76319

Psara
NTOG Traditional Guest House ✳✳
Psara
☎ 0272 61293

Vrondatos
Xenios Hotel ✳✳
Vrondatos
☎ 0271 93763

Chapter 10 •
The Dodecanese

Astipalea
Paradissos Hotel ✳
Astipalea Town
☎ 0242 61224

Kalymnos
Hotel Drossos ✳
Pothia
☎ 0243 47518

Delfini Hotel ✳
Mirties
☎ 0243 47514

Karpathos
Romantica Pension ✳✳
Karpathos Town
☎ 0245 22461

Kassos
Anessis Hotel ✳
Frei
☎ 0245 41201

Kastellorizo (Megisti)
Xenon Dimou Megisti Pension ✳✳
☎ 0241 29072

Leros
Alinda Hotel ✳
Alinda
☎ 0247 23266

Nissiros
Porfyris Hotel ✳
☎ 0242 31376

Patmos
Romeos Hotel ✳✳
Skala
☎ 0247 31962

Symi
Hotel Horio ✳✳✳
Gialos
☎ 0241 71800

Metapontis Pension ✳✳
Gialos
☎ 0241 71491

Tilos
Irini Hotel ✳
Livadia
☎ 0241 53293

A Note To The Reader

The accommodation and eating out lists in this book are based upon the authors' own experiences and therefore may contain an element of subjective opinion. The contents of this book are believed correct at the time of publication but details given may change. We welcome any information to ensure accuracy in this guide book and to help keep it up-to-date.

Please write to The Editor, Moorland Publishing Co Ltd, Moor Farm Road, Airfield Estate, Ashbourne, Derbyshire, DE6 1HD, England.

American and Canadian readers please write to The Editor, The Globe Pequot Press, 6 Business Park Road, PO Box 833, Old Saybrook, Connecticut 06475, USA.

MPC

The Globe Pequot press

Discover a New World
with
Off The Beaten Track Travel Guides

Austria
Explore the quiet valleys of Bregenzerwald in the west to
Carinthia and Burgenland in the east. From picturesque
villages in the Tannheimertal to the castles north of
Klagenfurt, including Burg Hochosterwitz. This dramatic
castle with its many gates stands on a 450ft high limestone
cliff and was built to withstand the Turkish army by the
man who brought the original Spanish horses to Austria.

Britain
Yes, there are places off the beaten track in even the more
populated areas of Britain. Even in the heavily visited
national parks there are beautiful places you could easily
miss — areas well known to locals but not visitors. This book
guides you to such regions to make your visit memorable.

Greece
Brimming with suggested excursions that range from
climbing Mitikas, the highest peak of Mount Olympus, the
abode of Zeus, to Monemvassia, a fortified medieval town
with extensive ruins of a former castle. This book enables
you to mix a restful holiday in the sun with the fascinating
culture and countryside or rural Greece.

Italy
Beyond the artistic wealth of Rome or Florence and the hill
towns of Tuscany lie many fascinating areas of this ancient
country just waiting to be discovered. From medieval towns
such as Ceriana in the Armea valley to quiet and
spectacular areas of the Italian Lakes and the Dolomites
further to the east. At the southern end of the country, the
book explores Calabria, the 'toe' of Italy as well as Sicily,
opening up a whole 'new' area.

Germany

Visit the little market town of Windorf on the north bank of the Danube (with its nature reserve) or the picturesque upper Danube Valley, which even most German's never visit! Or go further north to the Taubertal. Downstream of famous Rothenburg with its medieval castle walls are red sandstone-built villages to explore with such gems as the carved altar in Creglingen church, the finest work by Tilman Riemenschneider — the Master Carver of the Middle Ages. This book includes five areas in the former East Germany.

Portugal

Most visitors to Portugal head to the Algarve and its famous beaches, but even the eastern Algarve is relatively quiet compared to the more popular western area. However, the book also covers the attractive areas of northern Portugal where only the more discerning independent travellers may be found enjoying the delights of this lovely country.

Scandinavia

Covers Norway, Denmark, Sweden and Finland. There is so much to see in these countries that it is all too easy to concentrate on the main tourist areas. That would mean missing so many memorable places that are well worth visiting. For instance, there are still about sixty Viking churches that survive in Norway. Alternatively many private castles and even palaces in Denmark open their gardens to visitors. Here is your guide to ensure that you enjoy the Scandinavian experience to the full.

Spain

From the unique landscape of the Ebrodelta in Catalonia to the majestic Picos d'Europa in the north, the reader is presented with numerous things to see and exciting things to do. With the mix of cultures and climates, there are many possibilities for an endearing holiday for the independent traveller.

Switzerland

Switzerland offers much more than the high mountains and deep valleys with which it is traditionally associated. This book covers lesser known areas of the high mountains — with suggested walks in some cases. It also covers Ticino, the Swiss Lakeland area near to the Italian Lakes and tours over the border into the latter. In the north, the book covers the lesser known areas between Zurich and the Rhine Falls, plus the Lake Constance area, with its lovely little towns like Rorschach, on the edge of the lake.

Forthcoming:

Northern France
Southern France

Touring the ancient fishing port of Guethary, hiking in the Pyrennees and visiting the old archway in Vaucoulers (through which Joan of Arc led her troops), are just a few of the many opportunities these two books present.

Scotland

Heather-clad mountains, baronian castles and magnificent coastal scenery, all combined with a rich historical heritage, combine to make this an ideal 'off the beaten track' destination.

Ireland

Ireland not only has a dramatic coastline, quiet fishing harbours and unspoilt rural villages, but also the natural friendliness of its easy-going people. *Off the Beaten Track Ireland* will lead you to a memorable holiday in a country where the pace of life is more relaxing and definitely not hectic.

TRAVEL GUIDE LIST

Airline/Ferry details ....
....
....
....
....

Telephone No. ....

Tickets arrived ☐

Travel insurance ordered ☐

Car hire details ....
....
....

Visas arrived ☐

Passport ☐

Currency ☐

Travellers cheques ☐

Eurocheques ☐

Accommodation address ....
....
....
....

Telephone No. ....

Booking confirmed ☐

Maps required ....
....
....

DAILY ITINERARY

Date ....

Places visited

....
....
....
....
....
....

Accommodation ....
....
....
Telephone No. ....

Booking confirmed ☐

Notes: